Endings in

clinical practice

EFFECTIVE CLOSURE IN
DIVERSE SETTINGS

SECOND EDITION

Also Available from Lyceum Books, Inc.

Advisory Editor: Thomas M. Meenaghan, *New York University*

EVIDENCE-BASED PRACTICES FOR SOCIAL WORKERS: AN INTERDISCIPLINARY APPROACH, by Thomas O'Hare

CLINICAL ASSESSMENT FOR SOCIAL WORKERS: QUALITATIVE AND QUANTITATIVE METHODS, 2E, edited by Catheleen Jordan and Cynthia Franklin

HUMAN BEHAVIOR FOR SOCIAL WORK PRACTICE: A DEVELOPMENTAL-ECOLOGICAL FRAMEWORK, by Wendy L. Haight and Edward H. Taylor

WHAT IS PROFESSIONAL SOCIAL WORK?, by Malcolm Payne

THERAPEUTIC GAMES AND GUIDED IMAGERY FOR CHILDREN, ADOLESCENTS, AND THEIR FAMILIES, by Monit Cheung

ADVOCACY PRACTICE FOR SOCIAL JUSTICE, by Richard Hoefer

A PRACTICAL GUIDE TO SOCIAL SERVICE EVALUATION, by Carl F. Brun

MODERN SOCIAL WORK THEORY: A CRITICAL INTRODUCTION, 3E, by Malcolm Payne, foreword by Stephen C. Anderson

ETHICS IN END-OF-LIFE DECISIONS IN SOCIAL WORK PRACTICE, by Ellen Csikai and Elizabeth Chaitin

UNDERSTANDING SUBSTANCE ADDICTIONS: ASSESSMENT AND INTERVENTION, by Sophia Dziegelewski

RAISE UP A CHILD, by Edith Hudley, Wendy Haight, and Peggy Miller

MENTAL HEALTH IN LITERATURE: LITERARY LUNACY AND LUCIDITY, by Glenn Rohrer

FOREWORD BY THOMAS M. MEENAGHAN

Endings in clinical practice

EFFECTIVE CLOSURE IN DIVERSE SETTINGS
SECOND EDITION

JOSEPH WALSH
VIRGINIA COMMONWEALTH UNIVERSITY

LYCEUM
BOOKS, INC.
Chicago, Illinois

© Lyceum Books, Inc., 2007

Published by

LYCEUM BOOKS, INC.
5758 S. Blackstone Ave.
Chicago, Illinois 60637
773+643-1903 (Fax)
773+643-1902 (Phone)
lyceum@lyceumbooks.com
http://www.lyceumbooks.com

ISBN—1-933478-00-4 (pbk.): ISBN 13—978-1-933478-00-5

Library of Congress Cataloging-in-Publication Data

Walsh, Joseph (Joseph F.)
   Endings in clinical practice : effective closure in diverse settings \
Joseph Walsh. — 2nd ed.
      p. cm.
   Includes bibliographical references and index.
   ISBN—1-933478-00-4 (pbk.): ISBN 13—978-1-933478-00-5
   1. Psychotherapy—Termination. I. Title.
   [DNLM: 1. Psychotherapy—Case Reports. 2. Professional-Patient Relations—
Case Reports. WM 420 W2255e 2007]
   RC489.T45W355   2007
   616.89'14—dc22
                                                        2006034531

For my high school English teacher Barbara Share
(formerly Sister Barbara)
Your encouragement of my writing made an impression
that has lasted a lifetime.

Contents

Foreword

It is a rather unique opportunity for me to offer some introductory comments on this book. Professor Walsh was a student of mine many years ago when we were both at Ohio State University. Since then I have witnessed the evolution of his academic career, and of course his career's trajectory. I'm sure all his former professors feel as proud and honored as I do.

Endings in Clinical Practice will be of value and interest to students and practitioners for several important reasons. First, although the subject of endings is so relevant to practitioners and students, there is relatively little literature available. I've noticed that whenever this topic is offered to the professional community in lectures and discussions it always elicits strong interest and a great desire to talk about this important yet rather neglected aspect of practice. In my opinion, there is now a book that is both relevant and accessible.

Second, this manuscript does several things that address many valid criticisms of practice courses. Although the book contains much theory, it is practice-focused and people- and situation-specific. Rich in case studies and examples, the book affords students and academics opportunities to visualize, simulate, and discuss practice in real contexts.

Third, *Endings in Clinical Practice* presents several human behavior theory perspectives and demonstrates how they play out in different practice contexts. In this way the book really is an integration of human behavior theory and practice content.

Because *Endings in Clinical Practice* is practical and substantive, it helps contribute to our field moving from practices that stress assessment almost exclusively to effective interventions and also endings. For too long our field has been preoccupied with bickering over which religiously held theoretical system was right so that the assessment phase of practice often became the major focus of practice. By skillfully presenting different theories and then moving directly to practice imperatives, Professor Walsh deals with such issues as goal setting, defining and using resources, worker's roles, and assessing the impact of interventions. In short, his work reflects what best thinking and best practice suggest we should be doing—doing the best we can in a constructively critical manner.

Endings in Clinical Practice also is compatible with very recent trends linking clinical practice with program strategies. Obviously, this book is totally compatible with a practice environment that stresses results and accountability. But it also addresses spirituality and the quest for meaning, the need for practitioners to be thinkers and creators in their own practice, the reality that certain strategies may or may not work with certain groups or types of situations, and other topics that are crucial to effective intervention. Developments such as these are requiring the practitioner to note systematically what is going on in practice and then to participate in trying and testing new practice interventions. Professor Walsh's book is clearly supportive of the theme that practitioners have a responsibility to try to do better and to participate actively in more structured strategies.

By stressing the concepts of people living in social space with different backgrounds, strengths, and contexts, Professor Walsh encourages practitioners to realize that it is unlikely that a single theory-driven, a priori response has universal applicability. Rather, by stressing the complexity of life, Professor Walsh suggests that the nature of practice is affected by such considerations as the wonder about the activities and effects of practice. In this view of practice, practitioners need to be clear about their roles, their decision making, and their need to follow clients as well as to be the expert in professional relationships.

To return to my opening thoughts of having the opportunity to comment upon the academic work of a former student, let me close with one final observation. Although, of course, professors are pleased to see students learn and grow, it is even more heartening to watch such students become strong leaders within the field. For many years to come, I'm sure Professor Walsh and his scholarship will not only reflect the best in the field as it is but also help provide guideposts to where the field will go.

Thomas M. Meenaghan, Ph.D.
Professor
New York University

Preface to the Second Edition

Writing the first edition of *Endings in Clinical Practice* was great fun for me, because I thoroughly enjoy the topic and also got to spend so much time talking with clinical practitioners about their interesting experiences with endings. I am pleased that the book has been well received enough to merit a second edition. For this edition I have made no changes in chapter organization, and most of the major topics are the same, but I have added material to make some of the topic areas more comprehensive. Most significantly I have

- ◆ Added considerable new material to the chapter on endings with families
- ◆ Explored the issue of client suicide in more detail
- ◆ Included more content about the ways children and adolescents experience clinical endings
- ◆ Added material about the role of agency administrators in creating conditions so that practitioners can maximize their chances to experience positive endings with clients

In preparing this material I have added ten new case studies and a dozen or so references related to research studies on clinical endings.

In addition to the many people who helped with the first edition of the book, I add the names of Marcia Harrigan, associate dean at the Virginia Commonwealth University School of Social Work, who helped me develop the new material in the "Families" chapter, and Cynthia Weaver, associate professor at Marywood University, who made many helpful suggestions about what should be included in the second edition.

About the Author

Joseph Walsh, Ph.D., L. C. S. W. is professor of social work at Virginia Common-wealth University. He received his academic degrees from Ohio State University. He has been a direct services practitioner in the field of mental health since 1974, first in a psychiatric hospital and later in community mental health center settings. Professor Walsh has provided services to older adult and general outpatient populations but has specialized in services to persons with serious mental illness and their families. Since 1993 he has been at VCU, teaching courses in generalist practice, clinical practice, human behavior, research, and social theory. He continues to provide direct services to clients at the university counseling center and also at area shelters, clubhouses, and group homes. Professor Walsh was the 1998 recipient of the National Mental Health Association's George Goodman Brudney and Ruth P. Brudney Social Work Award, given annually to recognize significant contributions to the care and treatment of persons with mental illness. He is the author of four other books about clinical practice.

Preface

One spring afternoon several years ago a graduate student named Bethany raised an issue in my Clinical Practice class. Bethany was completing her field placement in the adolescent services program of a community mental health center. She was upset about a recent development with one of her clients, a high school student with a severe emotional disturbance. "The last time we met I told her that we had to end our work in four more weeks because we were both graduating," Bethany said. "It disrupted everything! She hadn't looked ahead that far. She got upset and said she didn't see the point of continuing if we had to end soon. I'm not sure what to do either. For the rest of that session we just looked at each other."

I was motivated to write this book as I watched my students, supervisees, and colleagues (not to mention myself) struggle at times with the ending stage of clinical intervention. Many students and other practitioners who have a firm grasp of practice theory and intervention techniques seem to feel less assured when it is time for them to end their work with clients. They receive little instruction in this area within their agencies or from their course texts. I believe this book will be of interest, then, to graduate and undergraduate students in human service fields and to practicing professionals, most of whom experience challenges with clinical endings and have little source material to guide them.

In contrast to Bethany's concerns, a faculty colleague once questioned the appropriateness of my focusing so much attention on clinical endings in my Practice classes. He said, "When I was working in social services, I'd draw up some sort of contract with my client, and when we were finished with the work we just shook hands and parted. It was never a big deal." Many clinical endings do proceed this smoothly, but in my own experience there are at least as many exceptions. The nature of the ending process is quite different depending on the agency setting, the client's problems and service needs, and the practitioner's intervention philosophy.

Why is it so important to carefully attend to the ending stage of a clinical intervention? I have written this book in an effort to answer that question. I provide some beginning reflections on the question here.

There have been significant changes in human service delivery practices during the past fifteen years corresponding with the establishment of managed health care. Accountability to third-party payers and clients has become a driving force in the social services field. All practitioners must provide their services in a manner that more clearly reflects structure, a short-term focus, and attention to measurable short- and long-term outcomes. This trend has had tremendous impact on clinical practice methods. Students must be taught more efficient ways of conducting assessments and interventions. There is a greater emphasis on specificity of behavioral goals and the generation of evidence that clients' positive changes will endure. Among the implications of these changes is that the issue of endings, or establishing positive closure to interventions, must be addressed earlier and more systematically by practitioners. Positive closure helps to ensure that clients will maintain their service gains.

A major challenge for Clinical Practice instructors is that students are interested in, and have concurrent field placements in, such diverse practice settings that it is difficult to organize educational topics that are relevant to them all. Inevitably some students complete their course work feeling that issues relevant to their areas of interest have not received sufficient emphasis. In this book I attempt to address this challenge by providing diverse examples of the clinical management of endings. Their variety should facilitate relevant classroom instruction as well as provide the working practitioner with new ideas for approaching clinical endings.

I believe that in the years to come, economic forces will continue to demand that helping professionals demonstrate effectiveness, efficiency, and practicality in their interventions. Skills in recording will assume greater importance as clear documentation becomes more highly valued by agency administrators. Professionals will likely use formal instruments for assessment and outcome measurement more so than in the past. Their performance evaluations will depend on their ability to demonstrate positive outcomes for clients. The process of clinical intervention may become somewhat more mechanized. Instructors will be challenged to enforce these trends while maintaining the humanitarian value base that attracts students into the helping professions. There will be an ongoing need for text materials that contribute to lively classroom and agency discussions about the knowledge, skills, and values required for competent clinical practice. This book is designed specifically to address both the human and technical aspects of the final phase of intervention.

Endings in Clinical Practice is comprehensive and can serve as a useful supplement to texts that emphasize other areas of clinical practice. One of the most appealing features of this book, in my view, is its inclusion of dozens of case illustrations about ending processes from a variety of practice settings. These include examples from my own practice and case material contributed by my current and former students and by many of the excellent working professionals I have known throughout my practice career. Another of the book's features is a consideration of the process of endings from ten widely used theoretical perspectives for clinical practice.

The book's eleven chapters are divided into three parts. Part 1, "An Overview of the Endings Process," presents material on the types of endings in clinical practice, both planned and unplanned; the importance of closure; and common ending tasks across fields of practice. Part 2, "Theoretical Perspectives on Endings," outlines ten theoretical perspectives, including ego psychological, object relations, existential, cognitive, behavioral, family systems, structural family, narrative, solution-focused, and group approaches. Part 3, "Endings across Service Settings," considers endings in more detail and in the context of agency influences. The chapters focus on client and practitioner reactions to endings, the many factors that influence their reactions, and termination rituals. In every chapter examples from a wide range of service settings are used as illustrations.

The practice settings that are represented in the book include public schools, substance abuse programs (for adolescents and adults), medical hospitals, a residential school for adolescents with severe emotional disturbances, community mental health centers, a physical rehabilitation hospital, hospice agencies, a university counseling center, a residential home for older adults, community-based service agencies for persons with serious mental illness, psychiatric hospitals, agencies that serve children with behavioral problems, a university child development clinic, a pastoral counseling agency, a prison, county social services departments, a community corrections program, a Catholic charities agency, therapeutic foster care agencies, a community services center, a psychiatric rehabilitation service, family services agencies, a juvenile corrections center, a center for perinatal addiction, housing agencies, a Head Start program, activity centers for older adults, a Meals on Wheels program, a veteran's administration center, a Travelers Aid agency, an Urban League agency, a domestic violence treatment agency, a wilderness challenge program, and private practice agencies for mental health counseling.

This book is both conceptual and practical in design. The comprehensive coverage of the subject makes it relevant to both beginning and advanced students and to working clinical practitioners. Part of my goal has been to include a broad assortment of strategies for ending that will enhance the practice repertoires of all clinical professionals. Readers can focus their attention on the book's content in several ways. Advanced practitioners may study the theoretical material in part 2 more extensively, while beginning students may prefer the overview of the ending process and the common tasks that must be addressed in all settings. Depending on their experiences and interests, readers may be drawn to different chapters and case illustrations. I believe that all readers will enjoy most of the case illustrations. I have presented them in a manner that is intended to enhance their generalizability.

Each chapter of the book includes text and case illustrations to support the major themes of the chapter. The cases are written in the first person so that all readers, even when not practicing in a particular setting, can enjoy reading about the challenges faced by the worker and be able to generalize some of the worker's decision-making processes to their own practices. Each illustration is organized with the following format:

1. The setting
2. The client
3. The challenge
4. How the challenge was resolved
5. Whether the process was successful (examples of both successful and unsuccessful outcomes are included)

6. What the worker learned about the endings process as a result of the experience

Classroom instructors should have no difficulty crafting a variety of assignments based on the text material. These can involve the application of concepts and practice tasks from the text to students' clinical setting.

In summary, the purpose of this book is to provide students and professionals with detailed instruction in the knowledge and skills required to ensure positive closure in clinical practice with individuals, families, and groups. I hope that readers will find this book to be the most comprehensive resource about its topic they have yet encountered. I hope they also find it to be entertaining!

Acknowledgments

This project was a labor of love for me because of the participation of so many wonderful people! At Lyceum Books, Inc., I would like to thank my publisher, David Follmer, for supporting the project and smoothly guiding it along from start to finish. Drs. Thomas Meenaghan of New York University (and, while at Ohio State many years ago, a professor of mine) and Irene Gutheil of Fordham University critiqued the original proposal and the work in progress. Dorothy Anderson was my copy editor, and her "light hand" made the process easy for me.

I owe special gratitude to two former MSW students. Bethany Barta actually inspired this book with her pertinent classroom comments and questions about clinical endings. Amy Carson proved to be an especially enthusiastic contributor and chapter reviewer.

Many of my colleagues at the Virginia Commonwealth University School of Social Work reviewed portions of the manuscript in draft form and provided me with helpful feedback. I want to especially acknowledge the help of Jacqueline Corcoran, who reviewed one chapter, provided a case vignette for another, and perhaps most importantly referred me to Lyceum Books, Inc., when I was working on the proposal. Other colleagues who reviewed chapters include Kia Bentley, Randi Buerlein, Rosemary Farmer, Marcia Harrigan, Pamela Kovacs, and Jane Reeves.

Finally I want to thank the many colleagues, former students, and community practitioners who shared their challenging experiences with clinical endings and taught me so much: Jan Altman, Linda Barker, Bethany Barta, Janice Berry Edwards, Joy Bressler, Carole Cadora, Kay Campbell, Amy Carson, Jacqueline Corcoran, Leavelle Cox, Jessica Cundari, Tim Davey, Jennifer Davis, Delores Dungee-Anderson, Rosemary Farmer, Marcia Harrigan, Marilyn Hartline, Joyce Hilliard, Tara Kanter, Leah Kilpatrick, Kathleen Koechlin, Pamela Kovacs, Cynthia Lucas, Mike Mason, Holly Matto, Katherine Meyersohn, Amy Morris, Kathy Orosz, Shannon Owens, Tracy Palmer, Gene Pembleton, Laura Rappaport, Jane Reeves, Karen Reynolds, Sherry Richards, Amy Rosenblum, Phil Rosenblum, Andy Slabaugh, Tracy Spahr, Melissa Taylor, Marie Fraelich, Kristi Vera, Amanda Waddel, and Trish Wenrich.

Part **1**

An Overview of the Endings Process

Chapter 1

Types of Endings

I begin by sharing two of my favorite stories about endings in clinical practice, both involving just one of my former clients. I once worked at a community mental health center where clients with serious mental disorders were sometimes seen for many years. Tara, only nineteen years old when we met, was one such client. She had a long history of sexual abuse by her father, and into her young adulthood she continued to passively enter into relationships with abusive men. Tara had low self-esteem and an unstable sense of identity. She was depressed, confused, and frequently suicidal. Tara had experienced dozens of short-term psychiatric hospitalizations prior to our first meeting. To her I was just one more in a series of social workers to whom she was referred after a hospitalization. She had not stayed involved with any professionals for longer than a few weeks.

I patiently tried to engage Tara in a working clinical relationship. Somehow I succeeded, but it was an on-and-off relationship. She frequently dropped out of treatment for weeks or even months. I probably asked my supervision group for help with Tara forty times! She would only return to my agency when convinced by a friend or hospital social worker to do so. Tara was never much of a talker—our sessions featured long silences that made me uncomfortable and left me uncertain about her moods, thoughts, and level of emotional stability. Still, we worked together for four years, and she improved a great deal. Each year, Tara was hospitalized only half as many times as the year before. She became able to end a long-term relationship with an abusive man, make some new friends, attend and graduate from nursing school, and find a responsible job in which she received excellent evaluations. Still, her self-esteem remained very low. She felt empty and worthless in spite of her outward achievements.

One of the great challenges I eventually faced with Tara was how to approach the issue of ending our work. Quite simply, I could not confidently devise a strategy or timing for our ending process. At her best, Tara experienced occasional crises related to her labile emotions and relationship problems. We both agreed that she was always at risk for problems of those types, so I had rarely considered how to end our work together in a planned way. Whenever I brought up the issue of her ending therapy Tara seemed ambivalent and said little. Eventually, I felt more strongly that we should end—that there wasn't much that I seemed to be contributing any longer to her quality of life. But being ambivalent, I decided to wait until she raised the issue of our ending. This didn't happen.

A few months later Tara dropped out of treatment again. Her missing an appointment was not unusual, but contrary to her usual pattern she did not later try to reach me and did not return my calls. She seemed to have disappeared. I was very concerned until one day at the agency I received the following letter from her:

> Dear Joe,
>
> I hope you are well. I am doing OK myself. I won't be coming back to see you anymore and I want to explain why. I feel like we've accomplished as much as we can together. I was afraid to tell you this, because I thought you would disagree. You think it is important for us to stay in contact and always make me feel like I have to keep coming in. I was afraid that I might hurt your feelings. So I thought I'd wait awhile before sending this and give you time to get used to not seeing me.
>
> Sincerely,
> Tara

In other words, I hadn't been able to manage ending my work with Tara, so she took matters into her own hands. I was impressed with Tara's initiative but was upset with myself for not having enough faith in her (or myself) to have recommended with conviction that we end our work. Besides, as she sensed, perhaps it was me who was having trouble with the end of our relationship! That seemed backward to what is supposed to happen in clinical relationships. I felt good that I had helped Tara, but unsettled about how our work ended.

But there is more to the story. Six months later, I took a new job at an agency out of state. After consulting with my supervisor, I wrote short letters to five of my former clients to announce my departure. These were clients who tended to come and go from the agency, sometimes with long breaks, and my supervisor suggested that it might be damaging to them if they tried to reach me in a crisis and learned that I was no longer available. Tara was one of those clients. I was not sure if she lived at the same address or what she was doing with her life, but in a few formal sentences I informed her that I was leaving. I told her that I was well and hoped that she was doing well too.

Two weeks later, very much to my surprise, I got a response. Tara wrote:

> Dear Joe,
>
> I was surprised to hear from you saying you were leaving the agency. You are a wonderful therapist and I know that wherever you go you will be an asset. You helped me change my life in many ways, all for the better. I hope you enjoy your new job and I know you will continue to change lives for the better.
>
> Sincerely,
> Tara

Now I experienced real closure with Tara. That is, we had an opportunity, however indirectly (and in only a few sentences), to mutually recognize that our work was over, to reflect on the course of that work, and see that it had been worthwhile. I did not need for her to say nice things about me (although I appreciated them). What affected me most about Tara's second letter, in combination with the first, was her implication that our work had indeed run its course and that it made sense for us to end our association when, and even how, we did so. I was able to put my bad feelings about mismanaging our initial ending behind me and think with more balance about the course of our relationship over the four years.

The Importance of Closure

All episodes of clinical practice, regardless of professional discipline or agency setting, include the stages of assessment, planning, intervention, and ending. The last stage is more often called termination, but that term has fallen out of favor somewhat, being associated since the 1980s with a well-known (and destructive) movie action figure. Every clinical practice textbook includes material about these stages (although they are sometimes categorized as more or fewer than four). Still, the topic of ending clinical intervention receives relatively little coverage, probably because the earlier phases of assessment and intervention are considered to require more knowledge and skill. No one denies the importance of the ending phase, but because it is conceptualized in large part as a process of consolidating gains already made, it receives less instructional and on-the-job supervisory attention.

Whether or not the ending of a clinical intervention is managed well can make the difference between successful and unsuccessful outcomes for the client *and* for the professional. Closure (a concept I alluded to earlier) is a process in which practitioners and clients bring their work to a mutually understood (not necessarily satisfactory) end, review their work together (successes and failures), perhaps acknowledge feelings about the relationship, and acquire an enhanced willingness to invest in future relationships.

The need to attend carefully to endings is more of a concern among professionals now that clinical intervention increasingly occurs in the context of short-term relationships. Practitioners have less time to establish a relationship of confidence and trust with a client and have less of an attachment on which to base closure after an intervention. If treatment gains are not consolidated; if the client cannot carry on with his or her new behaviors, cognitions, and affects after an intervention; and perhaps if the client's significant others are not prepared to assist in that process, the gains made during intervention may not persist. The example of my work with Tara demonstrates a few of the difficulties involved in ending clinical work and also highlights how the process is important to the professional as well as to the client. From his study of 132 practitioners at one agency, Baum (2005) concluded that considering variables within the following three domains can help practitioners assess the quality of a clinical ending: the source (client, practitioner, or an external source), the process (speed, control, choice, level of desire), and the perceived outcome from each person's perspective (failure or goal achievement).

Types of Endings

In the remainder of this chapter I review twenty types of endings that may occur in clinical practice. These are organized into three categories: unplanned endings initiated by the client, unplanned endings initiated by the practitioner, and planned endings. Clinical illustrations are included for some types of endings, particularly for those not addressed elsewhere in the book.

Unplanned Endings Initiated by the Client

In an unplanned ending, the client unexpectedly drops out of the intervention process. Even though the professional may have suspected that this might happen, the event is a surprise. The client never shares the reasons for this decision with the clinical worker, but it may be due to any of the following developments. It has been found, for example, that in university counseling centers most students complete only a handful of sessions, and close to 60 percent depart from therapy prematurely from the perspective of the practitioner (Hatchett, 2004).

The Client Feels That He or She Has Made Adequate Clinical Gains but Is Reluctant or Unable to Request an End to the Intervention   This was true of Tara in the earlier illustration. In these situations the practitioner understandably feels disappointed and puzzled, not knowing why the client has suddenly dropped out, and may assume that it is because of dissatisfaction with the practitioner or the intervention. But this is not always true—the client may well have gotten what he or she came for.

A review of the literature on client dropout supports this point. Most studies of individual and group interventions in a variety of settings indicate a 20- to 50-percent premature dropout rate (Sweet & Noones, 1989). Dropout rates for clients receiving alcohol and drug treatment tend to be even higher. For children and adolescents with behavioral problems the dropout rate is 40 to 60 percent (Kazdin & Wassell, 1998). Some of these clients undoubtedly had mixed feelings about their clinical involvement, but many others were satisfied with what they achieved. Among psychotherapy outpatients who left therapy at one community mental health center, 39 percent indicated no need for additional services, 35 percent indicated that environmental constraints (such as transportation problems and conflicts with work) precluded their ongoing participation, and only 26 percent noted a dislike of the service (Pekarik, 1983).

Pekarik and Finney-Owen (1987) surveyed 173 therapists and their clients at forty-three midwestern mental health agencies about their experiences with treatment dropout. Among their findings was that the projected duration of intervention was very different for the two groups. Practitioners anticipated that clients would be in treatment two to three times longer than the clients expected. Such a discrepancy can account for many clients' decisions to drop out because their problem has been adequately resolved. Indeed, 49 percent of them indicated this. In a study of 180 elderly clients at a community mental health center, Mosher-Ashley (1994) found that clients were twice as likely to end therapy as their practitioners. He speculated that the practitioners may have been reluctant to end intervention because of a protective attitude about elderly persons.

Dropout rates for students in college counseling centers are 25 to 50 percent, and several studies indicate that they, too, stop coming because their goals have been met. April and Nicholas (1997) surveyed dropouts from one center and learned that the students' counseling experiences tended to be positive. Participants stated that they would return to the counseling center in the future if needed and would refer friends there. Sander (1998) argues that young college students are in a stage of life where many relationships are transient, and they do not place importance on how those relationships end. The same author found, in another college counseling center, that clients who had relationship concerns tended to stay in therapy longer and to experience planned endings. Students with other issues were in therapy for shorter periods and did not as frequently have planned endings.

One study of adolescent clients with behavioral problems at a mental health agency found that while 79 percent who completed their intervention improved, 34 percent of those who dropped out also improved, as reported by their parents (Kazdin & Wassell, 1998). Their clinicians indicated that only 14 percent of these dropouts had improved, which again implies that clients and practitioners may approach intervention with different expectations. Fabricius and Green (1995) considered the issue of premature endings in child and adolescent psychoanalysis. They point out that there is a difference between principles from analytic theory that encourage long-term therapy and what is realistic with young people in practice. They assert that analysts will experience greater satisfaction from their work if they are flexible with their expectations about treatment and allow the child or adolescent to take the lead in matters of intervention depth and duration.

Practitioners' feelings about their competence can be enhanced if they understand more clearly that many treatment dropouts are satisfied with the clinical experience. One way for practitioners to minimize the negative impact of client dropout is to incorporate ongoing change measures into their intervention, rather than reserving such evaluations for a planned ending.

The Client Is Dissatisfied with the Absence of Perceived Gains
Clients also drop out of treatment because they are displeased with the course of the intervention. In the mental health agency study cited earlier, 26 percent of clients who dropped out did so for this reason (Pekarik, 1983). The dissatisfaction of these clients may have several sources, which are addressed in the clinical literature. Clients may perceive that their practitioners are ineffective, which

may be true in some situations. Clients who have symptoms of paranoia tend to withdraw from relationships with practitioners just as they do with other people in their lives (Sweet & Noones, 1989). One recent study of 128 outpatient mental health clients found that predictors of dropout included the client's having borderline personality disorder (featuring highly unstable interpersonal relationships), being female, having a tendency to act out in sessions, having interpersonal deficits, and having low levels of resources or social support (Marini, Semenzin, & Vignaga, 2005). In a similar vein, Minnix, Reitzel, and Repper (2005) found that the number of clinical scale elevations on the Minnesota Multiphasic Personality Inventory (indicating a range of symptoms of mood and behavioral instability) predicted premature termination. Clients who required excessive admiration and lacked remorse for the part they may play in their problem situations tend to be quickly dissatisfied with interventions and drop out (Hilsenroth, Holdwick, Castlebury, & Blais, 1998).

Client dropout is sometimes related to the practitioner's negative feelings about the client, particularly early in the course of the intervention (Shapiro, 1974). Further, generating a client's confidence is largely related to the practitioner's ability to articulate a rationale for his or her approach to intervention that is consistent with the client's expectations (Frank & Frank, 1993). Strean (1986), a psychodynamic practitioner, summarized other reasons therapists lose clients, including:

- ◆ Failure to listen carefully
- ◆ Answering questions too directly rather than helping clients identify their own answers
- ◆ Not being attentive to clients' indirect communications
- ◆ Reluctance to deal with clients' anger
- ◆ Indirectly acting out angry feelings toward clients
- ◆ Fearing any sexual feelings toward or from clients, normal or otherwise
- ◆ Failing to acknowledge clients' suspected negative feelings toward the practitioner
- ◆ Experiencing clients' problems as similar to one's own

If practitioners regularly take time to assess how they and their clients are responding to each other with regard to these topics, clients would be less likely to become dissatisfied with the intervention.

The Client Is Uncomfortable with the Practitioner's Personal Characteristics   Even a highly motivated client needs to feel comfortable with the practitioner before investing time, money, and energy in the process. The client must feel that the practitioner is empathetic and knowledgeable about his or her problem issues and also sensitive to issues related to age, gender, race, ethnicity, and perhaps sexual orientation (Bein, Torres, & Kurilla, 2000; Huey, 1999; Reis & Brown, 1999). Children may be reluctant to work with any practitioners because of their general discomfort with adults. Older adults may be reluctant to work with young counselors, perceiving them to be too young to understand issues of adult life. Female clients may want to see female practitioners because it is easier for them to talk with other women. Men may prefer to see female practitioners for the same reason! A gay male may only agree to see a gay practitioner, particularly if his concern is related to issues of sexual orientation. In one agency study of 527 clients, it was found that the interactions of client income and ethnicity differences between the client and practitioner, and therapist gender and ethnicity, were the most useful demographic predictors of premature termination (Williams, Ketring, & Salts, 2005). Agencies will often ask clients about their practitioner preferences, although they may not always be able to accommodate them. When clients feel that they are mismatched, they may drop out of the process.

Case Study: The Face That Will Never Look Old

My first job after graduate school was with a geriatric evaluation team at a county social services department. Our job was to make home visits with older adults who appeared to be experiencing emotional problems, most often depression. Physicians or families referred clients to us. We would assess the clients, usually provide short-term individual and family counseling, and make linkages to senior activity centers. I was twenty-six years old at the time.

I was assigned to work with a Mrs. Wooten, who was in her seventies. She was recovering from hip surgery and was said to be depressed about her slow progress and limited mobility. When I showed up at her apartment, she could not have been more hospitable. She offered me coffee and was very pleasant as I described the purpose of my visit. But when I began the formal assessment, she began laughing. She said, "You don't really think I'm going to talk about my personal life with you! Look at you! You're just a kid!" I'd heard about the possibility of this kind of client reaction, but I hadn't experienced it before. I responded, "Mrs. Wooten, I'm here to help you. I'd like to help you become more active and feel better about yourself." But she kept laughing and eventually said, "Tell your boss to send someone older. You seem like a very nice young man, but I can't talk to you about these things. You could be my grandson." Soon I realized I was not going to convince Mrs. Wooten that I had any knowledge or skills to help her. In fact, she couldn't accept me as a human service practitioner at all. I started talking with her more socially again. She offered me more snacks, just as she would her grandson. She knew I was disappointed when I left. On my way out, she said kindly, "You might try to find work in another department, because you have a face that will never look old."

Clients may end work with a practitioner of another race or ethnicity if they perceive basic value differences (Fong & Furuto, 2001). For example, Asian American clients tend to value family ties, family authority, deference to those with status, modesty, and a lack of aggressiveness. Hispanic clients value religion, the extended family, and distinct sex roles. Native American clients value patience, a slow pace, deference to authority, and mutual sibling responsibility. Persons from these groups may drop out of treatment if they perceive the practitioner to have essentially different values.

Case Study: The Jazz Pianist

I am a Caucasian male social worker at a mental health agency and have occasionally felt uncomfortable with African American male clients. I do not think of myself as racist, but I believe that racial differences can negatively affect practitioners and clients who work together. Also I am clinically less comfortable in general working with men than women. I raise the issue of racial difference with new clients when it exists to see if they have concerns about it. Usually they do not express any reservations. My problem, though, is that I am reluctant to raise the issue of race again during the intervention if I perceive that it might be a barrier between the client and myself. I don't want to risk insulting the client or imply that I am preoccupied with race. Maybe I'm off base about that, but it's how I feel.

Leon was a middle-aged and unemployed single African American male who came to our agency because of depression. He had chronic job problems, conflicts with women, and a strained relationship with his domineering father. He was rather well known around town as a talented jazz pianist. When we met he raised the issue of race himself, seeming suspicious that I might not be able to understand his life experiences. It was a constructive conversation, and we both seemed to feel satisfied. Every so often, though, he would challenge me again, wondering openly if I could empathize with him. This became difficult, because I did think that in many situations he placed himself in the victim role more than the evidence warranted, so to speak, using race as an excuse. But I was not comfortable saying this to him, because I was not sure that my perceptions were valid. Anyway, Leon dropped out of treatment after about six visits. I think he felt I was naive about the African American experience. I decided afterward that I needed to learn more about managing differences with my clients.

Client populations may approach their problems in certain ways that the practitioner must acknowledge in order to make a connection (Harper & Lantz, 1996). Those from lower socioeconomic classes may want to prioritize survival issues, focus on the present, attend to the consequences of actions rather than their causes, seek informality in the clinical relationship, and value concrete definitions of problems and solutions. Older adults tend to prefer active work on problems and the use of touch, reminiscence, and home visits. Clinical issues with children include respecting their resistance, patiently working through their distrust of strangers, setting boundaries on family communication, careful use of language and play, and respecting their short attention spans. Members of special populations are often sensitive to any negative worker reactions to their interpersonal styles but will not often articulate this.

In psychotherapy studies, socioeconomic factors are most consistently associated with client dropout (Zagayko, 1994). Up to 50 percent of clients in the lowest economic levels leave therapy prematurely. This appears to be related to the practitioners' attitudes as much as the clients' own attitudes described above. These dropouts are associated with clients' lack of perceived psychological mindedness, lesser attractiveness to the practitioner, and less positive prognosis.

The Client Is Frustrated with Agency Procedures or Environmental Constraints   A person who seeks professional help must be able to structure that activity into his or her daily schedule. Some clients face significant limitations on their time and availability, and these can sometimes lead to a decision to end their clinic participation. Of course, some ambivalent or involuntary clients cite these factors as excuses to end the intervention. Still, constraints are often legitimate. Researchers have identified several reasons for client dropout related to agency or environmental constraints. These include:

- The financial cost of the service, low insurance coverage, or not getting a fee reduction (Sweet & Noones, 1989)
- For older adults, the inability to receive home therapy (Mosher-Ashley, 1994)
- Conflicts with work schedules
- Problems securing transportation
- Family pressure to end the intervention (Pekarik & Finney-Owen, 1987)

Clients do not always articulate the range of agency and external pressures affecting them. They may perceive these factors to be extraneous to the intervention process. If practitioners monitor these pressures, however, they can be proactive in helping clients manage them.

Taking Advantage of a Perceived Opportunity to Drop Out during a Process of Involuntary Treatment   It is not always easy to identify an "involuntary" client, because many people have ambivalent feelings about entering into clinical relationships. Indeed, Hepworth, Rooney, and Larsen (2002) prefer the term "reluctant client" to capture the broad applicability of the concept. If a client's reluctance becomes strong, he or she may drop out of the intervention when an opportunity presents itself. For example, an adolescent may drop out when she learns that her parents will not really follow through with their threat to take her car away. A criminal offender on probation may drop out when he perceives that the practitioner will not recommend a return to jail for doing so. The practitioner who does not routinely assess clients' attitudes about intervention may experience these dropouts more frequently.

Confusion about the Practitioner's Intervention Methods   A client who does not understand the nature of the practitioner's methods and how they are supposed to help is likely to become confused, frustrated, and even angry, particularly if the intervention process moves more slowly than the client expects it should. Clients are less likely to drop out of treatment (and more likely to achieve goals) if the practitioner explains at the outset of the relationship the methods of intervention and a rationale for their utility (Frank & Frank, 1993).

Agency administrative procedures can sometimes clarify client expectations about intervention. One longitudinal study of 950 child and adolescent outpatients indicated that a 45.7-percent reduction in the early termination rate was achieved when the agency made changes in its clinical procedures, including fewer assessment sessions, more focused intervention techniques, and a shorter time interval between receipt of the referral and the first agency appointment (Lazaratou, Anagnostopoulos, & Viassopoulos, 2006).

The Unexpected Death of the Client   Some client deaths, such as those occurring in hospital and hospice settings, are anticipated by the practitioner and other members of the treatment team. When the client's death is known to be inevitable or a strong possibility, the practitioner can organize his or her interventions with that fact in mind and help the client and significant others (and him- or herself) plan for that event and its aftermath. Other deaths, however—including most suicides and deaths due to accidents in the client's outside life—are not anticipated. These endings may be particularly devastating to the practitioner. In the case of suicide, the practitioner may question his or her professional competence, be consumed by guilt, and feel unsure about how to approach the client's significant others, if at all. Even when the death is unrelated to the intervention, the practitioner will usually have a desire to bring a sense of closure to the relationship but perhaps not feel confident about how to do so.

Now we will move on to another category of unplanned endings—those initiated by the practitioner, about which the client may not be in agreement.

Unplanned Endings Initiated by the Practitioner

The practitioner may initiate endings intentionally, despite a client's failure to achieve his or her stated goals. This may occur in the following situations.

The Client Will Not Adhere to an Intervention Plan Deemed Reasonable by the Practitioner   Most clinical interventions require that the practitioner and client share responsibility for the change process. It is difficult to help a client who does not adhere to an intervention plan that he or she has agreed to and perhaps helped to write. In this circumstance, the practitioner should first consider that the plan may not be appropriate and, if not, revise it with the client. If the client still does not participate actively in the process, the practitioner may be justified in ending the attempted intervention. Clients who will not adhere to such plans are often ambivalent or involuntary and may require additional time to decide whether they want to invest in the help-seeking process.

The Client Abuses Boundaries in the Clinical Relationship   Boundaries are rules regarding the physical and emotional limits of relationships between practitioners and clients. They include rules about five aspects of those relationships (Bruhn, Levine, & Levine, 1993). Contact time refers to how much time the practitioner will spend in the company of the client, including their frequency of face-to-face, phone, and even e-mail interactions. Types of information to be shared include the range of topics they will discuss together. These may be limited to the client's formal concerns or may extend to other personal and social topics. Physical closeness refers to the practitioner's expectations about personal space when in the client's company, including how closely together the participants sit, their eye contact, use of touch, and range of nonverbal communications. Territory includes the range of physical spaces they may share. This may be limited to an office or might include the client's home, school, or other social settings. Emotional space refers to the extent to which they will share feelings about sensitive topics. The nature of clinical intervention does not give a practitioner a right to pry into all areas of the client's life, just as there are limits to what the client can ask the practitioner.

Boundaries vary depending on the practitioner, program, and type of client. While some boundaries are unspoken, practitioners should review boundaries with the client and the limits they imply about their interactions at the beginning of their work. If a client is unable to respect these limits (which make demands on the practitioner as well), it may be appropriate to end the intervention. Examples include clients who repeatedly call the practitioner at home without permission, come to the agency unannounced to demand meetings, or persist in questioning the practitioner about inappropriate personal topics such as his or her sex life.

The Client Engages in Unacceptable Disruptive Behavior   Clients are expected to observe rules and agency policies regarding general behavior. These rules are designed to ensure that all agency clients receive services in a relatively calm environment and that the behavior of some clients does not intrude upon the rights of other clients and staff. The client who monopolizes a group intervention or is overly aggressive or threatening may be asked to leave the group. The client who comes to appointments after drinking or using drugs may have services terminated. Disruptive clients are often warned about the effects of their actions before being dismissed from an agency.

Case Study: Out with a Bang

My client Dennis, a large twenty-two-year-old single man, had schizoaffective disorder, a mental illness. He was also a frightened, angry young man who often lashed out verbally at others in an intimidating manner. The staff in my case management program felt challenged not only to help Dennis adjust from hospital to community living but also to differentiate his illness-related behavior from his basic personality. We tolerated his verbal abuses largely because of his mental illness and our awareness that, in contrast to his bombastic presentation, he was actually fearful of other people. Still, Dennis could be so inappropriately aggressive with others that we had to set firm limits on his behavior. One limit was that he could not come to the agency, because he often ridiculed other clients in the waiting room. I would not meet Dennis at his apartment either, because he often made threatening remarks about having weapons nearby if I didn't "do right" by him. I was not afraid of Dennis but felt strongly that he needed to understand the seriousness of his antisocial behavior. I would only meet him in public places such as McDonald's, where he was far less likely to act out.

One day, upset by an argument with his mother, Dennis showed up at our agency. I was there but not immediately available. Dennis was not willing to wait—he demanded to see me! When the secretary hesitated, he positioned himself close to her face and screamed obscenities at her in full view of other clients and staff. The secretary ran to my office and beat on my door, telling me to come out and take care of Dennis. Of course I did so. I told him to leave immediately! He refused and began to threaten me in the same loud tone of voice. I had to shout at him even more loudly so that he would be quiet and hear my message. Suddenly realizing his mistake, Dennis left abruptly. I spent the next thirty minutes helping the secretary calm down.

That was Dennis's last visit. Even though he had a mental illness and needed help, we could not accommodate him in our particular setting. During the next few weeks he begged me to keep working with him, but I refused. My clinical director would not consider allowing him to remain on the agency caseload, and I supported the decision. I felt badly because in spite of it all I got along with Dennis as well as any practitioner had, and I actually like him. We suggested to Dennis and his mother where he could apply for similar services, but I don't know if he ever did.

The Practitioner Has Negative Feelings about the Client   Professionals do not like to admit that they might at times drive some clients away. It must be acknowledged, however, that at times a client may drop out of clinical intervention because of subtle, and perhaps unconscious, encouragement by the worker to do so (Hunsley, Aubrey, Vestervelt, & Vito, 1999).

While practitioners try to maintain a professional commitment to helping all clients, they are human beings with personal preferences and may not be equally interested in all types of clients. They may have difficulty generating enthusiasm for some presenting problems, diagnostic groups, or clients with certain personality characteristics. They may become frustrated with a client's behavior over the course of the intervention or become angry with a client. Practitioners' motivations may be affected by distracting issues in their own personal life or a desire to avoid dealing with clients' problems that are similar to their own. Psychodynamic practitioners summarize these feelings as negative countertransference reactions.

It is important for practitioners to engage in reflection and supervisory consultation to explore the reasons for such reactions. If these situations are not attended to, the professional may behave in ways that encourage the client to drop out—possibly without consciously realizing it. The practitioner may fail to explore the client's relevant problem issues as they arise, become overly confrontational, fail to explore a client's ambivalence, and in a variety of other subtle ways discourage the client's participation. A client who perceives the practitioner's negative attitudes may drop out, and the practitioner may feel relieved.

Case Study: She Wouldn't Pay Her Bill

It was only after she dropped out of therapy that I realized I had probably driven Patricia away. A physician, a colleague of mine who treated her for depression and addiction to an anti-anxiety drug, had referred Patricia to me. She was depressed, anxious, rather paranoid, and had many physical complaints. Her goals were to improve her mood and come to terms with her suspiciousness of other people.

Patricia was thirty-two and recently married when we met. I saw her for almost two years. We met on a weekly basis, although she occasionally took short breaks from our meetings. At those times she wanted to try functioning on her own, which was fine with me. In truth, I found her difficult to work with. Patricia tended to blame her troubles on other people or on her vague physical problems. She was reluctant to accept any responsibility for the part she played in her problems. None of her physical complaints were ever confirmed as diseases, but she persisted in seeing endocrinologists, gynecologists, and neurologists about them. Some of the diagnostic tests were inconclusive, which encouraged Patricia to stay focused on the physical symptoms. Also, she was always slow to pay her bill, and I tired of reminding her about this. Despite my negative feelings, I tried my best to help her, and in some ways I think I did. She said that I had helped her cope with the death of her father, make some career decisions, improve her social skills, and increase her confidence.

One afternoon Patricia was venting about the fact that her previous therapist, the physician, had done poor work with her. She made many derogatory remarks about this man that I perceived to be unfounded. This made me angry! It so happened that she was again several months behind in her payments to me. I confronted her quite sternly that day, stating that perhaps her comments about the physician represented her avoidance of dealing with her problems directly. I added that her failure to pay the bill seemed to be a reflection of her ambivalence about therapy. To my surprise, Patricia abruptly stood up and left, actually running out the door. The last thing she said, hysterically, was, "You'll get your money!" A few days later I got a letter from her, dated that same day. She wrote that I had seemed distant and angry. She claimed that I was attending to my own agendas that day rather than hers and that she had been insulted by my comments. She would never return because of my obviously negative feelings for her.

Patricia had always been extremely sensitive to nonverbal behaviors, and I think that she picked up on my feelings accurately that final day. But I had not been aware of those feelings myself! I think that I might have managed our relationship better with a clinical supervisor to help me with my reactions to Patricia—at the time I did not have supervision. I had never enjoyed working with Patricia, but I tried to be helpful. I think she was right—I had made those final comments as a way to vent my own anger rather than to serve her needs.

The Practitioner Is Frustrated with Other Job Stresses, Such As the Overwhelming Demands of a Large or Difficult Caseload   In many public agencies practitioners are required to carry high caseloads, many more clients than they can adequately serve. It is difficult to keep up with the clinical status of so many clients, so those with the most pressing needs often have the most contact with the practitioner. The professional's failure to follow up regularly with other clients, understandable as it may be, can result in the client "fading" from intervention. This may be a relief for the professional if it makes his or her caseload more manageable.

The Client Demonstrates a Lack of Expected Progress without the Perceived Potential to Make Future Progress   Some practitioners, despite their best efforts, are not able to help some clients. This may be due to the practitioner's lack of ability in the situation or the client's lack of willingness or readiness to follow through with appropriate change activities. It may be prudent for the practitioner to refer the client to another clinical worker or to suggest that the client pursue other means for resolving his or her concerns. These decisions should not be made impulsively but should follow client-practitioner discussion and perhaps supervisory consultation.

It should now be evident that there are many circumstances in which the ending of an intervention leaves the client or practitioner (or both) feeling that the process was incomplete or perhaps a failure. However, some strategies can increase the likelihood of the desired endings.

Planned Endings

Practitioners prefer planned endings—those that both parties can look ahead to and process. These occur in the following situations.

There Is Mutual Agreement That the Client Has Achieved His or Her Goals or Has Reached a Point of "Diminishing Returns"   When the client completely or substantially achieves his or her goals, the ending can be a satisfying experience for both the client and practitioner. In one survey, fifty-nine clinical social workers described their most common observations of client activities during these endings as reviewing progress, evaluating the therapy experience, and sharing feelings of pride, accomplishment, and independence (Fortune, 1987). The practitioners' reactions tended to be positive as well.

Sometimes, particularly if a client's goals are not concrete and the intervention is open-ended, it is difficult for the practitioner to decide when the client has achieved optimal growth. Private practitioners have the additional problem of weighing the issue of the client's relative growth against their concerns about income. Mathews (1989) provides a useful rule of thumb for these situations. Practitioners can ask themselves, "If I had a waiting list, would I still be seeing this client?" If the answer is no, it is probably time to end the intervention.

The Professional Must Observe Externally Imposed Time Limitations   Clinical practitioners classified as temporary staff, trainees, residents, and students begin their agency experiences with a clear understanding that they have a limited amount of time (measured in weeks, months, or perhaps years) to work there. They may need to observe time limits on their interventions even if such limits are not consistent with their theoretical orientations.

The Professional Utilizes Time-Limited Intervention Modalities (Based on Theory, Agency, or Managed-Care Mandates)   When clinical intervention is organized with attention to concrete end dates, the practitioner is likely to plan for that ending. Still, practitioners do not always adhere to such limits. In one study of fifty-nine clinical practitioners, 41 percent went beyond predetermined ending dates (Fortune, 1987). This was due to their perceptions of clients' incomplete progress, inability to cope on their own, presenting problems becoming worse, or stated desire to continue. In another study of ninety clients seen in a university counseling center, the lengthier interventions were associated with clients having borderline and histrionic personality traits, abandonment concerns, and intense anger (Hilsenroth et al., 1998).

The Professional Determines That She or He Is Not Competent to Help the Client with the Particular Problem Issue and Arranges for a Referral or Transfer   Practitioners have an ethical responsibility not to work with clients whose needs they cannot reasonably expect to meet, as illustrated in the following vignette. The practitioner may recognize the need to make a referral immediately or at some later time during the intervention.

Case Study: The Priest

Within the first fifteen minutes of my assessment of Tom I became overwhelmed. I had more than five years of experience as a psychotherapist but felt completely inadequate to help him! He was actually Father Tom, a priest who had been dismissed from his parish duties. His presenting problem was sexual addiction. He had been in long-term affairs with female parishioners for many years. Frankly, I was surprised that he avoided scandal for as long as he did. But Tom was a genuinely troubled man who realized he had destroyed his career and still could not control his compulsive behaviors.

I was not the first therapist Tom had seen. He had spent time in a nationally recognized inpatient program for sex addicts and was later followed by several well-known sex therapists in the eastern United States. He had wound up living with relatives in my city and, having no money, was seeking counseling at my public agency. We had no special programs and no staff with experience in sexual disorders. On top of it all, I was a member of a Catholic Church and was having trouble reconciling our client-therapist relationship with my ingrained attitudes about parishioner-priest relationships. I admitted to Tom during that hour that neither I nor anyone else at the agency had expertise in his problem area. I met with him several times to provide support but then arranged for him to be evaluated by a sex therapist in our city. I was able to arrange for a free initial evaluation, given Tom's financial condition. He seemed satisfied with the outcome.

The Practitioner Departs from the Setting (Often Necessitating a Transfer of the Client to Another Practitioner)   Because this reason for ending is so common, it is worth reviewing factors that help the new practitioner facilitate a successful transfer (Super, 1982). After receiving the "terminated" client, the new practitioner should:

Acknowledge the client's loss early in the first session
Deal with loss issues first, if the client raises them
Be sensitive to any subtle allusions to loss communicated by the client
Encourage discussion of the previous practitioner
Clearly communicate a willingness to work with client
Be self-aware of feelings of competition with the previous practitioner

Clinical transfers are not always successful, particularly when the client has been successful with and emotionally attached to the previous professional. Both practitioners need to carefully prepare the client for the change.

The Client Fires the Practitioner   Some clients who are dissatisfied with the services being provided by the clinical practitioner ask for a transfer. If the practitioner disagrees with the need for such a change, the ending can be awkward for both parties.

Case Study: The Pushy Psychologist

Times certainly do change. When I began working as a psychologist twenty years ago, the practitioner was considered to be the expert in all things clinical, including deciding whether he or she and the client were suited to work together. If a client was dissatisfied with the course of intervention and asked to see another counselor, the request was rarely taken seriously unless the practitioner agreed. Usually such a request was seen as a sign of the client's resistance to appropriate intervention. On a few occasions my clients requested intra-agency transfers. My supervisor and I always talked with the client separately about the request, but invariably the client was advised to keep working with me or seek services elsewhere. But now, with new practice theories, the emphasis on client empowerment, and legal developments, clients have a stronger voice in the treatments they receive. This includes their right to "fire," so to speak, one practitioner and begin working with another one at the same agency. This is what happened between Rita and myself.

Rita was a sixty-five-year-old divorced woman who lived alone and sought help for depression, concerns about her aging parents, and a strained relationship with her only child, a son. In my view, Rita was a dependent woman who had always been taken care of, first by her own parents and then by her son. She liked to ventilate her troubles, but she would not take action to resolve them. I knew that Rita needed time to discover and develop her self-care capacities. I thought I was quite patient with her. But I did include a task-oriented focus to my intervention because, as I told Rita, it was not productive for her to merely talk about her problems and their possible solutions. Rita said she agreed with my approach, but later she criticized me for "setting her up to fail" and "not understanding her limitations." Several months into our relationship she said that she wanted to work with another practitioner. We discussed her complaints but could not resolve them. In fact, things got personal, and she began to berate me about everything from my hair to my choice of shoes. I referred Rita to a conversation with my supervisor.

My supervisor's practice in these situations was to talk with me, talk with the client, talk with me again, and then make a recommendation. He understood my position that Rita's request was based on her anxiety about taking initiative and that granting a transfer would amount to our supporting her avoidance. At the same time, he was convinced that Rita would not work with me anymore, even if given no options at our agency. Considering the seriousness of her problems, he did not want Rita to be terminated. He recommended that she be transferred to another practitioner, a woman whom Rita might see as more nurturing even if she worked the same way I did. I did not contest the decision. I was angry but eventually I agreed that she had developed a dislike of me that would be difficult for her to overcome.

Rita and I did not have another conversation in my office. But our agency was small, and I saw her in the waiting room and hallways now and then. Initially, this was awkward for both of us. Eventually, though, it occurred to me that our seeing each other briefly in these ways was helpful. In time we learned to be cordial with one another. Looking back, I wish that I could have seen Rita privately one more time during her transfer, for just a few minutes. It might have helped both of us to look ahead and wish each other well.

The Expected Death of the Client   These endings are common in hospice agencies and other practice settings where services are provided to people with serious physical illnesses. An example of this powerful type of ending is included in the next chapter.

The Roles of Administrators in Clinical Endings

Another type of ending involves the worker's departure after agency administrators eliminate or downsize a program or otherwise lay off clinical staff. It is not often articulated that administrators can and should play a major role in the clinical endings that follow those actions (Harrigan, Fauri, & Netting, 1998). Administrators are responsible for maintaining continuity and service satisfaction for clients and staff when personnel changes occur. Policies and procedures should be in place to ensure that staff turnover does not place undue hardships on clients who need to be transferred. Closer to day-to-day clinical operations, managers (in addition to clinical supervisors) must oversee particular employee transitions and work to maintain agency morale. These tasks can be difficult when a program is downsized and staff must be laid off. Not only will the well-being of the clients of those particular staff be at risk, but if morale problems affect other clinical staff, their clients can be adversely affected as well.

Case Study: The Layoffs

The circumstances of my layoff were handled badly from the start. I was the adolescent services coordinator at a public social services agency that only employed about twenty clinical staff. Decisions and rumors emanating from the small executive staff meetings always circulated quickly. Being a public agency, staff was aware that our financial stability fluctuated from year to year. We had never experienced layoffs, however, when our executive director announced that because of funding shortfalls three staff would have to be let go. Those staff would be notified within two weeks.

Everyone fell into a panic, worried that he or she would be among the three people to be dismissed. I was certainly worried. I had seniority at the agency but felt vulnerable because of my high salary. For those few weeks none of the clinical staff seemed able to concentrate on their work. Rumors identified any of a dozen people as possible victims of the downsizing. Why did the executive director make his announcement and then let us all alone for two weeks? Agency morale nosedived, and the administrators were nowhere to be seen. Finally, I was told on a Friday afternoon that myself and two other staff who provided adolescent services were being let go. The director said that he had decided to eliminate the least financially viable of the agency's programs. I wasn't convinced that this was his actual reasoning. I suspected the decision might be in part personal. We argued for awhile, but clearly his decision was final. I was given seventy-five days' notice.

I always carried a full caseload of more than thirty clients. During the next two months I had to attend to their needs, try to manage my own anger and sadness, arrange transfers, and end my interventions. It wasn't easy. I had trouble controlling my feelings when meeting with clients, and I'm sure they noticed. I told them that I was being laid off because of the program being deleted; that I was not choosing voluntarily to leave. I was permitted to transfer them to other agency staff if they wished.

There were three interesting reactions I saw in my clients. Many of them expressed concern for me but returned pretty quickly to their own clinical problems. Other clients got more upset and talked about doing something to protest the director's decision. I discouraged their actions, and none of them ever did contact the director. Some clients actually gave me information about job openings in the area, which was thoughtful. I tried not to dwell on myself during sessions, but I'm sure that some of my clients could see that I was upset. I suspected that they began withholding information about themselves to protect me from more stress.

And what did the executive director do during this time? Nothing! He seemed to think that it was best to keep a distance from me and the other staff who were being dismissed. I really don't know what he or the other administrators could have done to make the layoff process go any better. I do think that it would have been helpful for them to maintain some connection with the staff rather than to isolate themselves. Perhaps they could have written a letter to all the clients explaining what was happening and reassuring them of the future of the agency. Agency morale stayed low for months afterward. Some staff, concerned about the long-term stability of the agency, found new jobs and left. That presented me with another problem—there were fewer people to transfer my clients to! The administrators ignored the fact that many clients felt insecure with the ongoing staff changes. They left it to the staff to take care of clinical issues. But to me this was an administrative issue as well. I will have more to say about the roles of administrators in chapter 10, in the section about practitioner reactions to client suicide.

Summary

This chapter reviewed many positive and negative circumstances in which clinical endings occur. Most practitioners experience all of these during their careers. We certainly prefer positive endings, but the manner in which clinical practice unfolds is unpredictable and often out of practitioners' control. All professions articulate ethical obligations for practitioners to do their best to facilitate interventions that end productively for their clients and themselves. The remainder of this book is dedicated to articulating such strategies. In the next chapter we look at examples of endings that were particularly powerful in helping clients realize their goals.

Chapter 2

The Importance of Closure

Building on our review of the many types of endings that occur in clinical practice, I focus in this chapter on how positive endings are significant to the well- being of both the client and practitioner. I elaborate on this topic with discussions of eight case vignettes. All of them have been provided by clinical practitioners as examples of situations in which the ending turned out unexpectedly to be the most important aspect of the intervention. The closure that was achieved served to resolve the clients' and practitioners' work on problem issues, work that had been unsatisfying during the earlier stages of intervention. The chapter concludes with general principles for practitioners and supervisors to follow in maximizing the chances for positive endings.

Understanding Closure

Closure, a central concept in this book, was briefly defined in the last chapter but is expanded upon here. The term characterizes an ending in which the practitioner and the client have the opportunity to:

◆ Bring their work to a mutually understood (but not necessarily satisfactory) end and to realize without ambiguity that the relationship is over

◆ Review the positive and negative aspects of their work (since all interventions will include some of both)

◆ Identify not merely what the client learned, but what they each learned from the clinical process

◆ Perhaps acknowledge mutual feelings about the relationship, if appropriate (professional boundaries always put limits on the practitioner's disclosures)

◆ Mutually experience an enhanced willingness to invest in future relationships and to use what was learned as a basis for moving forward with confidence into new relationships

In this chapter we see how these elements of closure were significant to the work of the practitioners as well as to their clients.

An ending might be successful without closure, that is, without all these issues being addressed. Following is a brief checklist of items for practitioners that helps to determine whether the intervention was positive or negative for the client:

1. Does the client show positive changes, such as fewer symptoms, fewer problems, improved behaviors, greater knowledge, and more stable moods?

2. Is the client satisfied that he or she got what he or she came for (whether or not the practitioner thinks the client got what he or she needed)?
3. Is the client interested in working toward any new postintervention goals on his or her own?
4. Does the client understand what he or she was doing prior to the intervention (with regard to the presenting issue) that wasn't working? Does he or she know how to avoid the recurrence of similar problems in the future?

The important point here is that it is not always essential for the practitioner and client to experience a sense of shared finality to their clinical work in order for the client to receive significant benefits from it.

The Power of Closure: Eight Illustrations

The vignettes presented in this chapter represent different types of clinical situations and challenges. They all involve work with either individuals or families. The first vignette describes how a practitioner who felt that she had "botched" her meeting with a couple was able to redeem herself with an intervention that produced a positive ending. In the next two vignettes, the clients unexpectedly brought objects to the final sessions that served as ideal discussion topics for processing those endings. Next are two stories of community rituals that provided moving contexts for separation. Two examples follow of client deaths that illustrate both the possibilities and problems involved in seeking closure with such a final ending. Finally, there is a story of a "bad" clinical ending that followed a "good" beginning, but the negative aspects of the ending were reversed at the last moment.

In the second and third illustrations the clients surprised their practitioners by bringing gifts to the final session. Unlike typical "thank you" items such as cards, the gifts symbolized for the practitioners the course of the clinical work they had shared with the client. The practitioners used these gifts as the basis for ending conversations that therapeutically summed up their work. In each case the clinician had already perceived the clinical experience as positive, but the unexpected events during the final session left them with an even deeper sense of satisfaction.

The practitioner in this vignette was having a bad day before meeting a new couple, and her frustrations spilled over into her session with them. To her credit, she was able to put the fiasco of that meeting behind her and, despite her initial doubts, help the client. The contrast between the first and final sessions helped her feel validated as a practitioner.

Case Study: Bad Beginning, Better Ending

My ending story involves a bad beginning. I first saw Tina, an overweight thirty-eight-year-old Caucasian woman, and her husband, Marshall, age thirty-five, for marital counseling. Unfortunately, I was caught in traffic and running late for their first appointment. After waiting for awhile, they had gone back to the receptionist to ask if there was a problem. When I finally came out to meet them, still flustered by my stress and the heat that day, they seemed angry with me and with each other. To make things worse, I had planned to videotape the session for supervision purposes. Explaining this procedure and getting the consent forms signed made our rushed meeting even more awkward. The session quickly collapsed into an angry interchange with Tina and Marshall screaming at each other. They ignored my attempts to get them to speak more calmly. They kept bringing up material from the past and arguing with each other in a repetitive, destructive way. I tried to intervene, to teach them some beginning communication skills, but my effort went unheeded. I felt that I had lost control of the session, never really having had control of it in the first place, and they didn't seem happy with me when they left. They did not seem to feel that they had gotten anything out of the meeting. I didn't think they would come back, and I blamed myself for poor preparation.

To my surprise, they returned for a second session. They were calmer, and I was able to get more information from them. Marshall, it turned out, was gay and had many affairs with men. Tina actually approved of this. Both of them had AIDS. Marshall had contracted the virus from sexual contact, and Tina had contracted it while using intravenous drugs several years ago. Tina had two adolescent children from a previous marriage who lived with their father. Although I was able to complete the assessment, the couple was not able to be clear about how they wanted their relationship to be different. Marshall kept saying that there wasn't any use in his coming to counseling, so we all agreed that Tina would come alone next time.

This is where the clinical work started happening. Tina revealed a history of ongoing sexual abuse by her father when she was a teenager. We worked on this issue using a trauma-focused, solution-focused approach. Tina was motivated for this work, so we made a great deal of progress in only four sessions. Tina processed her memories of the abuse, her relationship with her mother, and the impact of the abuse on her life. She came to understand that she married a gay man because she found sexual relationships threatening, and that her weight was protection against men being attracted to her. Her drug abuse was a cover-up for her pain. Tina learned how she could protect herself in other ways from men who might harm her, such as by setting appropriate boundaries with them.

We ended our work because I was leaving the agency, but Tina said that she was ready to stop anyway. Tina said that therapy had helped her to understand and resolve a lot of what had been driving her behavior. The day of our last session, she had gone to a job interview and came to the office dressed in business clothes. This ending was so striking to me because the beginning session, just one month earlier, had been so difficult and overwhelming. We spent the hour reflecting on Tina's progress. I asked her a series of questions about comparing her self-image, attitudes about her husband, and ideas for her future at the beginning and end of our work together. She no longer reported marital difficulties. We also talked about the course of her relationship with me. Tina admitted that she had felt hopeless after that first session. It had seemed to her that I wasn't going to be able to handle her and her husband. They both suspected that I was too young to understand them. Tina said that in the end she got a lot more out of our work than she had expected. The ending was quite gratifying to me.

Case Study: The Photo Collage

Allison was a twenty-six-year-old graduate student who came to our agency because she was overwhelmed with anxiety. She identified several family-of-origin issues as sources of her distress. Allison felt that her family life had always been chaotic. She had a brother just two years younger who was born with autism, and he was institutionalized when Allison was five. Her parents divorced when she was six and, in Allison's words, her world fell apart. She was raised by her mother, and they had little money. Having a positive sense of family was important to Allison, and its absence had always disturbed her. Allison was planning a career in child welfare work. She was also engaged to be married.

The theme of endings is often significant with clients at our agency. It is normal for college students to separate from their families, move away from their home communities, and experience new relationships that may end abruptly. Allison was distressed at this time because she saw her graduation and marriage as signifying a further separation from her family of origin. She was beginning a new career, planned to have children of her own, and might move farther away from her relatives. She wondered if her new family life would be better than her family of origin.

Allison was particularly concerned about her changing relationship with her brother. She had always been fond of him, visiting him regularly, but she also experienced guilt about the relationship. Had she been kind enough to him? Was it wrong to have felt embarrassed at times about having him in the family? Why was he disabled instead of her? How closely would she keep in contact with him after she was married? Her brother had been something of a family secret. Allison had learned from her parents that it was not appropriate to talk about him with outsiders. Of course, her brother was a major topic of her counseling with me.

Allison was a motivated, insightful client, and she seemed to benefit from her therapy. I helped her draw on her strengths to bring more structure to her life and manage some of her relationships with less emotional reactivity. Knowing her graduation date, I was able to implement a systematic termination process with her. Over a period of weeks we reviewed her progress and what she had learned about herself and her family relationships. I helped her look ahead to how she might sustain her gains.

During our final visit Allison surprised me. She had brought in a collage of photographs featuring herself and her brother, one that she had made many years ago. We had not talked about her doing this. But she wanted to share it with me, and she did so in depth. All the pictures featured the two of them when they were toddlers, before he was institutionalized. Allison pointed to each picture and told me a story associated with it. We spent half the session looking at and talking about the collage. I was touched at how Allison referred to her brother as such a beautiful child.

This act on Allison's part affirmed for me in a special way that our work had been important to her. I saw the collage as a gift to me, although it was not for me to keep and was probably not intended as such. Allison's decision to share the collage with me was a risk—she rarely showed it to anyone, fearing their negative reactions. It was a testament to her trust in me and her willingness to share something that she had believed was taboo to most others. It made this ending, which I already saw as positive, into an experience of joy that was quite motivating for my future clinical work.

Three characteristics of closure are evident in this example. First, the client's decision to focus the final session on a different topic than usual underscored her awareness that the clinical work was ending and that she wanted to recognize the event in a special way. Second, the client's bringing in such a personal item as the collage and allowing the practitioner entry into this intimate part of her life demonstrated that she was satisfied with the clinical experience and her relationship with the practitioner. Through a greater informality during that final hour the practitioner indirectly communicated her positive feelings about the client. Finally, the practitioner stated directly that this experience was highly rewarding and in that way contributed to her career motivation.

Case Study: The Pregnant Therapist

I became pregnant with my first child while working as a community mental health center therapist. I worked up until my final month of pregnancy. Many of my clients had interesting reactions to my condition, but I have an especially fond memory of its effect on my ending with a client named Brenna.

Brenna was forty-five, married but separated, and had a son and daughter. I worked at times with all three of them. In fact, I first saw her son, who was twenty-one, when he became a member of a therapy group I led with another worker. He had a dual diagnosis of mental illness and substance abuse. His participation at the agency was sporadic, but Brenna began coming to see me regularly for help with how she should respond to her son's troublesome behavior. I wound up meeting with Brenna about every two weeks for the next year, providing her with support so that she could manage the household. Brenna brought her daughter, age seventeen, along to see me for awhile because of conflicts between them. I did not take these lightly, but it seemed that her daughter was experiencing normal adolescent desires for autonomy. After about five sessions I did not feel that there was a need for her daughter to continue meeting with us. Brenna, however, seemed to benefit very much from her work with me. When I informed her, well in advance, of my last day prior to taking maternity leave, she decided to end her counseling.

Before our last meeting, Brenna called to ask if she could bring her daughter along to the session. I said sure, and later they arrived with a few packages. I opened them and was absolutely shocked to find an assortment of beautiful handmade baby clothes. Brenna and her daughter had made an afghan, a bib, booties, and a few other items. I was overwhelmed—they were so beautiful—and the act was so thoughtful! At first I didn't know what to say, except thank you. Then it occurred to me that I could use this moment and these items as a metaphor for their growth during the time that they had been seeing me.

I shared with them my observation that they had organized their joint effort to make the clothes so well. I asked detailed questions, such as, "Who made this?" "Who made that?" "How did you make it?" "Who chose the patterns?" "Who decided where to start?" I kept emphasizing that each item was a beautiful product and that making the baby clothes required careful teamwork between the two of them. They had done something together to be proud of, and they had not fought during the process. I put the activity into a context of representing how they had been able to come together to work toward a common goal while still being separate people. They were able to reflect on these themes with me, and they agreed that perhaps there was more common ground in their relationship than they had thought. I must add that I was surprised to learn that the project had been the daughter's idea, even though I had not seen her very often.

I wrote them a thank-you note shortly afterward. In the note I repeated the themes we had discussed in the last session and told them that I would think about them every time I used the clothes. Now, more than twenty years later, I still have those items and obviously still think about Brenna and her daughter. Their activity affirmed that the daughter and mother had valued their involvement with me, and the clothes-making process showed me that they had improved their relationship.

I know that the issue of accepting gifts from clients is controversial. I have worked at agencies where staff was strictly forbidden to do so and at others where staff was advised to use discretion in accepting or rejecting gifts. I think it was appropriate for me to accept these gifts. The process was so significant to the work that the mother had been doing with me that it would have been harsh not to accept them.

This practitioner and her clients experienced four characteristics of closure. The session described here was clearly their last, as the practitioner was beginning her maternity leave immediately afterward and would not be available for additional contact for some time. The clients stated their desire to end as well, so these two factors facilitated a clean break. The practitioner creatively used the theme of the mother and daughter's working together on the gift items as a means of reviewing the positive course of their intervention. It was partly for this reason that the practitioner decided to accept the gifts. The gifts were indications of the clients' positive feelings about their clinical experience and relationship. The practitioner's gracious acceptance of them, and her thoughtful discussion of each item, was an indirect communication of her own positive feelings. Finally, the practitioner helped the clients to see their gift-making project as evidence of their increased capacity for a positive relationship with each other (and, by extension, persons outside the family).

In many types of clinical intervention the practitioner attempts to initiate a process through which an isolated client becomes less reliant on formal service providers and becomes more integrated into natural community life with informal supports. The practitioners in the next two vignettes achieved success in this task and experienced a tremendous sense of closure, because they each had opportunities to watch their clients interact with the support systems they had helped to develop.

Case Study: From the Laundromat to the Park

I once supervised a social work student, named Jane, who devised a marvelous and creative ending plan with a client. It provides an example of how the end of the clinical relationship can be organized as a transition for the client who must move on from temporary formal supports to permanent natural supports. Jane's ending plan was based on a model of intervention I had used in my own work that focused on the development of indigenous community supports for clients.

The agency was a private multiservice community center located in an urban neighborhood in a large city. It provided programs and resources to help clients meet basic needs for food, shelter, and safety. A client in our job-training program complained to me one day about one of her neighbors. She said the woman stayed in her apartment all day long with a screaming infant. This client was concerned about possible child abuse or neglect. I asked Jane to investigate the situation with a home visit. This is how Jackie became involved with our agency.

Jackie was a twenty-eight-year-old African American single mother of a two-month-old son. She had worked as a maid for a wealthy family until she became pregnant. Her boyfriend, the father of her child, had abandoned her, and Jackie was fired from her job. Jackie had little money and was socially isolated. She was living on welfare benefits with nowhere to go and no one to turn to. Jackie was not abusing or neglecting her son, but she had many basic needs that were not being met. She was pleased to welcome Jane into her life, partly because the two women had so much in common. Jane was also African American and just a few years older than her client, and they shared similar backgrounds. Jane and Jackie became quite attached to each other. It was a testament to Jane's maturity as a practitioner that she realized the danger of her level of attachment to the client. She didn't want to become her client's friend, and she knew that Jackie might become too dependent on her. Jane understood that she needed to intervene with Jackie efficiently and then end their relationship.

Jane and Jackie worked together for two months, spending many hours together each week. Jane helped Jackie acquire additional money and other benefits to live on, but she focused primarily on her extreme social isolation. Jane wanted to help Jackie develop social supports and had several creative ways for bringing this about. First, all their early meetings took place in a neighborhood laundromat. This was the place where mothers with young children from the community were most likely to gather. Jackie met many other women there who had similar interests and life situations, and these women became her friends. After awhile, Jane targeted the neighborhood park as the site for their meetings. This was the second most popular gathering place for mothers with young children. The plan worked beautifully. Jackie's social isolation disappeared.

Soon, Jackie was functioning well as a member of her community. She felt good about herself, her friends, and her chances to be able to support herself and her young son. It was time to end the agency services. Jane wanted their ending to be a celebration of Jackie's progress. The two women organized a big picnic in the park for their last meeting. Jackie invited her new friends and their children. All six of the women who came brought food and party items. They all put a lot of preparation into the event, because they knew that it was special for Jackie, to recognize how far she had come. It was ironic that Jane, the practitioner, was the only member of the group who would be leaving! It was a joyful occasion for all the women. Jane felt sad but very proud. Before she left the park that day, Jane took Jackie aside for a few minutes to reflect on their work and their relationship and to affirm her progress. They hugged, and Jane drove off. Jackie stayed behind to help the other women clean up.

This unusual community-based ending was a carefully planned ritual that celebrated what the client had gained, especially her social skills and level of community involvement. Rather than Jackie's merely talking about what she had learned from the intervention process, she actually demonstrated it in her natural environment! It may have been a somewhat bittersweet ending for Jane, the practitioner, having to share Jackie's attention at this final meeting. But it was a relatively lengthy activity, and they did take time to privately share feelings about their time together. Jane was so pleased with the client's progress that she experienced a great reward—stronger faith in the power of her clinical work.

Case Study: A Spiritual Celebration

Probably my most moving ending experience occurred when I worked at an agency that served juvenile offenders. The agency provided educational services, day treatment, crisis intervention, and intensive home-based services. All the clients had criminal histories, and most were diagnosed with severe emotional disturbances. The courts usually referred the kids to us. All clinical staff provided a lot of case management and advocacy services for clients, doing whatever it took to get them productively involved in their communities. At the same time, we had to regularly file reports on their behavior to the probation officers, which made for a partially adversarial relationship. Almost all the clients were African American, and I was the only white worker in the agency.

I worked in the home-based program. One of my clients was Eddie, a nineteen-year-old African American male. He had spent the previous five years confined to a correctional facility for drug trafficking, weapons possession, and manslaughter. He was delivered directly from that facility into our program. I met Eddie along with his probation officer when he arrived home that day. Eddie was quite intimidating to me. He was big, muscular, intense, and sullen. Our relationship seemed to go nowhere for two weeks as I checked on him each day at his home. Eddie did not say a single word to me until I had spent about fourteen hours in his company. His family members, including grandmother, mother, and three sisters, were more friendly and approachable.

To my astonishment and delight, this turned out to be a successful intervention. During those first few weeks I talked to Eddie a lot in spite of the fact that he never responded. I tried to make him feel comfortable, to show respect for his family, and to affirm his reluctance to place any trust in me. I talked to an extent that was excessive even for me, a guy who can go on and on about nothing! I talked so much because it made me more anxious not to talk, and I hoped that Eddie would eventually warm up. Finally, he did begin to open up, very slowly. And he seemed to feel positively about my role. We spent a great deal of time together for the next nine months.

Most home-based work is intense, and I estimate that I spent seven hours per week with Eddie. I got to know all the people in his family very well and shared many meals with them. Eddie turned out to have many strengths, including a desire to turn his life around, and he made great progress. I helped him get his Graduate Equivalency Diploma and his driver's license, and I supported his cooperation with probationary expectations. Best of all, I was able to be a mentor for him. We went to the beach, the movies, and parks, and we did a lot of driving around, always talking about his thoughts and plans. After nine months he was ready to be released from probation.

Despite the intense interventions provided in our program, the only routine procedures in the ending phase involved a lot of paperwork. As you might guess, many clients are pleased to be finished with us when the time comes. Eddie had met his goals, and his paperwork was nearing completion, but I was concerned about feelings he might be having about our ending. Of course, I was concerned about my feelings, too. I wanted to arrange for some type of celebration. I called his grandmother and asked for her thoughts about our ending. She came up with a great idea—to hold a spiritual gathering in their home.

I had never participated in anything quite like this. The ceremony included Eddie, his grandmother, his mother, his three sisters, and several close friends and relatives. No other professional staff were invited. Eddie's grandmother and I co-led the ceremony, which lasted about ninety minutes. All of us took turns reflecting on Eddie's life up to that point, and we helped him look to his future. Many tears of joy were shed. I read a letter to Eddie in which I summed up my good feelings about our work and about the journey we had made together. I gave him the letter after I finished. There were frequent references to God and religion in the messages others shared. That was fine, but due to my discomfort with religious topics I downplayed that theme in my own contributions.

This was a stirring emotional experience for all of us. I learned that spirituality is an important part of the lives of many of our clients and should never be ignored by the professional. I was also helped to frame all of my endings with clients as "new beginnings," as corny as that might sound, because that theme was articulated by many of the guests. I was also reminded in this ceremony that clinical endings often affect more people than the client and professional, and practitioners should consider including some of these others in their final meetings.

Since we stopped working together I get a Christmas card from Eddie each year. Also, as a benefit for my agency, referrals from families in Eddie's neighborhood increased noticeably.

This elaborate ceremony touched on all five characteristics of closure. The event was organized to bring the clinical work, as well as the efforts of other significant members of Eddie's community, to a formal end. The client was in a sense "graduating" and returning to his social mainstream. The practitioner wrote and took the opportunity to read a letter that summarized the ups and downs of his relationship with Eddie, highlighting what he learned and commenting on his feelings about the client and his family. As the other persons present provided similar testimonials, Eddie's sense of his progress and worth was probably greatly affirmed. The practitioner was satisfied with the intervention, and his motivation to continue working with these types of clients was enhanced in a concrete way by the additional referrals from Eddie's neighborhood.

The next two illustrations involve expected client deaths. They were very sad occasions for the practitioner and the clients' significant others. They were also satisfying for the practitioners, however, because they succeeded in making the death experience more positive for the participants than it otherwise might have been. Notice in these examples that the practitioners did not withdraw emotionally, which might be tempting as a means of emotional self-protection. They remained fully involved in the clinical process until the end, risking themselves emotionally for the sake of their clients. It should be clear that in these difficult endings closure was dependent on the practitioners' focusing on the needs of the client system.

Case Study: A Second Chance for Closure

I was a hospital nurse working on the general pediatric unit when I met Zak, a nine-year-old boy with AIDS. He was first admitted to my unit for a related health problem that now I cannot remember. The pediatric unit had twenty-five beds, and each nurse was assigned four patients. Zak was by far the most active of my patients during the few weeks he was in the hospital. He had so much energy that he didn't seem ill. We "clicked" right away and enjoyed each other's company every day. He was friendly and affectionate, even though he was rather quiet. He liked to follow me around the unit and push the blood pressure machine up and down the hallway for me. I got to know his mother pretty well and also his younger brother, who unfortunately also had AIDS. His mother had adopted both boys.

Zak's illness was successfully treated, and he went home. About six months later, though, he was back and was more gravely ill this time. Zak now had end-stage AIDS, with pneumonia and a herpes outbreak. He was not eating. Zak didn't talk much at all this time. He was weak and probably depressed. I tried to rekindle our earlier relationship. I took him for wheelchair rides around the unit, and we spent time watching the boats in the river outside the window of the hospital. I talked with him as much as I ever did. He didn't talk back, so I playfully did his talking for him. This was not hard for me, because I am always chatty. I do remember thinking, though, that I was more attached to him than he was to me. I couldn't detect any evidence of our earlier bond. He behaved the same way toward everyone.

Well, the inevitable finally happened. Returning from a day off, I was told that Zak would probably die that day. Early in my shift another nurse came to get me and took me to his room, saying, "You are needed in there." I walked into Zak's room and found his mother, two doctors, and another nurse, all keeping a vigil. Ten minutes passed slowly. I struggled with whether or not I should say to Zak, "I love you!" as he went in and out of consciousness. I was experiencing a personal versus professional struggle, and despite my instinct I said nothing. I finally asked everyone to leave the room so that Zak's mother could be alone with him during his final few minutes.

After Zak died, and his mother left the room, I had the responsibility to take care of his body. I wanted some time to sit with Zak alone, and I got it while I waited for the priest to come. I talked to Zak, all the while regretting that I hadn't spoken to him just before he died. I learned afterward from another nurse that the night before, Zak had been hallucinating and was calling for me. This made me think that, despite his behavior in the past few weeks, he had been attached to me, too.

I thought that my involvement with the family would end after I attended Zak's funeral. Incredibly, I got another chance for closure with Zak. His mother called to invite me to lunch, saying she had something to give me. She said that during the few days before Zak died, he had told his mother he wanted to get me a special gift. He died before he could decide what to give me, but his mother had followed up on his wish and purchased for me a ring that contained the birthstones of each of her two sons. It was an incredible moment. I didn't care about the gift itself so much as the affirmation that my caring about this boy and his family was recognized. It validated for me the effort I had put into making Zak comfortable during his second hospital stay. I still feel badly that I didn't speak to Zak as he lay dying, but after that lunch meeting I was able to put the episode into a larger perspective and feel good about our relationship and about my work as a nurse.

An instructive aspect of this story is that the practitioner initially failed to achieve closure with the client and felt devastated as a result. Due to Zak's rapid decline and her own ambivalence related to the presence of other staff in the room, she was unable to have a final conversation with Zak. She was not able to express her thoughts about their relationship and their work together, although doing so immediately after his death was somewhat cathartic for her. Her reaction demonstrates why a practitioner who has many experiences of this type may lose some enthusiasm for clinical practice. Fortunately, this practitioner was eventually able to resolve her unfinished business indirectly with Zak's family. She learned that Zak probably knew he would die soon and had made plans to recognize the importance of their relationship with a special gift. She was also able to share with Zak's mother the thoughts and feelings that she would like to have shared with the boy, and in the end this helped her to feel affirmed.

Case Study: The Lonely Hobo

I was the first full-time social worker hired in the outpatient oncology clinic of a large public metropolitan hospital. I loved my job from the beginning even though the atmosphere was always rather chaotic. There were several subclinics in the department, and staff seemed to be constantly running back and forth between programs and patients. We often had fifty or more patients come through the clinic for cancer treatments each day. My job was to help patients acquire enough material and financial resources that they could get appropriate medical care and not need to stay in the hospital.

Mr. Burke was a patient of ours over an eight-month period. He was referred by a community nurse for evaluation of a skin cancer. While Mr. Burke eventually became well liked at the clinic, he was initially annoying to all the staff. He was a forty-two-year-old single Caucasian male who was homeless and illiterate. I was thirty-five at the time. During his first visits he looked and smelled bad. The doctors and nurses seemed to judge him negatively for those reasons. He was found to have malignant melanoma, and the prognosis was terminal. My job was to help Mr. Burke resolve his homelessness and find a safe environment for the duration of his illness.

Mr. Burke turned out to be a patient unlike any other I have known. Over time we developed a close relationship. I saw him on average once every two weeks, for about thirty minutes each time. I think he became attached to me because I showed him respect and communicated genuine interest in his welfare, which he was not accustomed to. He taught me so much about social work! Mr. Burke rejected almost all my efforts to find resources for him. He explained that he was homeless by choice, that he loved the freedom of traveling the country. His life routine was to settle in one area and work at construction or maintenance jobs long enough to finance his next travel episode. He was proudly and fiercely independent and in fact was a hard worker. He did not want charity from anyone. Of course, this was frustrating to me, because he would not cooperate with my efforts to secure such benefits as social security disability and Medicaid for him. Mr. Burke would allow me to find shelters for him, but he still slept outside under bridges when the weather was nice.

As the months went by, Mr. Burke's cancer steadily worsened. He came to the clinic every few weeks for his treatments, and we always talked. Staff became curious at the sight of this disheveled client having intense conversations with me, always addressing me respectfully as "Miss Risley." He began to grow on the doctors and nurses, and eventually he became a clinic favorite. Still, as Mr. Burke became weaker and in more pain, he could be difficult to manage. Like many cancer patients he feared debilitation, loss of control, and vulnerability. He could become angry and argumentative. On one noteworthy occasion I was called to intervene when he was making a big scene in a busy hallway, cursing at staff about something related to his treatment. As soon as I arrived and asked him to control himself he did so, addressing me as "Miss Risley," as always.

The end of our relationship was the most moving I have ever experienced. He was dying and a hospital inpatient. I was not his "official" social worker anymore, as he was being served in another department. But all the staff from my clinic had adopted this lonely man as family. I went to see him one afternoon, and we talked for about thirty minutes. Mr. Burke was very weak. He made a "confession" to me. He told me that he had been "a horrible person" in his life and told me about all the "bad things" he had done. He wondered if I could possibly like him, knowing those things. Of course I did. I had assessed many of his antisocial behaviors the first time we met. He then asked me, "Will I go to heaven?" I said I thought he would. Mr. Burke then told me how much I had meant to him during his illness, saying, "You were always there for me." Finally, this man who was less than two weeks from death said, "I will never forget you." Our visit ended then, and I barely made it out of his room before starting to cry.

What an emotional experience for me! I am so glad I decided to visit Mr. Burke that day. It served as a validation that the work I had done with him was worthwhile. Remember that, in the context of my job expectations, I had actually failed by not securing full and timely benefits for him and not placing him into an appropriate nursing facility. I think I already knew that my work had been good, but afterward I realized that the way we ended was important for my feeling affirmed. I also learned from this experience that there is often a moment in our work with clients when we must recognize that closure has occurred, even when further contact is possible. I could have gone back to see Mr. Burke again, but I chose not to, because during that last visit I felt that both of us had ended the relationship in a gratifying way.

In contrast to the previous vignette, this story is characterized by a spontaneous yet complete ending of the clinical intervention prior to the client's death. The final meeting was dramatically highlighted by the client's "confession" experience that very much resembles the sacramental practice within the Catholic religion. The client reviewed with the practitioner the successes and failures of his entire life, not merely their work together. Both persons acknowledged in powerful ways their feelings about the relationship. One hopes that the practitioner was able to tell Mr. Burke that his presentation had taught her much about the practice of good social work, as she states early in the narrative. It is also interesting to note that the practitioner could have visited the client again but recognized that they had so fittingly ended their relationship that there would be no benefit to additional contact.

This chapter's final illustration presents the ending of an intervention that was extremely frustrating for both the client and practitioner. The relationship between the two went from good to bad to even worse. The client finally quit in anger and then filed a grievance against the practitioner. Still, with the participation of the agency's clinical director, the relationship was ultimately resolved in a positive way. An important lesson from this vignette is that a third party can sometimes intervene to salvage a problematic ending. This theme leads into some closing thoughts for this chapter.

Case Study: The Grievance

Martell came to my counseling center to seek help in resolving concerns related to his sexual identity. The twenty-two-year-old African American man was coming to terms with the fact of his homosexuality. He was troubled by the impact of his coming out on his friends and employer. Martell was both lonely and felt at risk of being fired by an allegedly homophobic boss at the modeling agency where he worked as a photographer. He came to my agency because he had no friends in whom he could confide, and he was worried about being ostracized by his parents and brother. Martell was highly distressed from the time we met, but he was never suicidal and seemed motivated to work on resolving his sexual identity concerns.

Martell was initially open and reflective about the challenges of his lifestyle adjustment. We seemed to connect well, and he even said several times that he was pleased with my intervention approach. I encouraged Martell to reflect on his goals, values, and life dilemmas so that he might become able to generate his own solutions. I included an action-oriented approach to our problem solving in which he could seek out and test new social supports. I taught him stress management techniques to help him deal with interpersonal stress on the job. We worked along these lines for about two months, and I anticipated that he might complete his counseling in another few months.

What happened, however, is that Martell soon became impatient with his longer-term problems, such as the inability to persuade his good friends and family to accept him unconditionally as a gay man. As Martell became tenser, his thinking became more rigid. He began placing blame on others for his difficulties—his boss, his mother, his roommate, and finally me! For example, he wondered why I could not direct him to appropriate support resources more quickly. He began demanding quick solutions from me about his interpersonal problems, and he accused me of incompetence when I declined to give him direct advice. He asked to see a physician for a medication evaluation, failed to show up on three occasions, and then blamed me for failing to arrange a more convenient appointment. It seemed that Martell had become overwhelmed by the stresses related to his life changes. He had lost the ability to break them down into manageable parts.

Several nonproductive weeks went by, and after supervisory consultation I decided to keep meeting with Martell rather than suggest an alternative to our counseling. I cannot say that the sessions ever became productive again, because Martell typically began yelling at me partway through about my inability to understand him or to be helpful. I felt awkward, because it seemed that other staff at the agency could always hear him shouting. So why did I persist? My supervisor felt that in spite of the situation Martell felt a positive connection with me (otherwise, why would he keep coming in?) and that eventually we might become able to work constructively again. He was clearly not psychotic, and perhaps all his close relationships were like ours.

But this never happened. Martell lost his job due to insubordinate behavior (arguing with his boss about discrimination against gays) and was forced to move back home with his mother, two hours away. He was so upset about this negative turn of events that he filed a grievance against me at the agency. He met with the director and demanded that I be fired for incompetence. The director respectfully heard him out but defended my competence. Martell then demanded to see his record to make his case further. The director granted the request, as all clients at the agency have the right to see their records. Martell read my notes and picked out scores of statements with which he disagreed and felt were demeaning to him. He requested a second meeting with my director to review the notes and again demanded that I be fired.

What happened next was remarkable. The director agreed to meet with Martell and me together to process his complaints. He told Martell in advance that it would not be productive to go through the chart notes, because in the end it would amount to differences of opinion that probably could not be resolved. When we met the director was marvelous in his mediation role. He said that this was a time for all of us to share our opinions about what had transpired in the counseling and what could be done next to help Martell. Largely due to the presence of my boss, Martell did not lose his temper with me, even though he did not change his opinions about my behavior. I communicated to Martell that I always gave my best effort, was confident in my professional judgment, and would be agreeable to working with him again if he moved back to town. Martell started to raise specific complaints about his record and my actions. The director permitted Martell to speak for awhile but then reminded him that we wanted to help Martell develop a plan for ongoing care after he went home. My director had already looked into resources for Martell, formal and informal, and together we gave him this referral information. The director expressed genuine concern about Martell's future, as I did, and we invited Martell to keep in touch with us.

I walked Martell out to the lobby. He did not appear to be upset anymore. I like to think that despite his behavior he appreciated that I continued to meet with him after his anger became so prominent. We said little on that last day, but I wished Martell well and shook his hand. He returned the gesture and quietly left. It may seem like not much, but I was very moved by the peacefulness of our final parting. It was a more cordial interchange than we had shared in several months. I hope Martell is doing well today, although I did not hear from him again.

This intervention was not successful for Martell, although it could be argued from the practitioner's perspective that the client's expectations were not realistic. Still, this example demonstrates that a client and a practitioner can achieve closure without a positive outcome. With the supervisor's mediation, the two parties were able to proceed with a concluding session that included positive elements. The supervisor's presence promoted a far calmer atmosphere than was typical of the recent past. The practitioner acknowledged that his relationship with Martell had been difficult, while also noting that the client had achieved some successes during their time together. He was careful to frame this review, and explain his intervention actions, in a manner that was not defensive and did not place any blame on the client. At the end of the hour it seemed that Martell, due to the supervisor's encouragement, was prepared to seek out counseling services in his hometown. The practitioner felt great relief at the positive tone in this final session after so many earlier stresses and genuinely wanted to be available for Martell if he returned to the agency.

Summary

The purpose of this chapter has been to describe and illustrate the importance of closure in clinical practice. This book includes many suggestions for practitioners for achieving closure with clients. It must be emphasized, however, that self-awareness and the utilization of regular clinical supervision are the most important practices for attending to this and to other aspects of clinical intervention. Some general principles for practitioners and for supervisors to use in maximizing the chances for positive endings follow (Gabbard, 1995; Hepworth et al., 2002; Herlihy & Corey, 1997; Kocan, 1988; Minkoff, 1987; Nehls, 2000; Savage, 1987).

For practitioners:
- ◆ Set clear boundaries with your clients about what your clinical roles and activities will and will not include. Consistency of expectations is an excellent way to track the course of an intervention and to know when it should end. Clients should participate in establishing these boundaries. Clarify boundaries with clients over time, as they may change.
- ◆ Be aware of your emotional and physical needs as much as possible, and be wary of obtaining too much personal gratification from your work with clients. You may, for personal reasons, decide too soon or too late to end work with a client.

◆ Be aware of the client's previous experiences with significant endings of all types, in order to understand the meaning of the ending to the client and anticipate aspects of the process on which to focus.

◆ Promote the psychological separateness of the client. All interventions should be focused on the goal of making the client more self-sufficient and less reliant on professional services.

◆ Be educated about the client's cultural and community standards of behavior so as to understand what behaviors are reasonable to expect and encourage when formulating ending activities.

◆ Use peer consultation routinely (many practitioners learn more from their colleagues than from formally designated supervisors).

◆ Refer to professional codes of ethics when applicable for guidance in clinical decision making.

For supervisors:

◆ Promote clarity in staff roles. With role clarity, practitioners have an easier time determining what behaviors are appropriate in all of their activities with clients.

◆ Provide a safe forum for worker disclosure. Clinical dilemmas about ending are not always easy to discuss with another person unless trust is established.

◆ Pursue discussions of clinical dilemmas with guided exploration rather than cross-examination. The former practice encourages discussion, while the latter practice puts the worker on the defensive.

◆ Be proactive in helping the practitioner identify relationship concerns. Help the practitioner understand how his or her feelings may affect the ending of an intervention.

◆ Selectively use self-disclosure with the practitioner to normalize his or her feelings of uncertainty about how to end work with a client.

◆ Work with clinical staff and administrative staff to develop agency policies for processing certain kinds of difficult endings, such as those related to suicide, unexpected client deaths, litigious actions initiated by clients, and exceptional acting out by clients.

In the next chapter we consider the many ending tasks that practitioners must address in their efforts to promote closure.

Chapter 3

Tasks for Ending

Clinical intervention includes at least four phases—assessment, planning, intervention, and ending—and each phase has distinct tasks and areas of focus. The ending phase sometimes begins as early as the first session, particularly if the practitioner orients the client to an intervention strategy that utilizes concrete indicators of goal attainment. Even in those situations, however, attention to specific ending tasks may not begin until the practitioner perceives that the intervention is nearing completion. In fact, we can say that intervention includes both pretermination and termination activities. The former are activities addressed by the client and practitioner as the practitioner becomes aware of the approaching end and begins to focus the intervention in that direction. Termination activities emerge in the context of the practitioner and client discussing and agreeing on a specific ending strategy.

The ending phase of intervention represents the period when the practitioner helps the client prepare for functioning without the support of a professional, or at least the current professional. The practitioner is challenged to ensure that the client will maintain his or her gains after the relationship ends. All clinical practice theories have some unique perspectives on the process of ending intervention, and these will be described in later chapters. Across all theories, however, there are many common themes, which are the focus of this chapter. For example, the process of ending intervention always involves a "mini life review" for the client. The practitioner touches on aspects of the client's past, present, and future. The client's past is addressed as he or she is helped to reflect on how and why the presenting issue developed and how it affected his or her life. The present is addressed as the worker and client assess the client's current status with regard to the problem and the client's new knowledge, skills, or resources. Finally, the future is addressed as the client is helped to look ahead at maintenance or new growth strategies.

In this chapter we review the following common ending tasks and, through some examples, illustrate how the practitioner can manage them:

- ◆ Deciding when to actively implement the ending phase
- ◆ Timing the announcement of one's own leaving
- ◆ Anticipating the client's and one's own reactions
- ◆ Appropriately spacing the remaining sessions
- ◆ Shifting the intervention focus from "inside" to the "outside"
- ◆ Reviewing intervention gains
- ◆ Generalizing intervention gains
- ◆ Planning for goal maintenance and relapse prevention

- Addressing the client's remaining needs
- Linking the client with social supports
- Resolving the clinical relationship
- Formally evaluating the intervention (process and outcomes)
- Setting conditions and limits on future contact

We now turn to a detailed discussion of each of these tasks.

Deciding When to Actively Implement the Ending Phase

The practitioner and client know from the outset that their working relationship will end at some time. They may expect it to end very soon or at some indefinite and perhaps distant time. The practitioner may be very clear about this ("We are authorized to meet five times" or "I rarely see the need to work with clients more than ten times") or address the issue in general terms ("We can work together as long as it takes to resolve your problem"). Regardless of the particular circumstances, however, clients may or may not keep in mind that the end will happen or that it may be nearing. They are often too focused on their needs to think beyond the present. For this reason it is advisable for the practitioner to occasionally refer to an approximate timeline. And, the practitioner must bring the issue to the forefront when he or she perceives that the end is nearing.

Some practitioner guidelines for looking ahead to the ending phase of intervention (pretermination activities) include:

- Explaining any anticipated time limits (based on agency policy, insurance policy, or the worker's theoretical perspective) to the client during the first session
- Raising the topic of ending criteria during the periodic intervention plan update. The practitioner can address the issue as it pertains to the revised plan.
- In the absence of an automatic "prompt," periodically referring to the ending phase with some regularity (not necessarily at every session)
- Asking the client at the end of every session how he or she is experiencing the intervention, including movement toward goals. In this sense each session has an ending phase.
- Utilizing and referring to ongoing concrete measures of progress so that the client can literally see the end point, however near or far away

Several authors and researchers have gathered criteria from practitioners about when to move actively into the end phase of intervention. Northen (1994) writes that some clients indicate a desire or readiness to end through their words and actions. They exhibit increased confidence and share more reports with the practitioner of successes, satisfaction, and progress. Their communications become more relaxed. With family and group interventions the practitioner may notice members' increased mutual support and respect for each other's individuality.

Fortune's (1985, 1994) research on clinical endings found that practitioners based their decisions to end on various indicators of improved client behavior and intrapsychic functioning (representing external and internal changes), goal attainment, and a change in the focus of intervention toward topics less related to the presenting problem. Other criteria included the client's wishes, environmental changes that mandated ending the intervention, and the increased availability of external support. "Negative" ending criteria included a change in the clinical relationship toward the client's greater dependence, an absence of perceived client improvement, and restrictive agency policies. Kramer (1990) asserts that intuition is a legitimate ending criterion, defined as the practitioner's feeling or impression that the end is or should be approaching. He admits that this is hard to objectify. He adds that maintaining strict ending criteria may be clinically counterproductive. Doing so places theory at times above the client's well-being and elevates the practitioner to the level of an authority figure. He warns practitioners to distinguish between the client's readiness to end and the practitioner's desires.

Practitioners should be careful not to delay addressing relevant ending issues with clients after recognizing the onset of the final phase. This reluctance to move forward is unfortunately not uncommon and is usually related to practitioner ambivalence (Philip, 1994). Changes in practitioner behavior during the ending phase should include taking a more active stance in the relationship, suggesting a timeline, and setting posttermination boundaries. Some clients may experience these changes as controlling or rigid (Conway, 1999). Even in crisis intervention, however, practitioners should build in ample time for end-phase activities (Webb, 1985). One play therapist recommends that the practitioner announce the end of intervention at least four sessions before the final meeting (West, 1984). It should be presented in a way that makes the child feel special and frames the ending as similar to other endings in the child's life, such as the school term. The practitioner should space out the remaining sessions, allowing for gifts, cards, photographs, and treats, and for the child to get to know the practitioner more as a "regular" person.

More experienced practitioners and those in private practice tend to devote more time to the ending phase (Guy, French, Poelstra, & Brown, 1993). Analysts spend the most time on endings, while cognitive-behavioral therapists tend to permit more phone contacts as part of the process. Practitioners rated as highly empathetic are at risk to devote too much time to the ending phase with ambivalent clients, while structured practitioners tend to move through the process too quickly with avoidant clients (Holmes, 1997).

The guidelines presented earlier in this chapter are intended as ways the practitioner can remind the client that he or she is engaged in a process with limits. What follows are additional guidelines to help the practitioner decide when to formally implement ending activities:

By the halfway point (if not sooner) of strictly time-limited interventions, the practitioner should remind the client of their remaining time and continue to do so at each subsequent meeting.

When the practitioner determines that the client has reached a point of diminishing returns regarding progress toward goals, she or he should introduce a timeline for ending. Making this determination is difficult and should be done in consultation with the client and perhaps a supervisor.

When the practitioner assesses that remaining in treatment will serve only to sustain a client's maladaptive tendencies toward dependence, intervention should end. The client may have reached many of her or his goals or may cease working toward goals in order to postpone an ending.

If a client will be denied further agency services because of an inability or unwillingness to adhere to appropriate behavior limits (acting out, failing to adhere to a reasonable intervention agreement, missing appointments, not paying bills, and so on) the remaining time should be devoted to closure. Generally, depending on the nature of the violation, the client is warned one or more times so that the practitioner can raise the possibility of dismissal and attend to its possibility in organizing session content.

When the practitioner is leaving the agency, he or she should designate a time to begin making the announcement to clients in consultation with a supervisor. All clients should receive notification at approximately the same time.

The following vignette illustrates a clinical problem that developed when the departing practitioner failed to formulate an adequate ending plan with the client. Fortunately, the outcome was positive in spite of this oversight.

Case Study: Pen Pals

This ending experience made a lasting impression on me because it included an unusual strategy for trying to end with a long-term client, and it taught me the importance of being clear about an ending plan with the client and also myself.

A few years ago I divided my residence between Virginia and Massachusetts. I worked nine months each year as a school social worker in a facility for children with behavioral problems. I liked to work long-term with clients when possible, and I saw Nakia and her young son for fourteen months. Nakia was thirty-two years old, and Brad was seven. She was Caucasian, and her child was mixed. The father, no longer a part of their lives, was African American. Brad experienced behavioral problems related to his unstable background. I decided that focusing on Nakia's parenting and her other stresses would be the best way to help her son.

Nakia was initially a reluctant client. She was struggling to raise her self-esteem and overcome a tendency to enter into harmful relationships. She tended to get involved with people who took advantage of and sometimes abused her. Recently, she had developed a positive relationship with an older woman who became a "surrogate mother" to her. This woman acted as Nakia's "good parent," but this only reinforced Nakia's image of herself as a "bad parent." Nakia had been a substance abuser in the past but had overcome that problem.

I connected well with Nakia, and she enjoyed working with me. Nakia had primarily negative experiences with the many human service professionals she had known. She felt that they looked down on and discriminated against her because of her poverty and lifestyle. She perceived that they disapproved of her being unmarried and having a biracial child. Practitioners had accused her at times of being abusive to her own son. I liked Nakia, though, and affirmed her strengths and personal worth. She was motivated to do better for herself, had managed to stop using substances, and was trying to be a good parent. She was also successfully managing a small grocery store. We met weekly in therapy sessions for nine months, and Nakia progressed nicely. She developed better judgment and developed the self-confidence to resist abusive relationships.

I raised the issue of our ending with Nakia three months before my move to Massachusetts. I thought her progress was such that we could simply end our work before I left. But I miscalculated—Nakia was reluctant to let go. I tried for several months to locate another therapist for a transfer, but she rejected my recommendations, saying she could not trust other professionals. I was getting more anxious about our lack of a plan as the deadline approached.

Finally, Nakia asked if she could write letters to me—that is, conduct sessions by mail! I was not comfortable with the idea, but in the absence of alternatives I agreed to it. I thought that Nakia would write only a few letters until she got accustomed to functioning without my help. I was wrong, but to my surprise the process seemed to work well. Nakia wrote long, two- or three-page letters to me every few weeks about how she was managing her challenges. My clinical supervisor agreed that the process was helpful to the client and appropriate for me to continue. I always wrote back to Nakia. My letters were not long, but I commented on her thoughts and actions much as I would have done in person. The letters kept coming all summer long. I continued to use supervision to make sure I was handling the exchange appropriately.

Three months later I returned to Virginia and began seeing Nakia and her son again. We ended our contact permanently, though, just two months later. Nakia felt ready to end, and this time the process was uncomplicated. I reviewed Nakia's progress and the nature of our own relationship. I urged her to contact me again if she felt the need. She never did.

I learned some important lessons from this episode. I learned that you really need to end! I should have constructed a more focused plan for the ending. I should have clarified with Nakia whether the letters were intended to be a short-term part of an ending or to carry us over until fall. I also learned that my attachment to Nakia was clouding my judgment about how to address the transfer issue. It kept me from doing a better job of connecting her with someone else when I left. I guess I believed her that no one else could care about her. But a major achievement of her therapy was for her to learn otherwise.

Timing the Announcement of One's Leaving

When the practitioner is leaving and the client is staying, the practitioner must give thought to timing the announcement relative to the departure date. The practitioner should make the announcement sooner rather than later, although specific decisions will depend on the circumstances of the client and the nature of the service. Practitioners should always share at least the basic facts of their departure so that clients will not develop any unrealistic and perhaps harmful fantasies (for example, reflecting guilt) about those reasons (Siebold, 1991). They should be prepared for the possibility (but not necessity) of clients' anticipatory grief that may take the form of anxiety, avoidance, or denial.

It is not stated often enough that the practitioner should wait until he or she is ready to make the announcement to clients. The practitioner needs time to adjust to the upcoming change, particularly if leaving is a relatively recent development. The practitioner must reflect on his or her own feelings about the change, reflect on the ending needs of each client (they may be different), and maintain his or her standard energy level through the remaining meetings. The practitioner should seek support from peers if the process of leaving is stressful. Clients adjust at their own pace, and the practitioner should model how to say goodbye (Pearson, 1998).

The case illustration that follows describes a situation in which the practitioner's failure to remind the client about the short-term nature of their relationship resulted in a disastrous ending for both.

Case Study: What's the Point of Continuing?

Several years ago as a graduate student I had a field placement in the adolescent services program of a mental health center. Three months before the end of my placement I was assigned to work with an eighteen-year-old girl named Robyn. She was having difficulties related to conflict with her parents, her teachers, and her friends. Unlike many adolescents, the idea of counseling was not frightening to Robyn, and she was not opposed to meeting with me. It may have helped that I was only five years older than she was. Robyn was reserved during our first few meetings, but her willingness to share sensitive feelings developed quickly. It seemed to me at first that Robyn was experiencing typical adolescent rebelliousness, but later I understood that she had serious interpersonal problems. She had a fundamental inability to trust anyone. I decided that it would be important to use our own relationship as a point of focus as we explored her attitudes about other people. Robyn agreed to weekly meetings with me.

When we had met five times and had five sessions left, I reminded Robyn that my time at the agency was limited. I reminded her of the time-line, hoping that this would help us use our remaining time productively. To my surprise, Robyn became quite angry with me. She complained loudly in a very agitated tone of voice that there was no point in our continuing to meet if we had to end so soon. She added that this was further proof that relationships were not worth developing, because they are always transient and unreliable.

I wasn't prepared for her reaction. I tried to hide my own distress and shared my belief that she could make progress on her goals during the coming month. I assured Robyn that we would consult about a transfer to another practitioner as the end approached. She didn't accept this, or at least she had mixed feelings about it. Robyn came to our next four scheduled meetings, but she never talked much about her presenting problems again. Our momentum was destroyed—she was holding back. When I tried to draw her out, she complained again that there was no point in talking because I was leaving. I became more and more frustrated at our "wheel spinning" about this issue. I hate to admit this, but after a few weeks I really didn't want to keep meeting with Robyn either. I thought it might be best if I transferred her immediately to a full-time staff member. But I pressed on, trying unsuccessfully to reengage Robyn in a substantive intervention process. She did not show up for our final meeting, and I was relieved. I felt that we had gotten nowhere in our last four sessions.

In retrospect, I could have organized the ending issue as a therapy theme. I could have focused more consistently on us and how our relationship could be worthwhile even though it had to end. I could have posed a series of questions that were relevant to her presenting problems, for example: Why have we gotten along well up until now? How does it feel to have someone leave? Can we not keep parts of our relationships within us even as the other person moves on? What can we do together to make the best of the ending? Do relationships need to be permanent in order to be worthwhile? That approach might have helped, but I'm not sure. Robyn seemed to be looking for a permanency that was unrealistic. If I reminded her every few weeks about our time limits I guess we could have structured our work more suitably.

Anticipating the Client's and One's Own Reaction

A major theme in the literature about ending intervention is the importance of the practitioner's anticipating the client's reaction and attending to it. The practitioner should also reflect on her or his own reactions and process them in a manner that is therapeutic rather than harmful for the client (see chapters 9 and 10). The topic is included here to ensure the comprehensiveness of our task listing. The following case illustration underscores its importance.

Case Study: The Quiet Child

I've never forgotten an ending that occurred when I was in my first field placement as a graduate student of social work, many years ago. I was young and inexperienced (camp counseling had been my forte up to then) and was placed in an agency that provided temporary foster care for children. The agency, located in New York City, maintained a roster of foster parents who were paid to provide homes for children in emergency situations. The children might remain in foster care for six months to several years if the parent, for example, experienced a major medical or psychiatric illness.

I was assigned to work with a young boy named Alex, who was five years old. His mother had been admitted to a psychiatric hospital. Alex was placed with a couple who lived in Queens. He had a number of siblings who were placed elsewhere. I never knew them. I have vivid memories of riding the subway to Alex's foster home every two weeks to see how he was getting along. His house was a six-block walk from the subway stop. The neighborhood was bustling with small businesses, noisy traffic, and crowds of pedestrians. My routine was to spend time alone with Alex and also to talk with his foster mother. My visits were about an hour long, and I spent more time with the foster mother than with Alex.

My job was to help Alex make a good adjustment to his foster home and to help his foster mother promote his development. Alex was a challenge for me, not because of any active behavioral problems, but because he was so quiet. He was very shy—he never said anything at all or looked at me directly. My supervisor encouraged me to try to have conversations with Alex, to make him feel more comfortable over time, but this did not seem to work. Maybe that's why I spent more time talking with his foster mother. She said that Alex was creating no problems in the household but that he was always very quiet. She described him as timid, in fact. What I began to do in my time with Alex was play marbles. Every time I came for my visit we would play marbles on his living room floor. Alex was always willing to play, but still he never said anything. I didn't say much to him either.

I visited the home over a period of twelve weeks, so I probably saw Alex six times. My school year was ending, and I needed to end my work with Alex as well as my other clients. I wasn't sure how to go about this, since we never talked. My supervisor instructed me to end in a formal way, meaning that I should tell Alex and his foster mother in advance that my time with them was coming to an end and that another worker would take over for me. I did a fair job of this, I think, announcing my leaving and reminding the family of that fact over a period of several visits. On my last day I prepared to leave the house and head back to the subway. Nothing remarkable happened—that is, until I left.

I was four blocks away from their house, again making my way along the busy streets of Queens, when suddenly I had an impulse to turn around. I saw Alex, walking quietly down the street behind me, looking at me but still not making a sound. I was shocked and overwhelmed. This would have been a very threatening outing for Alex. I composed myself and walked Alex back home. I talked briefly to his foster mother again and then went on my way. I never saw or heard about the child again.

When I think back on this episode, there are many things I wish I had done differently. First of all, I know now that there are many strategies to use to communicate nonverbally with children. Play therapy might have been effective with Alex. I simply had no experience with children at that time. But what I learned from the experience about clinical endings is that I had discounted the meaning of our relationship to Alex because of his inability to communicate verbally with me. Besides that, I should have processed the experience of Alex's following me down the street more fully with Alex and his mother. I might also have done an informal follow-up to remind the child that I was still interested in how he was doing. I certainly never felt closure with this episode, which is why the experience has stayed with me over the years. Now that I work as an advisor to students in clinical field placements, I have come to realize that young practitioners frequently discount their importance to clients.

Appropriately Spacing the Remaining Sessions

Some practitioners adjust the frequency of sessions during the ending phase, often spacing them farther apart. For example, a practitioner and client may meet only half as often as usual for some period of time, and then perhaps even less frequently until they stop completely. The practitioner may give the client control over the scheduling, frequency, and length of meetings so that he or she is allowed to pull away at a comfortable pace. The practitioner should be careful not to interpret the client's pulling away during the end phase as resistance, as changes in the clinical routine may symbolize the client's taking more control of his or her life. The following vignette provides a good example of the value of the practitioner's structuring the final sessions.

Case Study: Jeremy's Last Four Visits

When interventions are intensive and long term, it is often difficult to know when to stop. I practice in a child guidance center where clients tend to be poor and have behavioral, substance abuse, and attention deficit disorders. Even when clients improve significantly, some serious problems may persist, often related to inadequate support resources. I think many of my colleagues, and sometimes myself, hang on to our clients too long.

I inherited Jeremy from a staff member who left the agency. Jeremy was a twelve-year-old African American boy with attention deficit disorder, adjustment disorder, and headaches that were believed to be stress related. When Jeremy was nine he endured the murder of his father and the imprisonment of his mother on drug offenses. He moved in with his grandmother, and his behavioral problems began. He had been an agency client for three years and had seen four clinical practitioners and two psychiatrists.

Shortly after I met Jeremy and his grandmother and reviewed his file, I saw that he was doing well and decided there was nothing left for the agency to do. He was tolerating his medications well, and his behavioral problems had diminished. He had been mainstreamed into the public school system and was getting decent grades. All staff at my agency are required to request Medicaid authorization for services, and I requested four more meetings over a two-month period. Included in the plan was my decision to see Jeremy and his grandmother together, which had not been done in the past. I thought this was a major oversight by the previous clinician, because, after all, they were living together in a parent-child relationship. The pair agreed to my plan for three family meetings and one individual session.

I gave the ending process a lot of thought, and it was well structured. During our joint sessions Jeremy was able to connect emotionally with his grandmother for the first time. He heard of her concerns and hopes for him and of her sadness about the family's tragedies. By their third session they were talking to each other rather than to me. I asked Jeremy and his grandmother to write letters to Jeremy's mom and dad, expressing how they felt about them and what they wanted them to know. They read the letters to each other during a session. Next I asked them to go to the cemetery and share a moment of silence with Jeremy's father. At his last session I presented Jeremy with a certificate that looked like a high school diploma, to recognize his accomplishments. I also wrote a personal letter to the family after they had ended, expressing my good feelings about their work. This was in addition to the generic letter we are required to send clients after they leave.

This experience affirmed for me the value of letting go. Ending is often a tough decision for the clinical worker, but in this case I felt good that I had been objective about their readiness to move on. I had empowered the grandmother and avoided getting trapped in the mind-set that services should continue only because they had been needed for so long. The way I spaced and structured the final four sessions seemed to sum up their progress and highlight their gains for each other.

Shifting the Intervention Focus from "Inside" to "Outside"

Clinical interventions are usually provided in a formal setting, removed from the everyday life of the client. The client comes to an agency; follows certain protocols regarding eligibility, fees, and other policies; and meets with a practitioner in a sometimes luxurious (but more often sparsely furnished) office. The practitioner may meet with the client in a different institution such as a school, prison, or substance abuse facility. The formal setting offers a temporary respite from that world. This is not a bad thing, because the "special" nature of the clinical setting supports the practitioner's credibility with the client (Frank & Frank, 1993). In most situations, however, the problems experienced by the client are "out there" in the "real" world. With some community-based intervention models, such as social rehabilitation for persons with mental illness and family preservation services, the practitioner actually does enter the client's natural environment. Typically, however, the tentative solutions developed by the client and practitioner need to be taken by the client back to the everyday world and tried out.

Intervention models differ in the emphasis they place on issues that are concretely related to the client's activities of daily living. They also vary in their emphasis on "practicing" in the natural environment what is discussed in the treatment setting. Practitioners who use interventions that are highly task focused articulate clear expectations that the client will regularly practice new skills and problem-solving techniques. In the ending phase, however, all practice models tend to make a shift toward taking what is discussed inside the confines of the office and applying it to the outside environment. Similarly, the practitioner may only support the client's discussing issues that have clear relevance to that environment. Even reflective, insight-oriented interventions become more concrete, focusing more on the client's present situation than his or her developmental needs (Goldstein, 1995). The practitioner may decide that no new material will be introduced into the intervention process. As examples, the person who has sought help adjusting to a medical condition may be encouraged to practice applying his or her new self-care knowledge and skills, and the person with chronic relationship difficulties may be asked to more carefully monitor how he or she deals with feelings of anger toward persons in authority.

This shift in focus is critical because it prepares clients to function in their everyday life, outside the formal setting, without the support of a professional. It represents the important transition of moving fully back into the natural environment.

Reviewing Intervention Gains

Part of the process of achieving closure in the client-practitioner relationship is looking back over the intervention and considering what the client has gained. This is a step toward a more formal evaluation, but it is more focused on helping the client informally review the worthwhile aspects of the intervention. The purpose of this task is to give clients an opportunity to step back and see, perhaps for the first time, what they have achieved. Intervention can be a difficult process for clients, and they may feel stress and anxiety as much as anything else, even as they make progress. The ending is an opportunity to "put the pieces back together" so that clients can get a holistic picture of the process. The practitioner may facilitate this task by:

- ◆ Reviewing past intervention plans, including the initial plan, as a frame of reference for what has happened and demonstrating (through cumulative review) what has transpired
- ◆ Sharing his or her own perceptions and memories of the process, focusing on key issues that indicated changes
- ◆ Asking clients questions to stimulate their own reflections on the process
- ◆ Encouraging or instructing clients to ask significant others (friends, family, and so on) about any changes they have observed since the beginning
- ◆ Inviting clients to review any writings they may have produced
- ◆ Asking clients to write a journal summarizing therapy experiences that they can review with the practitioner (this is elaborated in chapter 11 as an ending ritual)
- ◆ In the case of families or groups, asking other members to review with each other particular moments that indicated positive changes

In some instances, clients will not have made any significant gains, and there may be unfinished business. Even so, it is important to help clients feel positively about themselves and the future when preparing to move on.

Generalizing Intervention Gains

Anytime an individual faces a challenge or problem that he or she cannot manage without the assistance of a professional, the individual perceives some deficiency with regard to the capacity to problem solve or cope. This deficiency may involve a lack of knowledge or insight, a skill deficit, or cognitive rigidity. This is not to imply that there is something "wrong" with the client, but rather that there is an educational benefit to intervention that transcends particular presenting problems. What the client gains from the clinical intervention may be generalized to other current and future situations. Part of the ending process involves the practitioner's reviewing these new capabilities with the client and suggesting how they might be utilized in a variety of life situations. A few examples may help to clarify this point.

- ◆ High school students with "oppositional defiant disorder" may be referred to a group to learn how to more appropriately direct their anger toward teachers. In learning to constructively process negative emotions, they may be able to manage all relationships with adults more positively.
- ◆ A man is referred to an employees assistance program because of his inability to concentrate at work. With testing it is discovered that he has

attention deficit disorder, for which he is later prescribed medication. This not only improves his concentration on the job but also his ability to enjoy sustained interactions with his children.

♦ A woman who is depressed about a series of failed relationships learns that she has a pattern of self-criticism. When she learns through the practice of weighing the evidence for her self-statements to feel more positively about herself, she can be helped to see that all of her relationships can improve.

While the practitioner may help the client generalize throughout the intervention, doing so near the end is an important means of helping the client leave with confidence. The practitioner can facilitate discussion of this issue with the following types of questions and comments:

Let's step back and think about what you've accomplished here. How will you be able to use this in your life?

Are there other circumstances in which you might be able to use what you've learned here for your own benefit?

You've reviewed with me today what you have achieved in our work together. Let me add some of my own observations that go beyond what you've said. Let me know if you think this makes sense.

What have you learned about yourself in general that you can take with you?

Make a list of skills that you have learned as a result of completing tasks during our work together. Include on that list places where you might be able to use them.

You came here for help with a particular problem. Now that you are leaving, can you think of other problems that you might be able to avoid as a result of this experience?

Are you any smarter than you were when we started? In what ways?

The confidence of clients can only be bolstered by the realization that they are now equipped to manage more issues than those for which they initially sought clinical assistance.

Planning for Goal Maintenance and Relapse Prevention

The practitioner and client typically devote much time during their final sessions to looking ahead to the client's life after intervention with regard to managing recurrences of the presenting issue or stress. They anticipate what challenges the client is likely to face and how what he or she has learned can be maintained. The worker can help the client plan for these challenges by considering the following types of questions:

How might the issue be manifested?

Where might it occur?

How frequently may it occur?

What other persons and systems may be involved?

What are the client's current developmental needs?

What coping skills will the client need to manage the issue?

What normal stress may be anticipated related to the client's life transitions?

What cultural and social class factors may facilitate or impede the client's managing the issue?

What external resources does the client need?

What natural systems can the client mobilize to manage the issue?

What strengths and obstacles might the client experience in addressing his or her ongoing needs?

The practitioner may suggest specific activities for the client to implement. We will not consider any examples here, however. These will be discussed at length in part 3 in the context of their theoretical bases.

Addressing the Client's Remaining Needs

Particularly when an intervention is ongoing, the practitioner comes to know the client well. That is, the practitioner often knows what challenges the client faces in areas of his or her life that are not directly related to the presenting problem. As they finish working together, the practitioner should identify with the client any of these challenges that the client may need to address in the future, either with a new practitioner or alone. Returning to the structure of the initial assessment may help the practitioner process this issue. The range of client needs that the worker may address can be organized into a Maslowian hierarchy to include those of survival (food, clothing, income, transportation, health care), safety (housing adequacy, access to assistance), social needs (social groups, recreation), and self-improvement needs (support groups, counseling, education) (Maddi, 1996). When these are identified, the practitioner may use the same types of questions outlined earlier to help the client reflect on their significance.

Linking the Client with Social Supports

The client should be helped to identify all resources, formal and informal, that are available in the community for support after the intervention ends. Social supports can be defined as the interactions and relationships that provide clients with actual assistance or feelings of attachment to others (Walsh & Connelly, 1996). Social supports may be material or emotional. They promote physical health, mental health, coping capability, and community integration. Social supports provide clients and all people with a sense of attachment, validation of personal worth, feelings of community integration, sources of physical care, the opportunity to care for others, and practical assistance with the problems they encounter. They are parts of community systems that provide resources related to health care, housing, safety, education, personal and spiritual fulfillment, employment, legal justice, and even nutrition. Clients' indicators of social support may include a list of persons in their social or personal network, their reports of support experiences, or their perceptions of support adequacy (Vaux, 1988).

Clients' motivation to secure social supports is related to their attitudes about the communities in which they participate. Communities are people bound together by geography or network links who share common ties and interact with one another (Hutchison, 1999). A community may be based on geography but also on interactions with people who do not necessarily live in the client's immediate physical environment (for example, at a church or even over the Internet). A positive sense of community is the client's feeling that the members matter to one another and that their needs will be met by the mutual commitment to be together. Some clients, however, perceive their communities as settings for conflict. A client with the latter perspective will be much more cautious about following up with some linkages.

A challenge for practitioners is to learn how their clients use supports. Clients' linkage needs may be determined by reviewing their network clusters, or similar types of people with whom clients interact. These may include family of origin, extended family, current intimate relationships, work or school contacts, neighbors, informal community relationships (such as store clerks), church or religious contacts, club members, and other social contacts. Research indicates that social supports are most useful when they are spread over a variety of clusters. Client groups that are particularly vulnerable to social support deficits include chronically ill and elderly clients, disabled adults and children, homeless persons, persons living in rural isolation, culturally isolated persons, and abusive and neglectful parents (Hepworth et al., 2002).

Near the end of intervention, the practitioner and client can review the adequacy of the client's supports and mutually consider appropriate linkages. It may be useful to communicate with others (friends and family members) who may be helpful in the client's support acquisition (Northen, 1994). It is often desirable to begin this process early in the ending phase, if not before, so the client can have an opportunity to investigate linkages and share his or her experiences with them prior to the end of intervention.

Resolving the Clinical Relationship

A client may be pleased or sad (or both) that an intervention is ending. Regardless of the affective tone of the event, the practitioner should always address the nature and course of their relationship. Two topics for reflective discussion can help the practitioner develop this theme. The first is that everyone's life includes continual oscillations between togetherness and parting (Sanville, 1982). This experience should be affirmed as natural, as most relationships in life are relatively short term. Developing the ability to reflect on what one has gained and might take with one is a measure of maturity. Processing the end of the clinical relationship offers an opportunity for the client to experience a comfortable oscillation and models a positive way to manage endings in the future.

Related to this point is the practitioner's review of the client's typical methods of coping with separation and dependence. The practitioner may identify and affirm the client's ability to tolerate mixed feelings about relationships (Werbart, 1997). For example, during the intervention the client may have learned to accept and even express anger toward the practitioner and also learned that such feelings need not prohibit gratifying relationships. Discussing these topics helps the client to accept any mixed feelings related to separation as natural.

Formally Evaluating the Intervention (Process and Outcomes)

The purpose of any intervention is to help the client achieve a goal or set of goals that is formulated ideally by the client. Sometimes goals are set by an outside party that is encouraging or mandating the intervention. These goals can change over time. At the end of the intervention it is important for the practitioner and client to mutually evaluate the process. Two types of evaluation may be considered—one related to goal achievement and one related to how the practitioner and client worked together.

There are many ways to initiate an evaluation. Some agencies use standardized measures such as client satisfaction surveys. These tend to be closed ended in format and consist of lists of questions to which the client responds with checkmarks or short answers. Surveys may be given out at the time of the client's final visit with the practitioner or mailed to the client after the file is terminated. A problem with these surveys is that response rates tend to be low, and they tend to evoke biased favorable responses (Williams, Coyle, & Healy, 1998; Williams & Wilkinson, 1995). One might be particularly concerned about the validity of those forms that are collected by the client's own practitioner.

Still, a formal service evaluation completed in the company of the practitioner and including a discussion can facilitate a holistic review of the intervention process (Gutheil, 1993). The client's looking at and filling out a form objectifies the review of the clinical work for the client, providing the client with a level of detachment that can paradoxically elicit expressions of feeling. It gives the client permission to respond to such questions as what it felt like to ask for help, what he or she liked most and least about the process, and how he or she is planning for the future. The practitioner's comments about the client's responses leads to a process evaluation, in which practitioner and client discuss in more detail their experiences together.

A process evaluation can also be managed without a form and consist of a discussion between the client and worker. The types of questions that the practitioner might ask the client include:

How well did we work together?

Did the intervention take a longer time than you initially imagined? A shorter time?

What aspects of our work together did you find the most helpful? The least helpful?

What suggestions would you have for me as I work with clients in the future?

Do you feel that I understood your goals? Problems? Needs?

Did I respond appropriately to your questions?

How well were we able to communicate?

These questions can be used with group interventions as well and be facilitated by several members in addition to the leader. This method is based on the assumption that some group members are more likely to provide honest feedback about their experience privately to peers than directly to the leader. To organize this evaluation the practitioner asks for two or three group members to volunteer as liaisons between the group and practitioner. Prior to the evaluation session the practitioner meets with them privately for ten minutes and orients them to the task. During the designated session the leader excuses her- or himself early. The volunteers preside for the next twenty minutes or so and ask members to respond to and discuss the questions. These are offered only as guide questions—the group members may raise anything they want the leader to know. The volunteers document this feedback with notes, including content and the extent to which group members shared each perception. The leader returns to the group, and the liaison members review the material with the leader but do not identify the sources of the comments.

Setting Conditions and Limits on Future Contact

Once the practitioner and client have their final session, the client should understand how, when, and under what conditions he or she may initiate additional contact. The practitioner may offer no options about future contact or may informally invite the client to call if problems recur. Some practitioners actually schedule "booster" (occasional follow-up) sessions. Clients' anxiety about ending may be diminished greatly with the knowledge that they may see the practitioner again. Paradoxically, this knowledge may reduce the clients' need for the session! Nelson and Politano (1993) provide guidelines about the frequency of scheduling booster sessions for clients with personality disorders or traits. They recommend that planned follow-up sessions should be more frequent for schizoid (withdrawn), avoidant (interpersonally anxious), and borderline (unstable moods) clients, because they have more difficulty sustaining appropriate levels of social integration. Booster sessions should be fewer in number for dependent clients who have difficulty letting go.

This case illustration shows the kinds of headaches that can develop for the practitioner who has not been clear or firm enough with the client about post-intervention contact.

Case Study: The Client Who Wouldn't Go Away

The YWCA domestic violence program where I worked offers counseling to women who are in abusive relationships. Often the women are living with their abusers. Staff try to help them learn new ways to cope with the domestic situation, provide them with information about community support resources, educate them about the cycle of violence, and in general help them take better care of themselves. Counselors typically see clients weekly for an hour. I worked with Sofia at the agency for three months and had a very difficult experience ending with her.

Sofia, in her early thirties, was not reliable about keeping our appointments, but I was never upset about this. She was living with an abusive husband who monitored everything she did. I'd say he harassed her. He often followed her to appointments with me and waited for her outside. He listened in on her phone conversations at their house. Sofia had two young children she was concerned about. I'd say that she came in for seven out of the twelve times we scheduled meetings. When she missed a session I'd call Sofia on her cell phone to see how she was doing and reschedule a meeting. I think she benefited from her counseling with me. She learned how to protect herself and her children.

I was scheduled to leave the agency on a particular date because my internship was ending, and Sofia knew this. I told her of my plans when we first met. She did not show up for either of our last two scheduled appointments. I felt very unsettled about this. She had never missed two meetings in a row before. I wondered if this was a coincidence or Sofia's reluctance to say goodbye. I left without knowing the answer. I also felt bad that I did not know how she was getting along.

But that was not the end! Two months later Sofia called me—at my home! She said that she and her husband were divorcing, and I should expect a subpoena to her child custody hearing. In one way it was good to hear from Sofia, but I was mostly upset about her call and felt violated. She had gotten my number out of the phone book! During the next month as the court case approached Sofia called me three or four more times at home. She was afraid for her safety and felt that she didn't have any other support. I had mixed feelings about all of this. I didn't want to reject Sofia during her crisis, but I couldn't assume any official responsibility for her care. I kept asking her to call the YWCA or a local shelter for abused women. She always said she would, but she never did. This was a dangerous situation for me for liability reasons and because her husband might see me as Sofia's collaborator. My mistake was not to be more firm with Sofia that she needed to seek appropriate professional help and stop calling me.

The court date came, and I was present but was not called to testify. I saw Sofia there, and we talked briefly. She certainly had appreciated my support. A few weeks later she called me again for some help, but this time I was firm about her need to contact other agencies for assistance. She said she would do so, although I don't know if she followed through.

This was a very stressful experience for me. In retrospect, I should have been clear during Sofia's first phone call that I could not have any more contact with her. I crossed boundaries in that posttermination phase of our relationship in ways that were risky. I also learned that I should probably not have my phone number listed in the city directory when I work with certain types of clients.

Summary

The thirteen ending tasks described in this chapter can be utilized in clinical endings regardless of the practitioner's theoretical orientation. Not all practitioners attend openly to all of these, but the tasks tend to enter the practitioner's thinking in some fashion as the intervention moves toward conclusion. The ways in which these ending tasks are applied can be quite varied. This variety emerges from the clinician's practice theory and creativity and the needs of the client (individual, family, or group). It is important for us now to consider how to make choices for implementing these ending tasks. Having reviewed the types of endings, the importance of closure, and common ending tasks, we turn in the next chapters to an array of practice theories and see how they more specifically guide our efforts to achieve clinical closure.

Part 2

Theoretical Perspectives on Endings

Chapter 4

Reflective Theories

In this chapter, and the four chapters that follow, we consider how endings can be addressed from the perspectives of a variety of prominent clinical practice theories. All these theoretical perspectives have much in common with regard to our topic, but they also contain significant differences. It is not my intention to endorse one or several of these theories as inherently preferable for clinical practice but rather to provide an assortment so that you can make comparisons and get a sense of the breadth of current thinking about appropriate ways to end intervention. Those of you who utilize a theoretical framework described in the next five chapters may recognize some of the ending principles from that perspective, but I hope that you may get ideas for using ending procedures associated with other theories as well.

We first consider the broad issue of how working from a specific theoretical perspective is essential for the practitioner to competently organize all stages of an intervention. Next we review ego psychology and the ending processes that tend to be used from that perspective. We then consider object relations theory, which is related to ego psychology but places special emphasis on the client's relationship patterns. Object relations practitioners may use ending criteria from ego psychology but also draw on additional strategies. Finally, we review one type of existential theory and describe how its practitioners are somewhat less concerned with a "comfortable" process of closure. Three case illustrations are interspersed through the chapter.

The Relationship of Theory to Practice

Before beginning a review of specific theories, we need to reflect generally on what practice theory is, why it is relevant to our work, and why there are so many theories. One definition of practice theory is: a coherent set of ideas about human nature, including concepts of health, illness, normalcy, and deviance, that provide verifiable or established explanations for behavior and rationales for intervention (Frank & Frank, 1993). The value of utilizing a theory in clinical practice is that it provides us with a framework to:

◆ Predict and explain client behavior
◆ Generalize among clients and problem areas
◆ Bring order to intervention activities
◆ Identify knowledge gaps about clinical situations

There is also a potential harm of rigidly adhering to a practice theory. Because theories necessarily simplify human behavior, they are reductionistic and possibly antihumanistic, create self-fulfilling prophecies (we tend to see what we are looking for), and blind us to alternative understandings of behavior.

We all have a theoretical basis for our clinical practice. We work from assumptions and knowledge about human behavior, including our beliefs about the nature of problems and the nature of change. From this we develop logical strategies for how to help clients resolve their difficulties. Our choice of theory may be supported by research, the belief that it produces results with the least expenditure of time and money, its provision of useful intervention techniques, or its consistency with our values, knowledge, skills, and worldview. It is possible, however, that we may not be fully aware of, or be able to clearly articulate, our theoretical perspectives. Many practitioners cannot articulate a theory base because it has become a matter of habit (their approaches become automatic), they have not been challenged to do so, or they tend to absorb what their coworkers or supervisors do. This is not meant as a criticism, because many effective practitioners cannot articulate what they do in practice.

While we are thinking broadly about theory, it is also worthwhile to consider what "curative" factors all theories share. In their worldwide study of professional helpers, Frank and Frank (1993) identified the following common characteristics of effective interventions:

- ◆ The client perceives an emotionally charged, confiding relationship with the worker. The client perceives that the practitioner is competent and caring. The relationship is an antidote to alienation, enhances morale, and promotes the client's determination to persist in the face of difficulties.
- ◆ The setting of the intervention includes elements that help the client feel safe and arouses the expectation of help.
- ◆ Interventions are based on a comprehensible rationale and procedures that include an optimistic view of human nature. The practitioner's explanations are compatible with the client's view of the world and thus help the client make sense of his or her problems.
- ◆ Interventions are systematic and require the active participation of the practitioner and client, both of whom believe them to be valid means of restoring health or improving functioning. The client is provided with new opportunities for learning and success experiences to enhance his or her sense of mastery.

I hope you can see that the above discussion provides a useful starting point for appreciating the role of theory in clinical practice, including how it can help us to approach the ending of clinical interventions. It suggests that, while there is much argument among practitioners about the value and validity of various practice theories, one's ability to be effective with clients is largely due to feeling confident with whatever theories one utilizes.

Now we turn our attention to a sample of three specific theories and review how they can help practitioners to competently manage the final stage of intervention. These are loosely classified as "reflective" because they are less structured than many other theories and encourage clients to think freely about the problem situation. In doing so, clients can develop insight, or self-understanding, and gradually formulate their own solutions.

Reflective (Psychodynamic) Theories

Several prominent clinical practice theories derive from the psychodynamic perspective on human behavior. These include psychoanalysis, ego psychology, and object relations theory. All these theories focus attention on the deterministic functions of internal drives (toward pleasure and aggression, for example) and the influence of unconscious mental activity on human behavior. Our conscious mental functioning takes place within the ego, the part of personality that is responsible for negotiating between our internal needs and the demands of social living. This is where cognition occurs, but it is influenced by unconscious thoughts that are always directed toward drive satisfaction. Defense (or coping) mechanisms, which are unconscious distortions of reality, frequently come into play as we attempt to manage our interpersonal and other conflicts. A client's potential for personal growth or problem resolution may not always require attention to unconscious processes, but doing so often maximizes positive change. That is, change may require that we help the client uncover ideas and feelings that have tended to be kept out of consciousness. Freud's (1937) general criteria for the termination of therapy were that the patient was no longer suffering from symptoms of the presenting problem, the symptoms were not likely to reappear, and the patient was not likely to experience any further positive changes by continuing in therapy.

Ego Psychology

The theory of ego psychology evolved from psychoanalysis beginning in the 1930s (Goldstein, 1995; Schamess, 1996). Its development was related to the desire of some theorists to build a psychology of normal development, the influence of new humanistic ideas in the social sciences that emphasized adaptive capacities rather than pathology, and the American social value of pragmatism. The ego is a construct, a part of personality that is present from birth and serves the function of negotiating between internal needs and the outside world. It is the source of our attention, concentration, learning, memory, will, and perception.

Principles from ego psychology focus the practitioner's attention on ego development and adaptation throughout the life cycle. They call attention to the influence of one's past and present transactions with the environment on the quality of present functioning. Ego psychologists acknowledge the influence of unconscious thought processes on behavior, but the autonomy of the ego, and thus conscious thought processes, receives special emphasis (Goldstein, 1995). A unique idea in this theory is that all people possess a drive to mastery and competence. That is, we all have a fundamental inclination to come into harmony with our external environments.

When working from this theoretical perspective, the practitioner assesses the adequacy of the client's major ego functions, including reality testing, the exercise of appropriate control and direction of drives, defensive patterns, interpersonal relationships, and judgment in decision making, among others. The practitioner attends to the possibility of conflicts within the client or conflicts between the client and external world. The stress that a client (and all of us) experiences may result from excess environmental demands (an external focus), inadequate ego functioning (an internal focus), or reactions to normal life transitions (such as age and work transitions, parenthood, separation from significant others, and reactions to health problems).

Change is manifested in the client's ability to achieve greater mastery of challenges, crises, and life transitions. The goal of intervention is to improve the fit between the client's capabilities for coping and adaptation and environmental conditions. The client is helped to learn new problem-solving and coping skills to manage conflicts more effectively and to achieve insight or accurate self-understanding. Ego psychology incorporates two basic types of intervention techniques (Woods & Hollis, 2000). The practitioner chooses ego-sustaining techniques when assessing the client's ego functions as relatively intact. These techniques help the client to understand his or her motivations and behaviors more clearly and mobilize the client to resolve present difficulties. They include sustainment (developing and maintaining a positive relationship), exploration-description-ventilation (to encourage the client's emotional expressions for stress relief and to gain objectivity about problems), and person-situation reflection (so the client can arrive at solutions to present difficulties). The practitioner may also provide education to the client, often about environmental resources, and direct influence, particularly when the client is in crisis and temporarily unable to exercise good judgment about self-care issues.

The major ego-modification technique, which is used when clients experience maladaptive patterns of interpersonal functioning that require an exploration of unconscious processes, is developmental reflection. The clinical worker facilitates the client's self-understanding by exploring his or her personal history, providing new interpretations of relationship patterns, confronting maladaptive defenses, and guiding the client into corrective interpersonal experiences.

A major contribution of ego psychology (and other psychodynamic theories) to our understanding of intervention and ending processes is its emphasis on the importance of the relationship between the practitioner and client. The client's potential for change is facilitated by the worker's provision of empathy and support. When the client's problems are rooted in interpersonal conflicts, it may be important for the practitioner and client to regularly discuss their reactions to each other, as their relationship may become a basis for understanding the client's management of other significant relationships. The manner in which the client manages relationships may reflect unconscious processes, and ego psychology supports their exploration. Two concepts that have great relevance to relationship issues are transference and countertransference. They are also essential concepts in object relations theory.

Transference and Countertransference

The concepts of transference and countertransference emerged within psychodynamic theory during the early 1900s (Gabbard, 1995). They are critically important, as they call attention to the subtle impact of the worker-client relationship on all stages of the intervention. Transference was initially defined as a client's unconscious projection of feelings, thoughts, and wishes onto the practitioner, who comes to represent a person from the client's past, such as a parent, sibling, other relative, or teacher (Jacobs, 1999). The practitioner does not actually possess those characteristics, but the client assumes so. The concept gradually expanded to refer more broadly to all reactions that a client has to his or her clinical worker. These reactions may be based on patterns of interaction with similar types of people in the client's past or on the actual characteristics of the practitioner.

Countertransference was initially defined as a practitioner's unconscious reactions to the client's projections (Jacobs, 1999; Kocan, 1988). This concept has also broadened. It now refers to the effects of the practitioner's conscious and unconscious needs and wishes on his or her understanding of the client. It also refers to the conscious attitudes and tendencies that the worker has about categories of clients (such as being drawn to working with children or having an aversion to older adults). We will focus on the definitions that incorporate conscious elements of the process as they are consistent with most contemporary uses of the term (Gabbard, 1995).

Transference and countertransference are not exotic ideas. They exist in every relationship. We experience others not only in terms of an objective reality but also in terms of how we wish them to be or fear that they might be. These phenomena may be taken into account in every clinical encounter with regard to how they influence the clinician's perception and assessment of the client (and vice versa). The practitioners' awareness of their emotional reactions facilitates the intervention process as it helps them to better understand the rationale behind the clinical decisions they are making.

To better understand these terms we also need to review the common defense mechanism of projection. This occurs when we unconsciously experience a feeling about another person with which we are not comfortable, and in order to avoid "owning" the emotion we attribute it to that other person. For example, if I feel that being angry with my best friend is wrong, when we are in conflict I may decide that he is in fact angry with me. If I am ambivalent about how to work with a client, I may assume that the client is ambivalent.

Practitioners are not always open to exploring their negative countertransference reactions. One reason is that we tend to be reluctant to admit that we can have negative feelings about clients (Mehlman & Glickauf-Hughes, 1994). Still, if we accept the universal human conflicts of independence versus dependence, interaction versus isolation, and activity versus passivity (Kanter, 1988), we should expect to experience mixed emotions during intensive work with any client. Our reluctance to process any negative feelings with clients may reinforce their fears that such affects cannot be constructively managed. Of course, countertransference reactions may be positive and assist our ability to persevere with a client. Examining these feelings is critical during the ending stage of intervention, because they influence the practitioner's behaviors. When we understand countertransference we can manage it and ensure that the ending is processed in a manner consistent with the client's best interest.

Common Countertransferences

Countertransference reactions are problematic only when they cause the practitioner's clinical decision making, including decisions of when and how to manage the ending, to be based on factors related to his or her feelings rather than the client's goals. Following are some common countertransference reactions that practitioners may experience (Hepworth et al., 2002; Kocan, 1988; Schoenwolf, 1993).

♦ Dreading or eagerly anticipating seeing a client
♦ A differential promptness of response to a client's behaviors (such as returning phone calls or responding to missed appointments)
♦ Talking or thinking excessively about a client during nonwork hours
♦ Having trouble understanding a client's conflicts
♦ Being bored with a client
♦ Feeling angry with a client for nonspecific reasons
♦ Being unduly impressed with a client
♦ Feeling defensive or hurt by a client's criticisms
♦ Doing tasks for clients that they are capable of doing for themselves
♦ Feeling uncomfortable about discussing certain topics with a client

In summary, practitioners who work from the theoretical bases of ego psychology or object relations theory should carefully monitor their own and their clients' transferences as they relate to ending the clinical work. The practitioner will want to feel confident that decisions to end or not to end are related to the client's current status with regard to the presenting problem rather than to feelings that they might be experiencing about one another.

Endings in Ego Psychology

Given the abstract nature of ego psychology's assessment and intervention concepts, it should not be surprising that determining an appropriate end point is not always easy. One feature of all the reflective theories is that they encourage the practitioner to consider problem issues and outcomes in the context of a client's overall ego functioning rather than focusing only on the discrete presenting event. Termination can be a lengthy process, sometimes up to one year long when the practitioner wishes to gradually wean the client from the relationship (Firestein, 2001). While its guidelines for the ending process are less clearly defined in comparison to other theories, ego psychology can provide a relatively concrete focus for ending when practitioners limit their attention to the presenting concerns and utilize ego-supportive interventions.

Many prominent clinical theorists have articulated guidelines for ending. The intervention may be ready to end when the client reaches a point where he or she is able to tolerate suffering and occasional depression (Hartmann, 1964), develops a capacity for love and work (Freud, 1937), or achieves a stable sense of identity, ego, drive control, and developmental maturity (Blanck & Blanck, 1979). Robb and Cameron (1998) write that the ending phase should be introduced when the client demonstrates reduced symptoms and improvements in relationships and develops greater self-acceptance, greater insight, and a tolerance for negative emotions. Levin (1998) emphasizes that termination is part of the client's educational experience in that it teaches the client a greater mastery of progression through life cycle transitions. Because of this, the process should focus on the client's mastery of current and past separations. The ending phase should call forth the client's strengths for coping. It is also recommended that the psychodynamic practitioner not proceed with intervention beyond a point of diminishing returns (Schachter, Martin, Gundle, & O'Neil, 1997).

Many theorists describe the ending stage as a period of heightened feeling for both parties, a stage that represents a significant loss. It is a reenactment of earlier relationship endings and as such suggests a process of loss and grieving (Orgel, 2000). The practitioner may be saddened by the loss of the professional role and perhaps even resent the care the client has received if it is better than the care the clinical worker has received in her or his life! The client and worker may, in a desire to continue their mutually gratifying relationship, subconsciously collude to ignore the evidence that the intervention is nearing completion and delay the process (Robb & Cameron, 1998). For this reason, the practitioner should always be alert to transference and countertransference feelings that emerge at the end.

Though the criteria for ego psychological endings seem to be vague, Fortune, Pearlingi, and Rochelle (1991) also found in their general survey of practitioners that 50 percent attend to global rather than specific client improvement factors as their criteria for ending. For example, the practitioners reported that the end occurred when clients felt better or had worked through unconscious conflicts. The practitioners did note both intrapsychic and external considerations and also the cost-benefit issue of potential future gains. But they gave relatively little weight to clients' concrete resolution of presenting problems.

Otto Rank, who worked in the first half of the twentieth century, made a major contribution to the process of therapy endings from the psychodynamic perspective. He understood that the practitioner did not always have the luxury of open-ended analysis and thus should organize the intervention around a process of working toward predetermined ending criteria, specifically the client's acquisition of separation and individuation capabilities (Lieberman, 1985). By conceptualizing during the initial assessment what a positive ending would represent for the client, the therapist could organize the intervention accordingly. Rank's work foreshadowed innovations in brief therapy, in which the practitioner needs to observe externally imposed limits in planning the scope of his or her intervention.

As is true with most theories, psychodynamic practitioners recognize problems with unplanned terminations, such as a lack of opportunity to integrate therapeutic gains or resolve many issues of ego functioning and the transference. In the case of transfers, which are planned, clients may experience problems with a new therapist if they carry over unresolved issues from the previous one. With respect to this point, unplanned termination has been called "disenfranchised grief" (Levin, 1998). Forced terminations, defined as those that must end sooner than initially anticipated, should feature a strengths orientation. The practitioner should focus on the client's potential for adaptation and growth, mastery and maturation, and attachment to others. The therapist must express a full range of feelings and be positive about the client's future (Siebold, 1991).

While the tapering of meetings during the ending stage is common in all theories, some psychodynamic practitioners do not observe this practice. This is shown in two of the case illustrations that follow, and the reasons will be described there. Practitioners also tend to deemphasize the utility of follow-up sessions after ending, but there are some exceptions. Several possible advantages of follow-ups is that they reactivate the client's self-reflection, complete the process of de-idealization of the practitioner, and bolster the client's sense of self (Sczecsody, 1999). A posttermination meeting may help the practitioner to stabilize, assess, and consider the possibility of a client's further participation in clinical work with the useful perspective of distance.

In addition to evaluating the extent to which the presenting problem or challenge has been resolved, the practitioner should review the status of each relevant ego function that has been a focus of intervention and discuss these with the client. It will be important to communicate to the client that further strengthening of ego functions is possible after the work they have done together ends. The practitioner should help the client to devise strategies for continued self-reflection.

The client should be helped to review his or her past, present, and future with regard to the presenting problem. A brief life review can strengthen the client's sense of identity. The client's recent past can be addressed with a review of the intervention process. The client's present situation is reflected in his or her current status, focusing on new knowledge and skills. This can provide the client with evidence of positive change even if the process has not been completely successful. Looking ahead to the client's potential growth opportunities outside the clinical setting helps him or her look constructively toward the future.

Additional ending principles are provided later, but they can be understood more clearly after a review of object relations theory.

Object Relations Theory

The term "object relations" is a rather unfortunate one, as it has a mechanistic tone and is confusing to many students and practitioners. It generally refers to interpersonal relations. Object relations is also an ego function, but this theory (or group of theories) focuses on the processes by which we learn to form and manage relationships with our primary caregivers and the ways in which those patterns tend to persist throughout life (St. Clair, 1999). People who have recurrent interpersonal problems may have a fundamental inability to form and sustain relationships and have great difficulty with trust and intimacy. Their sense of self outside of relationships may be quite fragile. Clients with these characteristics may be assessed as having deficits in object (interpersonal) relations and sometimes personality disorders, defined as inflexible patterns of perceiving and relating to the environment and oneself that cause significant distress (American Psychiatric Association, 2001).

Object relations theory helps us to understand how our earliest relationships set these patterns into action and also how they can be changed. It enhances our understanding of the role of the relationship in clinical practice and how it must be monitored throughout intervention. The client's relationship with the worker is subject to the same dynamics as any other, and thus the worker may use it as a model. I will summarize some basic concepts of object relations theory that have significance for the process of ending relationships. The theory is similar in many respects to ego psychology in its attention to such phenomena as unconscious processes and defense mechanisms.

Object relations theorists assert that healthy development requires a nurturing early environment, that we are relationship seeking from birth, and that we internalize (or permanently adopt) our early relationship patterns. There are stages in our early development of object relations, each of which must be successfully resolved to ensure our future capacity to have satisfying relationships. In the state of object (again, interpersonal) constancy we internalize the images of caring others within our psychological selves. When we have internalized the sense of the availability and permanence of caring others while also developing a sense of ourselves as separate beings, we are capable of developing satisfying, trusting relationships. When our moving through infancy fails to unfold in a supportive environment, however, due perhaps to inconsistent caregiving or deprivation, we may develop a poor sense of self. We may become overly dependent on others, extremely anxious when alone, and fundamentally unable to trust others. When a practitioner is helping a client with such problems, the goals of intervention will include enhanced insight (described earlier as developmental reflection) related to interpersonal style and helping the client to develop realistic expectations about new relationships. Often the client will perceive the clinical relationship in the same distorted ways as he or she perceives other relationships in his or her life, which makes the course of that relationship an excellent basis on which to focus the intervention.

Endings in Object Relations Theory

All the ending issues related to ego psychology apply to object relations theory. With its focus on relationships, however, there is a special emphasis in object relations theory on the need to help the client achieve object constancy and separate from the practitioner as a unique person, rather than another person whom the practitioner represents (Frank, 1999). The practitioner and client should move into the ending stage when the client develops insight into relationship patterns and is able to approach new relationships as unique rather than as repetitions of earlier ones. The client's ability to end the clinical relationship in a positive manner and separate from the supportive "object" constitutes a test of his or her ability to appropriately manage future interpersonal conflicts and losses. Both parties should reflect on and discuss transference and countertransference issues. The practitioner should address the ending in a particularly delicate manner, as it includes the possibility for reawakening the client's sense of feeling abandoned by significant others. Ending principles related to these points include the following.

The practitioner can develop a theme for the ending that everyone's life includes continual oscillations between togetherness and parting (Sanville, 1982). This experience should be affirmed as natural. The clinical relationship and its ending offer opportunities for the client to experience increasingly comfortable oscillations and thus to master ambivalence about relationships. To promote the client's management of this issue, he or she may be given more control over the scheduling, frequency, and length of meetings. In this context the practitioner should not interpret evidence of the client's pulling away as resistance, as any changes in clinical routine may symbolize the client's taking more control of his or her life.

Clients should be helped to review their methods of coping with separation, dependence, and any related negative emotions, such as anger. The worker may identify and affirm clients' emerging ability to tolerate ambivalence as feelings of both love and hate toward the same person (Werbart, 1997). During intervention, clients may have learned to accept and express anger toward the practitioner and learned that such feelings do not prohibit a gratifying relationship. Discussing this topic helps clients to process the inevitably mixed feelings related to separation from significant others.

The client should be helped to review the evolution of his or her transference reactions. For example, how did the client view the practitioner when they began their work? On what were these impressions based? How did these impressions change over time? The client should be helped to see the practitioner as a "real" person rather than a manifestation of some "type." In this way clients are reminded that each new relationship is unique and that they may be hampered in their ability to develop good relationships with unfounded expectations of what other people are going to be like.

The following two vignettes describe endings from the ego psychology/ object relations perspectives. The first of these focuses on the process by which the practitioner and client determined that they were reaching an end point and then how they completed their work together. The second example focuses more specifically on the final session and the delicate interaction that occurred between the two parties as they considered how to address one final, significant issue. Both illustrations represent positive endings.

Case Study: The Distressed Wife

I provided psychotherapy to Shirley for two and a half years. She was thirty years old and experiencing depression related to marital problems. We met twice weekly, as I subscribed to an intensive therapy model in my private practice at that time. I use ego psychology intervention concepts in my work. I want to emphasize that, in my view, the issue of ending is intentionally not addressed in detail as a distinct stage in psychodynamic therapy. Therapy is as educational as it is treatment focused, so there is usually not a specific time when the client "should" end. Clients often decide to end therapy for external reasons such as moving or taking on a new job rather than because of what is going on in therapy.

Shirley progressed well in our work together. We addressed the ways in which her personality style contributed to the strained marital relationship and how she might make changes in that regard. Shirley had been raised in her family of origin to play the role of the altruist, or caregiver. She believed that she needed to put the needs of others before her own. Consistent with this worldview, Shirley had become a nurse. She married a man who was very bright and talented but also rather self-absorbed, not sensitive to her needs. Even though Shirley was accustomed to being a caregiver, she eventually became depressed because her needs were not being met in the marriage. She wanted children, for example, and her husband kept putting this off. Further, he was verbally abusive to her at times. He was also reluctant to participate in therapy. He felt that their problems were not serious, and he was preoccupied with his career.

In therapy I promoted Shirley's use of person-situation and developmental reflection strategies to increase her self-understanding, including becoming more clear about her needs and goals. She benefited from this approach. Over time she developed a higher sense of self-worth and became able to speak more assertively to her own needs in the marriage. The marriage improved as Shirley's husband, initially upset with her assertiveness, became more attentive and appreciative of her qualities. They stayed together and began a family. I never actively explored Shirley's transference with me, even though I was a man of approximately the same age as her husband. I do think that I modeled what a man such as her husband could be like. I respected her point of view, encouraged her personal development, affirmed her rights within relationships, and supported her use of compromise in the marriage. So it was a positive transference, and because of that fact I did not believe it merited open exploration.

Shirley finally suggested that we consider ending the therapy. I had not brought up the idea before, but it made sense to me. She decided to end when she recognized that she was an equal in her marriage, that the relationship was good and likely to stay that way, and that she did not need my consultation anymore in making decisions. We could have met further, because, as I said, therapy can be educational. She might have acquired additional benefits, but it was not necessary to her well-being. We agreed on a two-month ending process. During those eight weeks we discussed her current concerns but also where she had started out, where she was now, what she had learned, and what the triggers of her relationship conflicts were. In contrast to what many therapists do during the ending process, we did not taper our visits. She did not "practice" not being in therapy, which to me is what tapering amounts to. My view is that the end of therapy does not need to be dragged out. When it is over, it is over. Shirley was satisfied with the process and the outcome. I invited her to call me in the future if she wanted additional assistance.

Nine months later I had three more sessions with Shirley. She had called to report an upsurge in conflicts with her husband. She made it clear that she was only seeking brief consultation. In those meetings we reviewed what she had learned over the course of our intensive work. Shirley was reminded of her personal qualities. She was satisfied with this "refresher" series and planned to stay in her marriage. One year later, she again called to say that she was doing well, but that she and her husband were interested in enhancing their marriage with couples' therapy. I supported the idea and gave her a referral.

Case Study: The Champagne Toast

I worked with Sylvia using psychodynamic therapy (as described in the first case example). Sylvia was a thirty-five-year-old mental health professional who was depressed about relationship problems that represented an unsatisfying life pattern for her. I intervened with Sylvia using reflective techniques, including person-situation reflection and developmental reflection. I asked a lot of questions and did not give her any concrete advice. I encouraged Sylvia to explore the meanings behind her thoughts and behaviors so that she could come to understand herself better, to uncover her unconscious motivations at a manageable pace. She had a positive transference toward me. As a female professional, I think I modeled certain qualities that she wanted to develop. Sylvia made steady progress. We met twice weekly for about two years before she indicated that she was feeling well enough to consider ending our work. She wanted to do this gradually, and the process unfolded over a period of six months.

Our last session was memorable, as it pertains to the issue of celebrations as well as to how endings are managed within psychodynamic theory. Sylvia came to our last meeting with a small shopping bag. She sat down in her chair and took out a bottle of champagne and two glasses, which she placed on the small table next to her chair. She said nothing about this action but seemed to be waiting for me to react. Of course, I was struck by the unusual gesture, but I did not say anything about it. I wanted her to bring up whatever she had in mind. In psychodynamic therapy the client is always expected to take the lead. Our final session proceeded, and the hour was coming to a close. I still had not mentioned the champagne and neither had she.

Sylvia finally began to talk with some difficulty about what her therapy and our relationship had meant to her. Her voice shook, and she stammered. Expressing herself directly had been a problem for her all along, but she was actually able to do it that day very well. Later she thanked me for not bringing up the topic of the champagne. She said, "If you had asked me about the champagne, I would have suggested that we open the bottle and toast our work. But then I would not have had to really express my feelings about our work. I need to learn to do that. So I'm glad that you never brought it up."

It was interesting that Sylvia had brought a celebratory gift to our final meeting as an avoidance strategy. This is why I believe that gifts should not be routinely accepted or acknowledged by the practitioner. If Sylvia had brought up the issue herself and offered to pour us some champagne, I still would have asked her first to talk about what the gesture meant. I still would have gone for her feelings. That was a large part of our work together and an important part of the analytic approach.

Now we turn to the final reflective theory and consider what it may add to an understanding of the ending stage.

Existential Theory

Practice principles related to existentialism and spirituality have become more prominent in the helping professions during the past ten years (Hora, 1996; Willis, 1994). We will consider the broader concept of existentialism here. Existentialism has many definitions, but it can be understood as a person's search for, and adherence to, meanings, purposes, and commitments in life (Krill,

1996). It may or may not include a religious system (Fromm, 1967). A basic tenet of existential philosophy is that we are all free to make whatever commitments to other persons, causes, and values are consistent with our nature. Some existential writers assert that we create what is meaningful in our lives, and others assert that we discover meaning. The idea of creation implies that our meanings are highly individualistic, that they emerge within each of us and reflect our unique interests and values. The perspective of discovery holds that there are at least some meanings that reflect a reality that exists independently of us. We are thus challenged to discover meanings that exist objectively. Both views can be held simultaneously, as a person might consider some purposes to be objective and others to be based on individual meaning constructions.

Existential meanings can include one's investment in belief systems, social concerns, creative pursuits, the hope of a better future, and personal relationships. These concerns arise from or help us to manage anxieties that are inevitably produced by our confrontations with issues of death, the possibility of isolation, our freedom to make choices and the responsibilities involved in choice, and concerns about our place in the world (Yalom, 1980). Coming to terms with these issues is a challenge for all people. We do not necessarily confront them on a daily basis, but they have fundamental influence on how we organize our lives.

Human behavior theorists point out that we have certain emotional experiences that can serve as signals of our existential struggles (Lazarus & Lazarus, 1994). These may underlie the presenting problems of many clients. Anxiety may result from perceived threats to our sense of identity or future well-being and from our facing life and death concerns. It is powered by our struggle to maintain close connections with others, a process that is often threatened by the fragile nature of life. Guilt results from thoughts we have or actions we take that are in violation of our standards of conduct, especially when other persons who are important to us observe them, that is, we have not behaved in accordance with an important personal value. Shame is similar to guilt but refers more specifically to our failure to live up to a personal ideal. It may not be noticed by or directly affect another person, but it is within our own awareness. It is also important to emphasize here that we experience positive emotions such as happiness and joy when we behave in ways that affirm our existential values. Existential interventions include the following principles:

◆ To engage the client more fully in life activity
◆ To encourage the client to look externally for solutions to problems rather than focus on the self (or balance these two areas)
◆ To encourage the client to care about something outside the self
◆ To remove obstacles to the client's inclinations to look externally for solutions

It is not appropriate to raise existential issues with clients in all practice situations (May & Yalom, 1995). They may not be appropriate for clients who are

absorbed in immediate problems for which they are seeking practical assistance. Issues of meaning and purpose may become appropriate topics during
intervention, however, when a client is troubled more vaguely by strong negative emotions or demonstrates inclinations to look beyond the self and the immediate situation in understanding personal dilemmas.

Logotherapy is an existential practice theory that is based on psychodynamic theory (Frankl, 1988). In it, the will to meaning, a basic and enduring
tendency to obtain what satisfies a person's nature, is conceptualized as a universal drive. All of us use this drive to either create or discover meaning and purpose in life beyond our basic physical survival. Despite the existence of this
drive, many people do not often reflect on their existential purposes. This is because recognizing these issues is always accompanied by an awareness of vulnerability to tragedy, anxiety, and loss. Our inevitable experiences with suffering, guilt, and death can result in a repression of the will to meaning. The drive
may be relegated to the unconscious (this is similar to the use of repression in
psychodynamic theory). Instead of accepting and grappling with the essence of
our lives, we may become consciously preoccupied with less threatening, more
superficial aspects of life. This is never a satisfactory resolution to the problem
of vulnerability, however. No drive can be completely suppressed, and when
doing so, we will experience ongoing distress in the form of symptoms of mental and emotional problems.

When appropriate, a task of the clinician is to help the client develop insight to become aware of his or her ultimate values and commitments, including those existential impulses that have been pushed out of awareness. This
process will result in the client's personal growth, but it will be in part painful.
The client will need to accept more fully his or her vulnerability to the uncer-
tainties of life. Relief cannot be a primary goal of intervention, because the
essence of living includes the frequent experience of distress. The practitioner
must remind the client that focusing on existential concerns cannot be managed comfortably. The worker will not shield the client from the possibilities of
risk and loss involved in making and sustaining commitments.

Endings in Existential Theory

The process of ending intervention in existential practice is slightly different from the theories described earlier. The client will (hopefully) have resolved
his or her presenting concerns but also learned, or been reminded, that most solutions involve new risks. It is certainly true that what the client gains from
being more fully involved with commitments can be highly beneficial. But the
practitioner will emphasize throughout the intervention that the client must become able to openly experience and manage the pain of separation and loss.
The clinical worker may observe many of the principles from ego psychology
and object relations theory in the process of ending. He or she may be less nurturing, however, and less inclined to try to minimize the possibility that the

client will have difficulty with the end of the clinical experience. Certainly, in the vignette that follows, the practitioner was not inclined to minimize the client's anxieties as they related to the end of their relationship.

The following vignette represents the existential approach to ending. The client was in a state of significant distress, and the practitioner essentially gave him the choice of whether he wanted to keep himself there or take certain risks that might eventually result in his feeling more interpersonally connected. This was not a positive ending from the client's perspective, although the practitioner saw it differently.

Case Study: A Midlife Crisis

As an existential practitioner, I have much empathy for the pain my clients experience. I think this comes across in my work with them, as I recognize and praise their strength in dealing with life struggles. But I do not suggest that their pain can be taken away or that there might be safe risks that one can take in life. To live is to risk, and to risk is to often fail. But not to risk is to become emotionally dead. I expect my clients to eventually face these harsh aspects of life, and I help them decide how they can summon their strengths to risk more satisfying changes. The will to meaning is a concept that recognizes the desire we all have to find meaning in spite of uncertainty.

John was a forty-four-year-old man who had experienced a series of losses in the past few years. First, his wife of twenty years divorced him and immediately became involved in a lesbian relationship. Next, the printing business of which he was the founder and sole nonclerical employee began a downward spiral, as he could not stay competitive with the new computer technologies. Finally, John's only child, a son, graduated from college and left the country to work with the Peace Corps. Each of these losses was devastating, and they threw John into a state of depression. He reluctantly agreed to ongoing clinical intervention following a brief psychiatric hospitalization.

Almost anyone would become depressed by the kinds of losses John experienced. Given his background, however, their impact was more profound. John had long ago learned to be suspicious of other people. He was an insecure child who received a stern upbringing from achievement-oriented parents. He grew up in the shadow of an older brother who was, in his view, the "all-American kid." John had been an angry, insecure youngster. From the time he completed high school, he gave up trying to develop close relationships with others and became a loner. He intended from the beginning that his printing business would be a solo venture. He quickly married a woman about whom he felt ambivalent. John wanted to be close to someone and in retrospect believed that she was much like him with regard to intimacy problems. They established a superficially secure household.

Once John felt comfortable with our relationship, I shared my assessment with him. I added my observations that he wanted to find purpose in his life within relationships of mutual caring, but most of his major life decisions (regarding jobs, where to live, and who to spend time with) were based on a desire to avoid close contact with others. He assumed that rejection and pain were inevitable if he allowed himself to become involved with other people. As a result he did not manage any relationships well. John was a nice-looking and articulate man, and he did attract people. He could be friendly up to the point where he might be expected to make a commitment. Then he abruptly terminated the relationship by avoidance or with some hostile action. John often justified his rejection of others by asserting his intellectual superiority, which was in fact a mask for interpersonal inadequacy. He managed formal relationships best and thus was most comfortable at work.

I helped John look to others for emotional support in a variety of contexts such as church, work, and family. I became John's major supporter and confidante as he began to risk more honest participation in those relationships. My acknowledgement of the inevitable anxiety associated with risk actually helped John to feel better about himself. He had always assumed that emotional struggles were evidence of maladjustment. But when I challenged John to become more open with others, he was always ready to recount the many times he had been betrayed. I became more confrontational with John as I could see his ingrained tendency to rationalize why he could not do anything differently. Even as he tended to discount my suggested strategies for addressing his problems, I saw evidence of John's desire to change in his continued attendance at our weekly sessions.

When the time came for the intervention to end because of agency time limits, John's anxieties returned. He did not feel "strong enough" to carry on with social and vocational reintegration. He cited my refusal to petition the agency for additional meetings as evidence that he should never trust anyone. I was patient with John's anger but did not change my mind about the issue. I summarized the many indicators of John's progress and affirmed his capacity to function adequately. I told him that he was looking for a security that I could never provide. John even expressed vague suicidal ideas, but after evaluating his emotional status I concluded that he was not at significant risk of self-harm. John's mood stabilized somewhat near the end of our work, but he did not show up for the planned final session. He left a message that he needed to attend to a family matter.

From the perspective of existential theory, it was predictable that our ending would be difficult for John. He might wonder if his ability to confide in me was a fluke. He might be concerned that in natural settings his anxieties might overwhelm him and that with any failures he might lose the positive momentum he had generated. John might also feel hurt to realize at its end that his relationship with me had always been a formal one. I felt that with his increased insight and ability to take initiatives, John was likely to maintain an improved level of functioning. I tried to communicate this to John through the ending process. John was not able to hear this assertion of confidence from me, but he might have appreciated it in the future if he maintained his sense of interpersonal competence.

It should be evident from this example how the existential practitioner is less nurturing but no less thoughtful during the end stage of intervention.

Summary

A practice theory is a coherent set of ideas for organizing both clinical assessment and intervention. All practitioners work from one or more theoretical perspectives depending on their training, habits, or the needs of particular clients. Every practice theory includes guidelines for how to approach the ending stage of intervention. In this chapter we have considered the perspectives of three psychodynamic (reflective) theories and articulated five ending strategies that derive from them. These strategies are relatively nonspecific compared to other theories we review in the next four chapters. The timing of their implementation depends on practitioners' ongoing assessment of their clients' progress and potential for future gains.

Chapter 5

Cognitive-Behavior Theory

The cognitive and behavior theories present different perspectives on human behavior. Practitioners may use one or the other as a guiding framework for clinical practice, but the theories are often integrated into a holistic approach to working with clients. Cognitive theory focuses on the rationality of one's thinking patterns and the connections among thoughts, feelings, and behaviors. It also emphasizes the client's need to practice new skills and complete "homework" assignments between sessions. Behavior theory is not so much concerned with internal processes but provides advanced strategies for changing the reinforcers of human behavior. These theories are quite different from the reflective theories discussed in chapter 4, as they deny the significance of unconscious mental processes. However, reflective discussion of here-and-now issues is still critical.

From the cognitive perspective, conscious thoughts rather than unconscious impulses are the primary determinants of our feelings and behavior (Beck, 1995; Granvold, 1994; Greenberger & Padesky, 1995; Lantz, 1996). Thoughts and feelings are separate mental processes. Most of our emotional experiences and behaviors are a result of what we think, tell ourselves, and believe about ourselves. Many mental, emotional, and behavioral problems are the result of cognitive misperceptions (beliefs that are not supported by external evidence) that can be adjusted. Behavior theory takes the trend in cognitive theory of deemphasizing innate drives and unconscious thinking even further (Granvold, 1994; Wilson, 2000; Wodarski & Bagarozzi, 1979). The practitioner using behavior theory does not deny the reality of internal mental activity but makes few or no inferences about it. Behavior therapists focus on observable behavior and contingency management (that is, reinforcements and punishments). Thoughts and emotions are conceptualized as behaviors that are also subject to reinforcement contingencies. Reinforcement is environmental feedback that encourages a person's continuation of a behavior, and punishment is feedback that discourages the continuation of a behavior. Problem resolution is a process of changing specific behavior reinforcements.

Each theory offers some distinct perspectives to the ending process, but again they have much in common in that regard. Three case illustrations focus on the cognitive-behavioral perspective to ending intervention.

Cognitive Theory

Major Concepts

Cognitive theory, which entered the human services during the 1950s, incorporates several central concepts. Cognitive structure refers to our internal biological mechanisms for organizing the input we acquire from the environment. These may be innate but are not located (as far as we know) in a specific area of the brain. Within that structure we internalize and store propositions, or basic assumptions regarding the environment and ourselves. These can and do change, but not easily—they tend to be rigid. Cognitive operations refer to our information-processing procedures—how we take input from the environment, combine it with our assumptions about the world, arrive at some conclusion, and then store it as knowledge. These procedures are learned but occur automatically. The results of these operations are cognitive products. These include our beliefs, attitudes, values, and judgments about the world. There is nothing necessarily true in a factual sense about these products, but we tend to see them as such because they make sense to us. All these processes can be summarized as cognitive schema—our internalized representation of the world, or systematic patterns of thinking, acting, and solving problems.

So long as our cognitive style helps us to achieve our goals, it is considered healthy. However, our thinking patterns can feature acquired distortions in thought processing or cognitive biases that dismiss relevant environmental information from our judgment. These may lead in turn to maladaptive emotional responses. So how do we define "rational" thinking? This can be understood as thinking that is based on external evidence, is life preserving, keeps us directed toward personal goals, and decreases our internal conflicts. It is important to understand, too, that not all unpleasant emotions are dysfunctional, and not all pleasant emotions are functional.

Within cognitive theory there are no innate drives or motivations that propel us to act toward others in particular ways. Human action always includes the possibility of choice. We may be predetermined to act in certain ways because of the nature of our schema, but this can be adjusted through our acquisition of new information or our reasoning. Our capacity to effectively adapt to the social world unfolds over time with the biological maturation of our cognitive capacities. Piaget's work is the best-known account of the process by which we develop the capacity for abstract reasoning from childhood through adolescence and early adulthood (Maier, 1978). Natural biological changes in our physical and neurological development are necessary for cognitive development to proceed.

Nature of Problems and Change

Many problems in living result from misconceptions (conclusions that are based too much on internalized patterns of thought and not enough on available external evidence) that people have about themselves, other people, and life situations. These misconceptions may give rise to problematic feelings and behaviors. Such problems may develop for three general reasons. The first of these is the simplest—the person has not acquired the information necessary to manage a novel situation. This is often evident in the lives of children and adolescents. They face many situations at school, at play, and with their families that they have not experienced before, and they are understandably not sure how to respond to them. This lack of information is known as a cognitive deficit.

The other two sources of problems are more complex and are related to personal schemas that are too rigid to manage a novel situation. The concept of causal attribution refers to three sets of assumptions, or core beliefs, that we carry about the sources of power in our lives. First, we might assume that situations in which we find ourselves are more or less changeable. Second, we might see the source of power to make changes as existing within ourselves or outside of ourselves. Finally, we might assume that our experiences are limited in their implications to the specific situation or that they have global implications. For example, if I am unable to provide for my family during a time of temporary unemployment, I might assume that I am a thoroughly incapable parent.

The final sources of problems are cognitive distortions of reality related to faulty or rigid cognitive information-processing patterns. Because of our thinking habits we often interpret new situations in biased ways. We all utilize cognitive distortions at times, and they may not always create difficulty for us. Following are the common cognitive distortions:

Absolute thinking—the tendency to view experiences in a polarized manner, as all good or all bad, and failing to understand that experiences can be a mixture of both

Overgeneralization—when deficiencies in one area of our lives necessarily imply deficiencies in other areas

Selective abstraction—focusing only on the negative aspects of a situation and consequently overlooking its positive aspects

Arbitrary inference—reaching a negative conclusion about a situation despite a lack of sufficient evidence

Magnification—creating large problems out of small ones

Minimization—making large problems small and thus not dealing adequately with them

In cognitive theory, change can occur in three ways. It may involve the practitioner's changing the personal goals of a client so that they are more consistent with his or her cognitive inclinations, adjusting cognitive assumptions (beliefs, expectations, meanings attached to events), and adjusting cognitive processes (selection of input, memory and retrieval, thought patterns). Even though many of our beliefs are irrational and distorted, our potential to correct these beliefs in light of contradictory evidence is great. In clinical assessment, the practitioner must assess the client's schema, identify any faulty thinking patterns or cognitive deficits, and consider the evidence supporting a client's beliefs in judging their validity. During intervention, the practitioner utilizes techniques to help the client adjust his or her cognitive processes in ways that will better facilitate goal attainment. In doing so, the client will also experience more positive emotions.

Intervention Principles

Cognitive interventions focus more on present than past behavior. The past is important for discovering the origins of a client's thinking patterns, but it is present thinking that motivates behavior. The nature of the practitioner-client relationship is important, as it must catalyze the client's difficult process of questioning some basic assumptions and considering new schematic patterns. The practitioner must demonstrate positive regard for the client while alternately functioning as a model, coach, collaborator, and trusted representative of "objective" thinking. The practitioner is active in cognitive intervention, much more so than in the reflective theories, participating in discussions and the mutual development of change strategies.

There are many particular strategies for cognitive intervention, but they all fit into three general categories. The first of these is cognitive restructuring. The practitioner assesses the client's patterns of thinking, determines with the client that some of them are not effective for managing important life challenges, and through a series of discussions and exercises helps the client to experiment with alternative ways of approaching challenges that will promote goal attainment. Some strategies toward this end include:

Didactic teaching—filling information gaps for the client

Attribution training—helping the client to understand that his or her emotional life and potential for goal attainment have more to do with thought patterns than the client might believe

Self-instruction training—helping the client utilize self-talk to rehearse or maintain new patterns of thought in certain situations

The dysfunctional thought record—a paper-and-pencil technique for the client to distinguish the effects of automatic thoughts on emotional reactions and to learn substitute ways of thinking for automatic ones

Double standard technique—helping clients see that they hold themselves more accountable for problems than they would other persons accountable in the same situation

Point-counterpoint technique—debating with the client the relative arguments for and against a certain belief that is based on external evidence and also the costs and benefits to the client for maintaining certain attitudes

Helping the client develop more functional imagery, or mental pictures, to cope more effectively with problem situations

The second category of cognitive interventions is coping skills training. The practitioner helps the client learn and practice new or more effective ways of dealing with stress. All of these involve step-by-step procedures for the client to master new skills, and these must be rehearsed and practiced by the client to ensure mastery. Some techniques include:

Social skills training—such as communication and assertiveness training

Stress management skills—such as strategies for overcoming stress or minimizing the effects of stress that cannot be eradicated

Relaxation training—such as deep breathing and muscle relaxation

The third category for intervention is problem solving. Some clients experience stress because they lack effective problem-solving skills. By changing general patterns of addressing problems and learning to be more creative in addressing them, the client can become more capable of managing the present problem and perhaps other challenges in the future. The steps in problem solving include helping the client to:

Specify the nature of the presenting problem

Analyze the problem and identify the needs of any significant others

Brainstorm a range of possible solutions

Evaluate each alternative and select the most promising one

Implement the selected option

Evaluate the outcome

Either end or go back to the "selection" step

It should be evident that cognitive interventions require the client to be active in resolving his or her problems and that the client needs to practice solution strategies while in treatment. The practitioner must develop skills for understanding when client change is sufficient and intervention can end.

Preparing the Client for Ending

There are seven ongoing (sometimes called pretermination) activities that the practitioner can initiate to facilitate the formal ending process when that time arrives. All these strategies reflect three themes—practicing new cognitive patterns, skills, and behavior; increasing the client's confidence about taking over his or her own "intervention"; and preparing for the possibility of relapse. These activities, many of which are drawn from Ludgate (1995) and Nelson and Politano (1993), are described in the following sections. Not all of these are specific to cognitive theory. They are consistent with the approach, but some can be used with theoretical approaches described in later chapters.

Initiate a Collaborative Stance to Intervention   At the outset of their relationship, the practitioner should introduce a theme of collaborative problem solving in which the client plays a major role in decision making about the intervention process. The client should be encouraged to identify target behaviors and set goals, contribute to session agendas, design homework activities, and give feedback about the practitioner's own actions. This collaborative atmosphere will facilitate a gradual shift during the intervention toward the client's independent work on maintenance and relapse-prevention activities. To promote this atmosphere the practitioner needs to recognize the client's capacity to function as a "partner." The client's expertise in articulating concerns and strategies for how he or she might productively address them must be acknowledged.

Keep the Ending at the Forefront   As part of the client's orientation to cognitive intervention, the practitioner should stress that client and practitioner are working together for a limited amount of time toward an end point. The client should be reminded that he or she has strengths on which to build and that the overarching goal of intervention is for the client to acquire new coping strategies that can be used without the practitioner's assistance.

Review Progress Regularly   Whatever intervention techniques are utilized, practitioners must help clients review their new skills and behaviors both during sessions (perhaps with role plays) and through homework assignments. Clients should consider how their new skills can help them manage presenting problems and also other life situations. To reinforce their learning, clients should also be asked on a regular basis to identify the generalizable principles of cognitive therapy.

Encourage Self-Monitoring   Clients can be given a variety of self-rating scales to monitor their thinking, emotions, and behavior changes. Many such scales, such as depression and anxiety inventories, are available in the literature (Beck, 1995), and others can be constructed by the practitioner and client. For example, the practitioner may link particular client behaviors at ten-point intervals on a self-rating scale from 0 (least desirable) to 100 (most desirable). Clients can record their progress from week to week, and the ratings can become the focus of sessions with the practitioner. As intervention progresses, clients can be given greater responsibility for developing, scoring, and interpreting these scales. Graphing results may be useful for clients who respond to visual information.

Provide Skills with Broad Applicability   Clients should be taught the process of problem solving, rather than focusing only on specific problem situations (Hepworth et al., 2002). The practitioner should exploit every opportunity to transfer new knowledge and skills from one situation to others. This process should include a discussion of the common intervention principles that may be generalized across problem situations after each situation-specific intervention. Such common tools may include testing automatic thoughts, generating alternative response options, anxiety reduction methods, activity monitoring, and problem-solving skills. The specific steps in problem solving were outlined earlier in this chapter. This process helps the clients assume responsibility for self-directed problem solving.

Increase Emphasis on Between-Session Behavior   Cognitive intervention always stresses the importance of homework and between-session activity, but this focus should become even more pronounced as the intervention proceeds. The intervention emphasis shifts from collaborative problem solving within sessions to the practitioner's supervision of the client's application of these methods in the natural environment. In this way clients gradually assume greater responsibility for helping themselves and can perceive the movement of intervention.

Identify Relapse Risks   During intervention the practitioner helps the client to identify the major risk factors for relapse. He or she reviews the possibility of relapse or failure with each intervention strategy. The client can be encouraged to monitor these identified relapse risks and make plans for how to respond to them. The client's participation in this exercise represents an important step toward self-control. As a part of this process it is useful for the client to imagine a setback and predict what he or she will be thinking at that point, based on previous experiences. Such anticipatory self-statements give clues to the client's belief system, and any maladaptive cognitive responses can be addressed in advance of an actual setback. This can help the client identify cognitive distortions, and the practitioner can help the client respond in more functional ways.

Ending Activities

The seven additional activities that follow can be implemented when the practitioner and client explicitly recognize that they are ready to formally end the intervention.

Explore Thoughts Regarding Termination   As noted earlier, the ending process should be discussed at times throughout intervention, but it should receive more attention as the work progresses. The practitioner may raise questions with the client such as: "To what extent do you think you have achieved your goals?" "Have you given any thought about ending?" "What are your thoughts about ending our work?" "How does the immediate future, after we finish, look to you?" The practitioner should provide his or her own thoughts about ending as well, and it is possible that the two parties will have a different perspective. Whether to end the intervention may need to be negotiated. If the practitioner feels strongly that it is time to end but the client wishes to continue, the practitioner should explore the client's automatic thoughts behind the reluctance to end. Of course, the practitioner's own reluctance to end with the client may be an issue as well, requiring that the practitioner consult with a supervisor or engage in self-reflection about his or her own cognitive biases.

Reduce Session Frequency The gradual tapering of sessions is a common ending activity and does not seem to reflect a particular theoretical perspective. This action can be framed as rehearsal for the eventual ending—an experiment to evaluate the client's progress and level of self-reliance. There can be much variety, of course, in how the strategy is implemented, for example, when it begins relative to the anticipated end point and at what interval sessions are scheduled. Practitioners and clients often decide to space their meetings further apart as the final ending point approaches. This tapering should be done collaboratively, as it may stir anxiety in some clients who are concerned about their ability to function effectively without the practitioner's support.

Support the Client's Sense of Self-Efficacy Cognitive intervention is usually focused on helping the client develop the sense of competence for problem solving. As the intervention nears an end, the practitioner should emphasize the client's self-efficacy even more so—not to instill false confidence but to celebrate changes the client has made. The client's skills in self-instruction, self-reinforcement, environmental control, and modeling can be reviewed. To facilitate the client's sense of self-efficacy and readiness to end intervention, the practitioner can ask such questions as: "What have you achieved in our work together?" "What is different now, and what did you specifically do to make this happen?" and "What have you learned, and what tools do you now have to work on your problems in the future?" These questions are intended to help the client reflect on his or her strengths and overcome any concerns about inadequacy. They can be used as the basis for discussions or as homework assignments. For example, the client can be asked to maintain a journal of the changes she or he has made during the intervention and the personal strengths applied when making those changes.

Proactively Plan for Responding to Relapse The practitioner should discuss with clients the nature of their difficulties and behaviors over the course of treatment, and then consider the likelihood of relapse after treatment ends. This is done throughout the intervention, but it is important to place more emphasis on the issue during the ending stage to prepare clients for self-monitoring. There is always a chance of relapse, and its occurrence should be normalized. If clients understand that life after treatment will not be problem free, they will be less likely to feel overwhelmed if relapses do occur and will feel more prepared to end. The practitioner should introduce the notion of prolapse—that movement forward may be accelerated after the client experiences a relapse (Ludgate, 1995). This is the positive side of backsliding. The practitioner can help clients consider that when they find themselves back-

sliding, they can stop what they are doing, examine the situation, identify automatic thoughts that may be mediating the situation-affect link, and initiate coping strategies. The purpose of this activity is to help clients become sensitive to
the subtle changes in mood, thinking, or behavior that precede a more significant relapse.

In the case of depression, for example, it is common for clients to find themselves experiencing the negative mood almost "out of the blue." They become
unable to help themselves recover until it is too late. Almost always there are
subtle signs of the recurrence of depression. Some clients use self-monitoring
instruments to monitor their moods, but the process of recognizing early warning signs should be personalized with each client. Signs may include subtle
changes such as social withdrawal and irritability. Such questions as: "What are
high-risk situations for you?" "When are the times that you think you might slip
back if you are not careful?" and "What situations might put you back into a depressed state?" help clients identify the more obvious high-risk situations.

Once risk situations are identified, the client and worker can discuss the
range of coping strategies that the client may implement. These strategies should
be discussed in detail and listed in order of priority. For example, when faced
with the temptation to use alcohol in a given situation, a client with a drinking
problem may first try "strategy one"—refusing the invitation to have a drink. If
that does not resolve the client's discomfort or cannot be used in the situation,
"strategy two," leaving the room, might be utilized, and so on. In this way the
client develops lists of response alternatives that preclude him or her from having to think through the process during a time of challenge. The practitioner
should also help the client develop criteria for deciding whether to recontact
the practitioner. For example, "strategy five" on a response list may be to call the
practitioner, given the fact that the first four coping strategies have not worked.
Clients may be encouraged to write out these response lists and carry them in a
wallet or purse for ready reference.

When relapses occur near the end of the intervention, the practitioner
must convey to the client that the fact of relapse is not as significant as the
client's reaction to it. If the client becomes discouraged, the practitioner should
explore the client's core thoughts behind this feeling in case new cognitive distortions have emerged. The client may believe, for example, that there should be
no relapses. The practitioner can set up a win-win situation for the client by
stating, "Old habits die hard, and certain negative thoughts are likely to recur.
Dealing with them successfully is the best outcome, but if we cannot, relapses
give us useful information about the kind of thinking that keeps us distressed
and can be adjusted."

Involve the Client's Significant Others Cognitive intervention strategies may be used when working with families or couples. It may also be appropriate at times to consult with or enlist the participation of the client's significant others during the end stage of intervention. The client may request such

involvement to ensure that he or she will be supported in efforts to maintain intervention gains. Family members, partners, or friends can be brought into one or more sessions to be educated about the nature, course, and treatment of the client's problem issue; the rationale and strategies of cognitive intervention; the early warning signs of relapse; and strategies they might use in the client's ongoing recovery process. Such participation can be conceptualized largely as educational, so that the significant others can understand the client's needs and ongoing goals related to the intervention experience.

Plan a "Self-Therapy" Program　In addition to considering the specific relapse situations that may arise, the practitioner can help the client devise an ongoing plan for maintaining healthy cognitive practices. Investigating and uncovering beliefs about therapeutic progress and self-efficacy can facilitate a self-therapy focus once the intervention ends. The client's program may include daily breathing exercises, the regular practice of writing down troubling thoughts, reading over therapy notes on a regular basis, doing one fun activity every day, breaking down challenging tasks into small steps, and using a structured problem-solving process when challenged. Some cognitive practitioners urge clients to set regular appointments with themselves! With this option, clients can review the week, engage in formal self-monitoring, target problems for work during the coming week, consider relapse triggers, and set up new homework tasks.

Consider Booster Sessions　Many practitioners invite clients to return for one or several booster sessions. These may be optional or recommended. When recommended, the sessions may be conceptualized as a part of the tapering-off process described earlier. When optional, the invitation is extended to help reassure the client who is anxious about ending that, if old problems emerge, the practitioner will be available to help. Some practitioners find that this invitation to return actually reduces the likelihood that the client will do so. That is, the reassurance increases the client's sense of security. Some clients do, however, return for short periods. The practitioner needs to be clear before the client ends whether such a return will be considered a "boost" or may include the possibility of resuming longer-term intervention.

In a booster session, the practitioner should focus with the client on the following questions:

What has gone well?

What problems have arisen?

How might the client have coped better?

What additional problems might arise? How likely are they?

What has the client done to maintain progress?

What gets in the way of the client's positive functioning, and what else might he or she do to minimize this?

What goals does the client have? What plans has the client made for working toward them?

It is possible that a client will unexpectedly experience a high level of environmental stress immediately following intervention. One or more follow-up sessions may be required to address this. The practitioner should acknowledge that no repertoire of coping strategies is sufficient to control all contingencies in anyone's life. As with crisis intervention, it is important for the client to mobilize his or her interpersonal and material supports until relief is achieved. The practitioner and client can then review the situation and, in the tradition of anticipatory guidance, plan ahead for managing future crises.

It is sometimes recommended that booster sessions should be encouraged for persons who are isolative by nature, because they will have fewer natural supports available (Kupers, 1988). Sessions should perhaps be offered less often for clients who will tend to use them to maintain an inappropriate dependency.

The following illustration provides a good example of a practitioner's attention to the end stage of a cognitive intervention.

Case Study: The Mama's Girl

I am a private practitioner and have a contract with a local company's employee assistance program (EAP). I often work from a cognitive theory perspective with those clients because they are usually limited to ten sessions. Joyce, a thirty-seven-year-old African American woman, was referred by the EAP to get help for her depression. She lived with her mother, whom she described as her best friend. Joyce had no other close relationships, although she was involved with a man who, in her own words, treated her badly. In fact, Joyce had never had any other close relationships. She was lonely, and because she always felt insecure, Joyce was afraid of losing her job, without a clear reason. She had symptoms that met the diagnosis of major depression. Joyce made it clear that she did not want to take any medication.

When I have a limited number of sessions with a client, I institute ending activities right at the beginning. I help the client be clear about what he or she wants to accomplish, and we set priorities for those goals. I review clients' progress each week and remind them how much time we have left to work. In Joyce's case, this approach worked out very well.

Joyce had developed a lifelong cognitive schema in which she believed she was not attractive, that no one could be interested in her, that she needed to accept any man who showed interest in her, and that her mother needed her as a companion and caregiver. Perhaps most seriously, Joyce believed that she could not be helped. She had never sought help for her problems because of this belief. After eliciting these cognitive patterns during the assessment, I educated Joyce about cognitive theory and the possibility that she was living with cognitive distortions. I initiated a process by which we examined each of her beliefs with regard to the evidence in her environment that supported them. At first Joyce was withdrawn and flat during our conversations, but soon she responded to my strategy and showed much motivation to participate in the process. It seemed to make sense to her. We developed specific plans for each session, and I always gave Joyce written homework tasks such as the dysfunctional thought record so that she could check out the validity of her beliefs and test out new perceptions of herself with new behaviors.

In cognitive therapy, clients are ready to end when they become able to reflect on cognitive assumptions on their own, when they can independently maintain cognitive restructuring practices they have developed with the help of a professional. Part of the ending process, then, involves showing the clients that they are becoming capable of managing their lives more successfully. By the fourth session Joyce was able to accept that she did not have to make commitments to others simply because they were interested in her. She broke up with the man she had been seeing! At the time of our third session, she got an offer for a much better job in a city five hundred miles away. By our fifth session her confidence was such that she could consider that offer. One of the highlights of our work came after I suggested that she talk to her mother about the implications of her moving. Joyce did so, and her mother made it clear that she did not need Joyce. In fact, she had felt all along that Joyce had needed her! Her mother was dating a man and managing her own money, and she encouraged Joyce to take the job!

By the tenth session, Joyce had learned very well how to unravel her own automatic thought patterns and determine when they represented distortions. As I said, we had been planning for the end all along, and during our final meeting we reviewed in detail the process by which Joyce had become able to think for herself. We arranged one follow-up contact—Joyce would call me after she moved and got settled in her new city. She did call me, three weeks later, and left a message on my answering machine. She said that the move had not been as difficult as she had imagined. This woman who had once been so flat laughed and added, "I wonder why I don't feel so depressed anymore?"

In this example the practitioner utilized a collaborative relationship with the client, maintained a focus on the end point of the intervention, reviewed the client's progress weekly, and encouraged the client to self-monitor her cognitive and behavioral changes. When the end was nearing the practitioner highlighted the client's self-efficacy and, before she moved, arranged for one follow-up contact.

Now we turn to behavior theory, introduced earlier in this chapter as a perspective that relies primarily on observable evidence in the process of assessment and intervention.

Behavior Theory

Behaviorism has been prominent in the social sciences since the first half of the twentieth century, but it became a popular theory among clinical practitioners in the 1960s. Behaviorism reflected the new emphasis in social science on empiricism (observable evidence) in evaluating the outcomes of intervention. Today's service delivery environment, with its focus on outcome indicators, owes a great debt to the behaviorists, who remain the most proficient group of practitioners in measuring intervention outcomes (Granvold, 1994).

The basic principles and assumptions of behavior theory are as follows:

Behavior is what a person does, thinks, or feels that can be observed.

People are motivated by nature to seek pleasure and avoid pain.

Behavior is amenable to change.

People behave based on their learning.

People are likely to behave in ways that produce encouraging responses.

People often learn by watching others behave and interact.

Assessment must focus on observable events with a minimum of practitioner interpretation.

Behaviors must be operationalized, or defined in terms of measurable variables.

Intervention focuses on influencing reinforcements or punishments for client behaviors.

Thoughts and feelings are behaviors that are subject to reinforcement principles.

Consistent and immediate reinforcement produces change most rapidly.

The simplest explanations for behavior are preferred.

Practitioners must avoid reification (giving life to esoteric concepts such as the ego) and the search for "ultimate" causes.

Inferences about mental activity must be minimized because they cannot be observed directly.

The practitioner must be seen as competent and trustworthy, particularly if he or she will be asking the client to engage in behaviors that are not initially comfortable. For the same reason, the client must be a collaborator in developing behavioral interventions.

Strict behaviorists make few assumptions about the internal or psychological nature of the individual. You will recall, for example, that ego psychology has much to say about psychosocial development, and cognitive theory postulates some principles of schematic development. Behaviorists assume that people are motivated to seek pleasure and avoid pain and that all behavior is related to reinforcement contingencies of basic and social survival. They acknowledge that genetic and biological influences are relevant to one's physical and trait development but otherwise offer no developmental concepts.

The Nature of Problems and Change

Within behavior theory the nature of problems for which clients seek professional help is always the existence of negative reinforcement contingencies (those that perpetuate problem behavior) and an absence of positive contingencies. All behavior, whether functional or problematic, is influenced by the same principles of conditioning. The nature of change is simply the rearrangement of reinforcement contingencies so that more desirable or functional behaviors will result. Behavior is changed through the application of action-oriented interventions. For the practitioner this always includes the concrete measurement of behavioral responses.

The goals of intervention are to help the client achieve new, desirable behaviors by manipulating the environment. For example, if a child behaves in school in ways that are disruptive to the classroom process (from the perspective of the teacher), the practitioner can devise a plan in which those negative behaviors are extinguished and new, more acceptable classroom behaviors are reinforced. One of the great challenges in behavior therapy, however, is to identify the specific responses that are reinforcing to the client among the many responses that he or she receives following a behavior. In the example cited, the teacher's displeasure with acting-out behaviors might serve as punishment to some students but as reinforcement to others.

Intervention Principles

The process of intervention in behavior theory is quite systematic and includes the following steps:

The client's problems are stated in behavioral terms.

Measurable objectives related to problem reduction are developed.

The practitioner and client gather baseline data on the problem behavior.

The steps required to reach problem resolution are specified in graduated terms (moving from easier to more difficult).

The client's personal and environmental resources for making changes are specified.

Relevant significant others who will participate in the intervention plan, if any, are identified and sought out for consultation (often as reinforcers).

Possible obstacles to goal achievement are identified in advance.

An appropriate intervention strategy is chosen, always with the participation of the client and with an emphasis on positive consequences of behaviors.

The practitioner, client, or other persons collect data about the client's activities.

The client's behavior changes are documented on a regular basis.

The intervention process is evaluated regularly.

The intervention ends after the client achieves his or her goals with the likelihood of goal maintenance.

There are many interventions from which the behavioral practitioner may select, depending on the client's presenting problem, the client's preferences, and the time and resources available to the practitioner. Following are some of these interventions:

Modeling. The client watches a model, someone he or she would like to emulate, perform a desired behavior in order to learn the behavior and become motivated to perform it. The behavior is broken down into its component parts so that the client understands the skill and can rehearse it. For example, members of an adolescent group may watch a video by a music celebrity in which strategies for refusing drugs are described. The client practices the new behaviors, perhaps in the artificial setting of the agency and with the practitioner, prior to implementing the behavior in its natural setting. In group settings, peer support is a major reinforcer.

Manipulation of reinforcers (positive and negative). The practitioner helps the client and significant other persons in the client's environment devise methods for identifying behavioral reinforcers and then organizing the environment in such a way that the reinforcers or punishments for a behavior will tend to increase or decrease its occurrence.

Stimulus control (rearranging antecedents). In contrast to the manipulating reinforcers intervention, the client and practitioner alter the conditions that precede a client's target behavior. For example, the misbehaving classroom student described earlier may be moved to a classroom with fewer students so that there is less of an incentive to behave in ways that will impress those students.

Exposure. The client, in a series of graduated steps that require closer contact with a dreaded but desired situation, acquires mastery of the challenge. In short, the client masters the situation little by little. Often, relaxation techniques such as deep breathing are used to facilitate this process.

Shaping. The client's behavior gradually moves from its baseline state to the goal by the reinforcement of behaviors that approximate the desired behavior. That is, a client who is seeking help for controlling his or her angry outbursts can be rewarded in some ways (praise, attention) whenever he or she is less volatile. These rewards become more prominent as the client comes closer to the desired behavior. The client (for example, a person with mental retardation) may not even be aware of the process.

As with cognitive interventions, the practitioner seeks to help the client achieve specified goals and maintains the intervention until they both are confident that it will persist. When that point is reached, the practitioner moves into the ending stage.

Endings in Behavior Theory

Ideally, ending intervention in behavior theory is a process of fading. That is, after an intervention has been underway for some length of time and the client has acquired the desired new behaviors, any artificial supports (including the practitioner and the reinforcement schedule) are gradually eliminated (or faded). This includes reducing the frequency of meetings between the client and practitioner. The fading process helps the practitioner to determine whether the artificial reinforcements are still necessary and to what degree. It is hoped that the new behaviors will continue with the client's development of natural reinforcers. As part of the fading process, the practitioner may address the ending tasks described earlier with regard to cognitive theory, particularly those of incorporating the theme of ending as a regular agenda item, reviewing progress regularly, encouraging self-monitoring, planning for response to relapse, reducing session frequency, planning for goal maintenance, and booster sessions.

We will now see how the cognitive and behavior theories can be combined and then review several examples of how endings can be approached from this holistic perspective.

Cognitive-Behavior Theory

Strict behavioral practitioners will not incorporate aspects of cognitive theory into their practice, because it involves attention to internal processes that cannot be observed. Behavioral approaches can be highly effective by themselves, particularly when working with client populations that have limited cognitive skills, such as young children and persons with cognitive disabilities. Cognitive practitioners, however, who rely on the client's completion of out-of-session tasks and homework assignments, can incorporate aspects of behavior theory into their work as a means of introducing comprehensive task activities. In order to effectively prescribe and help clients follow through with homework assignments, the cognitive practitioner should adopt procedures from behavior theory that bring rigor to that process. The clinical vignettes that follow involve this combined theoretical approach and illustrate how endings can be managed when using cognitive-behavioral interventions.

The two vignettes presented here are drawn from caseloads at the same facility. The Child and Adolescent Treatment Center (CATC) is an urban inpatient residential facility for children and adolescents with severe emotional disturbances. The facility adheres to a structured cognitive-behavioral theoretical perspective. The facility's procedures provide excellent examples of the importance of planning for a client's ending.

CATC houses up to fifteen children and twenty adolescent boys and girls. The focus of the program is family and community reintegration. The cognitive, educational, and behavioral interventions emphasize improving coping and life skills to help the child or adolescent successfully return to the community. Services include case management; parent support and education; individual, family, and group therapy; medication management; nursing care; recreation, art, music, and occupational therapy; and community integration activities. The average length of stay for residents in this facility is six to nine months.

When new residents enter the program they are required to establish three primary goals. These often involve learning to follow rules, progressing in school, and developing more socially appropriate behaviors. Staff make a concerted effort to keep residents' families involved in all facets of the program. Staff also keep residents involved with their home communities so that the treatment experience does not represent a complete break with their natural environments. Residents earn points for positive behaviors that can move them from starting points at level three to levels two and one and then to graduation (discharge). All staff, including teachers, clinical professionals, and even housekeeping and dietary staff, share responsibility for awarding points on a daily chart for a resident's behaviors. Points are awarded to a resident every thirty minutes during the day for the successful completion of whatever task she or he has been prescribed (including waking and going to bed on time, using appropriate hygiene, attending and participating in school, using appropriate social skills, attending and participating in treatment groups, and so on).

Staff attend carefully to the process of a resident's termination from the facility. Residents are considered to be ready for discharge when they can earn 80 percent of their possible daily points consistently for a period of two to three months. A formal termination plan is initiated thirty days from the resident's projected discharge date. During that final month staff take extra time to talk with the resident about his or her overall progress and additional changes the client may make after discharge. All persons from the client's community who will participate in the resident's discharge plan (family, friends, and teachers) are encouraged to participate in the process. For example, a social worker will accompany the resident to the new community school to visit the principal and discuss the resident's course of treatment. Over a period of two weeks the resident will attend the community school alternately with the facility's school, spending two days at a time at each one.

When possible, staff discharge residents during natural breaks in their community life. Discharges may be more frequent at the end of an academic year or during the December holidays. Staff anticipate that the resident's behaviors may regress during the final month because of anxiety associated with the upcoming change. Staff "rally the forces," providing the resident with much support. They increase the fervor of their cognitive strategies—helping the child to recognize his or her power and reminding the child to use positive self-statements. Staff assure the child that they do and will continue to care about him or her even as the child is leaving. The child will be invited to come back and visit after discharge (many former residents do so). During the regular group interventions there is a greater focus on the child's emotions in addition to his or her behaviors. Finally, each resident has a graduation party. The extravagance of the party depends on the child's program level. The party is a festive occasion when residents and staff have a chance to state publicly what the child has accomplished and what he or she has meant to the program.

With this introduction to CATC, we now look at two clients who participated in the program—one who had a positive ending experience, and another who did not.

Case Study: The Boy with the Feeding Tube

I work as a case manager at CATC. As a member of the day shift, I help run groups and escort residents on community outings. I also participate with the treatment team in residents' program planning. One of our clients was Eddie, a twelve-year-old African American boy with serious physical and emotional problems. His physical problems included sickle cell anemia and anorexia. He had not been eating appropriately for several years, and before he was admitted here a physician had inserted a feeding tube into his arm. Each day nutrients were fed into this tube. Soon after his admission I noticed that Eddie used the excuse of his sickle cell illness to avoid many normal responsibilities, including attending school, and to manipulate others to do things for him. Eddie also exhibited oppositional behavior. He tended to defy authority figures and throw objects when upset. He also experienced school phobia, having been out of school for several months at the time of his admission, and his behavior was infantile in some ways. For example, he purposely spoke with a very high voice and a limited vocabulary, appearing to some people like he might be only five or six years old. We were concerned about the boy's prognosis, because his problems were long standing, and he seemed physically fragile. On the positive side, his mother was supportive of the treatment program—she would cooperate fully with staff and be in regular contact with us.

A primary staff goal during Eddie's nine-month stay was to stabilize him medically and emotionally to a point that his feeding tube could be removed. This would require that his weight, which often fell below seventy pounds, rise to eighty pounds and stay there for two months. His other target behaviors, to which Eddie agreed, were to give up his childish voice and acquire a "normal" one, become able to express himself rather than throw objects when upset, and seek a medical exam when feeling sick rather than retreating to his room.

We try to give residents as much control over their intervention as possible, so Eddie was asked to take a dietary supplement every day and to fill what was termed a "healthy plate" of food at mealtimes. He received points for how well he filled his plate and how well he ate. He also earned points for attending and participating in groups, interacting with his peers in appropriate ways, using a normal speaking voice, expressing his feelings, not throwing objects, and not retreating to his room or asking to go home when he felt sick. Like many of our residents, Eddie was slow to get involved in the program, and he often refused to participate in activities and go to school. Still, he was accustomed to manipulating others to do what he wanted through negative behaviors, and this was not working for him at CATC. On the other hand, he received a great deal of positive attention for his healthy behaviors. One key to the success of behavioral interventions is that they must be applied consistently, and we were able to do so because of our frequent team meetings. Eddie gradually became compliant with the program. He eventually responded to positive feedback more than I initially thought he would. Besides our behavioral interventions we also tried to teach Eddie about appropriate ways to get attention, make friends, and take care of himself. After the first three months in the program Eddie went home sick only two more times!

Even though Eddie did well at our center, he never made it to level one. He couldn't maintain his points at an 80-percent level quite long enough to get that promotion. One problem was that his weight fell below eighty pounds occasionally. But the feeding tube was removed, and Eddie's overall progress was good enough after eight months that he was considered ready for discharge. During the ending phase of Eddie's stay, his transition back to the community became the staff's focus. His mother, whose participation was in my opinion the key to Eddie's progress, had been learning from the therapists since the beginning how to implement behavioral management strategies with Eddie at home. For example, she learned how to reward his cleaning his room, taking care of the yard, doing his homework, and getting out to school each day. The nurses taught her about Eddie's illnesses so that she would be able to respond to his concerns without overreacting, which she had done in the past. I was highly involved in some of Eddie's transition activities. I went to Eddie's home with him several times per week during the final month to help him understand his mother's different approach to running the household and to validate that it was healthy for him. Because Eddie was going home at the end of the academic year, we spent more time outside the facility helping him to connect with summer activities. I helped him get signed up for baseball. I even met with some of Eddie's friends to plan some activities for them with Eddie after he returned home.

Eddie hadn't made level one, but he still had a nice party when he left. We didn't worry too much about his backsliding when he left. His mother's preparations for his coming home had a lot to do with that. And while Eddie had come to like our facility and program, he was always focused on going home. Perhaps because he lived nearby and knew we would always be here he felt comfortable with the change. Actually, it may have been harder on the staff that Eddie was leaving than it was on him. He had become a staff favorite! I think that the discharge parties are good for staff as well as the residents to help us to manage our sense of loss.

Many cognitive-behavioral ending strategies were employed with Eddie. Staff allowed him to have input into his goal setting, and he was given feedback about his progress on a daily basis, verbally and through the point system. Eddie was encouraged to monitor his own behaviors during his group interventions, and through the program milieu he was provided with an array of new knowledge and skills. His major "significant other," his mother, was a key participant in the program. During his final month in the program, staff praised Eddie's acquisition of new skills and his improved self-efficacy. Staff also contacted various community members to participate in his discharge plan and showed Eddie how he could maintain his gains. As a kind of "booster" plan, Eddie was reminded that he was welcome to visit staff and his peers at the facility after he left.

Case Study: The Aggressive Adolescent

Curtis, age sixteen, was an ambivalent client throughout his five-month stay, but this is pretty much the norm at CATC. He had serious problems with aggressive behavior related to his anger and had participated unsuccessfully in several less comprehensive programs before coming to us. Curtis came from a poor household that included only himself and his mother. She was overwhelmed by the trouble he so often got into and was feeling desperate. There were few relatives nearby. My role as the social worker was to meet with his mother and help her learn how she might have a better relationship with Curtis as well as uphold reasonable expectations for his behavior. His target behaviors were to become able to adhere to rules, give other people their personal space (rather than become physically aggressive with them), and share his feelings when upset rather than shutting down.

After Curtis was admitted to CATC he went through a "honeymoon period" of about two months. Many residents feel relief from outside pressures when they first arrive, and they also take time to assess the facility and make a positive impression on staff. Eventually we began to see more of Curtis's negative behaviors. At first they were school related, as he became oppositional with his teachers. He refused to do school work and became angry and sullen when confronted about this. When Curtis began to have trouble earning points with his behavior, we responded by writing down our expectations for him each day and increasing our limits on his behavior. But Curtis became even more aggressive and stated clearly that he wanted out! Our response was to ask him to show us that he was ready to go home by successfully completing the program. Unfortunately, he also made it clear to his mother during our biweekly meetings that he wanted out. He had an ability to shake her resolve by complaining to her about the program and the staff.

Our interventions intensified during his fourth month, when we began to provide Curtis with one-on-one supervision. There was a staff member with him at all times whose task it was to supervise his behavior and encourage his positive program participation. We thought that he would settle down, but unfortunately he did not. The extreme behaviors he finally exhibited were hitting a staff member, hitting a peer, and being caught hiding glass in his room, which we saw as a potential weapon. Curtis was put on restriction—virtual isolation from his peers. When this happens we immediately institute a program of reentry whereby the resident can move back into the regular program. By earning enough points the resident can return to level three.

The key to all of this was the ongoing participation and support of his mother. During our meetings I stressed the importance of her supporting our work with Curtis. I asked her to tell Curtis that she expected him to stay at CATC until he met his goals. But this is where the intervention eventually fell apart. His mother had been exasperated with him prior to program admission, and she continued to feel that way as he experienced difficulty with us. Curtis could manipulate his mother by promising to be a better son if he came home and complaining about what he perceived as harsh treatment from us. During the sixth month his mother suddenly dropped out of contact with me. She was worn out again, it seemed. Without her support we could not continue intervention and needed to discharge Curtis back home.

The ending of this intervention was complicated by the fact that his mother did not make herself available for discharge planning. We wanted to send her son home, but we could not just drop him off without her acknowledgment of the plan. We left several phone messages and sent several letters but had no response. Finally, we sent a certified letter to her address, letting her know when we would be bringing Curtis home. It was a particularly difficult ending, because there was no coordination with his mother about his ongoing needs. Our desire for continuity with the client's family and neighborhood was lost.

What could we have done to make Curtis's ending process more constructive? I'm not sure, because his mother's refusal to participate limited our options. Engaging the mother more fully in the program philosophy and supporting her desire to set limits might have been beneficial. Unfortunately, she had few supports in her own life to help with these decisions. Staff spent a great deal of time with Curtis prior to his discharge, asking him to reconsider his decision to leave. We also tried to help him look ahead to his life after he returned home, but he had tuned us out by that point. We pointed out his positive qualities and that he had shown the ability to make some responsible decisions while he was with us. We also shared information with the other residents about Curtis's pending discharge so that they could say goodbye. Few of them chose to do so, because he had been rather quiet and alienated for several months by that time. This was a type of discharge that left all of us feeling bad. We had failed to help a resident and could not arrange for a positive, gradual transition back to his home. These endings are quite emotionally draining for me and help me understand why the ceremonies we usually provide for discharged residents are so important for all of us.

Intervention with Curtis failed largely because he never made a commitment to the program, and his mother was ambivalent about her role in it. For Curtis's discharge, staff attempted to initiate the same types of activities they had employed with Eddie. His mother's lack of participation, however, compromised their efforts to reintegrate the client into his home community. Staff encouraged Curtis to think ahead to his life after discharge and emphasized his strengths and adaptability. They also encouraged other facility residents to say goodbye to Curtis. But it was difficult to reach closure with this client who had not been an active participant in the process.

Summary

Cognitive theory and behavior theory represent two approaches to clinical intervention that can be provided separately or combined into a single intervention perspective. Compared to the reflective theories described in chapter 4, much empirical research has been done to support the efficacy of these intervention approaches for a variety of client populations (Chambless, 1998). Because these are structured interventions, the practitioner can build ending activities into the process from the beginning. In this chapter we reviewed fourteen elements of the ending process in cognitive theory, ten of which are directly applicable to behavior theory as well. The case vignettes illustrate how the practitioner can work to bring such interventions to closure.

Chapter 6

The Solution-Focused and Narrative Theories

The solution-focused and narrative therapies are the newest approaches to clinical practice presented in this book. They have some elements in common, as both derive from the broader social theory of constructivism. This is a different approach to understanding human behavior and the nature of change than we have considered thus far. I begin this chapter with an overview of social constructionism and then describe how the solution-focused and narrative interventions reflect this perspective on the self and the social world. I then consider how the end of intervention is approached from each perspective.

Social Constructivism

The theory of social constructivism maintains that there is no objective reality that we can all apprehend and agree on (Rodwell, 1998). We share a physical reality, but what that reality means to us (including our perspectives on relationships, social situations, and ourselves) is a mental creation. We apply internal assumptions and beliefs acquired from prior experiences to the input we receive from the environment. This perspective is consistent with cognitive theory as presented in chapter 5, but social constructivism incorporates fewer assumptions about human nature.

All of us are born with certain biological and temperamental qualities that influence our abilities to integrate sensory perceptions, but we become active participants in the process of making sense of the world early in life. It is the interaction of what we bring to social situations and what those situations present to us that produce our evolving view of reality. These subjective processes shape our sense of self, competence, and contentment. Our satisfactory interpersonal functioning depends on maintaining many patterns of shared meaning with others.

A major implication of this theory is that our presumed knowledge about ourselves and others is wholly subjective. We cannot make generalizable assertions about the nature of the self and social world. In contrast, psychodynamic theories assume the existence of common psychosexual or psychosocial stages, and practitioners use that knowledge to assess clients' social functioning. Cognitive theorists maintain that there are stages of cognitive and moral development that are relevant to assessment and intervention. In social constructivism the notion of a common human nature is deemphasized. Practice theories that reflect this perspective feature less emphasis on clinical assessment, because the practitioner does not rely on knowledge of developmental stages as significant to problem development or intervention.

In summary, social constructivism holds that:

◆ Reality is humanly constructed.
◆ Meaning is constructed both internally and socially.
◆ Truth is relative to one's frame of reference.
◆ Knowledge is a set of assumptions.
◆ Knowledge building is an interpretive process that tests shared beliefs.

This short introduction is sufficient to provide a background for the practice theories we now turn to.

Solution-Focused Therapy

Solution-focused therapy is a short-term approach to intervention in which the practitioner and client attend to solutions or exceptions to problems more so than to the problems themselves (Corcoran, 2000; De Jong & Berg, 2002; O'Hanlon & Weiner-Davis, 1989). The principles that underlie solution-focused therapy originated in the fields of strategic therapy, brief therapy, and crisis intervention. Its focus is on helping clients identify their strengths and amplify them so that they can be applied as solutions to presenting problems. There is a deemphasis on "problem talk" and an emphasis on "solution talk." The model is clearly oriented toward the future.

Major Concepts and the Nature of Change

The solution-focused perspective includes few assumptions about human nature. It assumes that people want to change, are suggestible, and can develop resources to solve their problems. The nature of problems is as follows (O'Connell, 1998):

Problems result from patterns of behavior that have been reinforced.

People are often constrained from change and finding solutions by narrow views of their problems.

Problems can be resolved without understanding their causes.

Rigid beliefs, assumptions, and attitudes prevent people from noticing new information in their environments that can provide solutions to their problems.

There is no "right" way to view any problem or solution.

Problems are not so ubiquitous as people tend to assume.

The concept of selective attention is relevant to solution-focused intervention. That is, people benefit significantly from learning to recognize when a problem is not happening. Identifying solutions that follow the discovery of these exceptions is considered to be easier and more effective than focusing on problems.

Significant change can be achieved for most clinical problems in a relatively brief period of time. The nature of change is as follows (O'Hanlon & Weiner-Davis, 1989):

Change is constant; it is always happening, whether we recognize it or not.

Change is facilitated by reinterpreting situations and acquiring new ideas and information about them.

There is no difference between symptomatic and underlying change; all change is equally significant.

A small change sets ongoing change processes in motion.

Rapid change is possible.

The goals of intervention in solution-focused therapy are for clients to:
Focus on solutions to problems
Discover exceptions to problems (times when they are not happening)
Learn to act and think differently
Become more aware of their strengths and resources

Assessment and Intervention Principles

Solution-focused therapy focuses on specific behaviors that are achievable within a brief time period. Practitioners do not claim to possess "special" problem-solving strategies but present themselves as collaborators. They assure their clients that they can work together to discover effective solutions. The client defines the goals; the practitioner helps the client select goals that are achievable and frames them in ways that are concrete and workable. The practitioner builds the client's sense of efficacy and normalizes the problem so the client feels less overwhelmed. She or he affirms the client's perspectives on problems and solutions but presents alternative viewpoints that may free the client from typical patterns of behavior.

There is not a clear demarcation between assessment and intervention. The assessment process involves the practitioner's questioning of the client about the problem situation. This is different from the broad social histories suggested in other clinical approaches, as it is limited to questions directly related to the problem issue. The practitioner inquires about (Corcoran, 2000):
The client's perceptions of the problem
The client's attributions of its causes
How the problem affects the client
What the client has tried already to resolve the problem
What the client is doing to keep things from getting worse
How the client has coped

The client's experiences with other helpers (formal and informal)
Nonproblem times, or exceptions

The practitioner externalizes the client's problem and makes it something apart from rather than within the client. For example, if a client is depressed, the practitioner focuses on aspects of the environment that create or sustain the negative feeling. In situations where the client has a physical illness or disability, the worker focuses on aspects of the environment that contribute to or inhibit his or her ability to cope. This process of externalization gives the client a greater sense of control. The practitioner also explores exceptions to the client's presenting problems. These questions initiate the intervention stage, as they bring ideas about solutions to the client's attention. This also contributes to the later formulation of specific intervention tasks. The practitioner identifies exceptions with the following types of questions:

What was different in the past when the problem wasn't a problem?

Are there times when you have been able to stand up to, or not be dominated by, the problem? How did you make that happen? What were you thinking? When did it happen? Where did it happen? Who was there? How did they have a part in creating that? What did you think and feel as a result of doing that?

What are you doing when the symptom isn't happening?

What do you want to continue to happen?

Practitioners do not falsify clients' reality through the above interventions. They do not "make up" strengths or distort situations in order to make clients feel better. Rather, they identify qualities that clients can realistically bring to bear on the problem situation.

After goals are developed and exceptions are identified, the client is encouraged to do more of what he or she was doing when the problem was not happening (DeJong & Berg, 2002). Intervention tasks may be developed with the "miracle" question. The client is asked to imagine that, during the night while asleep, the presenting problem went away, but he or she did not know this at the time. What, then, would the client notice the next day that would provide evidence of problem resolution? The client's answers to this question provide indicators of change that can be incorporated into tasks intended to create those indicators in real life. These tasks can relate to the client's personal functioning, interactions with others, or interactions with resource systems. They are based on existing strengths or on new strengths and resources that the client can develop.

The client's progress is often measured with scaling techniques. The practitioner helps the client scale goals on a 1-to-10 continuum. The practitioner asks the client during each meeting to indicate where he or she is on the scale and what needs to happen in order to advance to higher points on the scale.

Endings in Solution-Focused Therapy

In solution-focused therapy the practitioner focuses on the ending almost from the beginning of intervention, as goal setting and solution finding orient the client toward change within a brief time period. That is, the practitioner should enter the relationship with a view of how best to facilitate an optimal ending (Kieffer, 2006). The practitioner should ask him- or herself during the assessment: "What would it take for the client not to feel the urge to come to treatment right now?" The practitioner and client may or may not begin with a limited number of sessions in mind, but progress is monitored each time they meet. Once a client has achieved his or her concrete goals, they either set new goals or discuss plans for ending. This is clinically appropriate, because it is assumed that the achievement of even small changes will lead to further positive changes in the client's life. The ending focuses on helping clients identify strategies to maintain changes and the momentum to continue working on change. The practitioner introduces a language of possibility to replace earlier language of the certainty of change. A focus on the future emerges early in the intervention with such questions as "Tell me what will be different when our time here has been successful," and "What will you be doing when the problem is no longer with you?"

Following are examples of questions the practitioner may use during the end stage of intervention (O'Connell, 1998):

What will you do to make sure you do not need to come back and see me?

How confident do you feel about following the plan of action?

What help will you need to persist with the plan?

What do you expect your hardest challenge to be?

What do you think the possible obstacles might be, and how will you overcome them?

What do you need to remember if things get difficult for you again?

What will be the benefits for you that will make the effort worth it?

Who is going to be able to help you? Who do you feel will be more a part of the problem?

How long do you think it will take before you feel this is not a big problem any longer?

How will you remind yourself about the things that you know help?

With all the changes you are making, what will you tell me about yourself if I run into you at a convenience store six months from now?

The practitioner must be careful to end the intervention collaboratively, because clients do not always perceive the process as such. In their study of couples who had completed therapy, Metcalf and Thomas (1994) found that clients and practitioners gave different perspectives on the presenting problem, and that some clients felt that the intervention had ended too soon because the practitioner forced the process. The researchers concluded that practitioners should be less quick to assume collaboration and ask more directly and routinely whether families are getting what they want. Practitioners should also take care to present a comfortable enough environment that clients will share their feelings about the process, including the desire for a lengthier intervention.

The following vignette provides an example of a successful solution-focused intervention and ending with an individual client.

Case Study: The Journalist

Felicia was a twenty-three-year-old single female recreation therapist who came to see me through her employee assistance program. She had a pressing request—she needed to overcome her inability to express her feelings toward men immediately! Felicia explained that she had a lifelong problem of being unable to express feelings of affection to men. This had ruined her chances for many relationships with boys and young men over the years. Whenever she cared about a man she apparently became tongue tied to the point of avoiding intimate conversations altogether. Because she was quiet by nature, the men interpreted her reticence as indifference and did not pursue the relationship. Felicia was devastated in these situations but had never been able to make any progress with the problem. On the other hand, Felicia had many close female friends and had no trouble communicating with them. I saw nothing about Felicia's appearance or manner of presentation that would repel men or women. As a man, I found her to be bright, interesting, and nice looking. She communicated her feelings clearly to me.

I wondered if Felicia experienced any exceptions over the years to her inability to communicate with potential boyfriends. She could not think of any, and then she described what she considered to be the source of her problem. Her father was a domineering, unexpressive individual who punished his two daughters for any displays of emotion. Felicia had learned to be more expressive with women through the example of her mother. I told Felicia that I appreciated her willingness to disclose this information but that it would have limited relevance to our work together. That is, her existing strengths and potential resources should be sufficient for her goal achievement.

Continuing on the theme of seeking exceptions, I reminded Felicia that verbal communication was not the only way to express feelings to others. I asked her if she was able to be effectively expressive in other ways, not to men but to people in general. After thinking for awhile she responded that she was a pretty good writer. She could express herself well in writing, because she was alone at those times and could think carefully about what she wanted to say. In fact, she had kept a journal for several years. I asked

Felicia if she ever sent letters or shared any of her writings with men. She had not done so, but the idea furthered our discussion about her strengths as a writer.

Felicia decided that she might be able to discuss her feelings with her boyfriend verbally if he learned in advance what they were. She could arrange this by first writing her boyfriend a letter in which she expressed what she wanted to say. She would include her reason for sending the letter since it would probably surprise him. She would end the letter by saying she wanted to keep their date on Friday to discuss what was in the letter. I supported Felicia's plan and praised her creativity in formulating this strategy. I asked her to return in a week to talk about the process. I reminded her that the letter may or may not help achieve her goal, and that she should not consider the plan to be a "sure thing." I believed that there might be other ways to tap Felicia's strengths to achieve her goal.

A week later Felicia told me that the letter worked perfectly. She had felt comfortable writing the five-page document and only mildly anxious about putting it in the mailbox. Her boyfriend called her after reading the letter to say how much he appreciated it and that he would be excited to see her the following day. The date went well, and their relationship was continuing. Felicia added that since the ice had been broken with her boyfriend it had become easier to share her feelings verbally.

This was wonderful to hear, and what Felicia said next surprised me. Feeling good about the incident with her boyfriend, she had decided to write a letter to her father as well, expressing anger at how he had treated her and her sister over the years and asking that he talk with her about this in person. He had agreed, and Felicia spent an afternoon with him, talking through their relationship. She said her father was quite upset by what Felicia had to say but that they communicated well. Felicia said she planned to continue talking about these issues with her dad. It seemed that within one week Felicia had become a better communicator than I was!

Our relationship ended that day. I gave Felicia the option of coming back a few more times so that we could monitor her progress, but she turned me down, saying she had achieved her goals. As part of the ending process I asked Felicia a series of questions intended to encourage her to look ahead toward ways of sustaining her achievements. I asked how confident she felt about continuing with her strategy for improving her verbal expressiveness. Felicia responded that because her strategy of writing letters had been effective, she would continue to use it when she felt unable to communicate verbally. She was also planning to regularly reflect in her journal on her capacity for clear communication with men and women. I could see that Felicia had new confidence in her ability to manage herself interpersonally.

Next I asked Felicia to consider any obstacles she might experience relative to her ongoing interpersonal success and how she might manage them. Felicia quickly admitted that she was not sure how her "verbal confidence" would respond during and after arguments with her boyfriend and with her father. She planned to use letters in these instances, since those had proven successful, and she also planned to consult more openly with her good friends about these concerns. Felicia also planned to read more books about relationships. She had read such books in the past with little success but hoped that they might prove more useful since her confidence was greater. She framed verbal communication as a skill requiring practice.

My final question with clients is: "With all the changes you are making, what will you tell me about yourself if I run into you on the street in six months?" Felicia will tell me that she is continuing to work on her communication skills. As a result she will also tell me that she has more close male friends (not necessarily a boyfriend) and is in regular contact with her parents. She will no longer be feeling inadequate in her relationships. She will say that she has improved in her ability to manage disagreements with friends. I congratulated Felicia on her success and told her that she could call if her problems recurred. She thanked me for my help and left the session.

Felicia had learned an effective way to communicate her feelings that eliminated a presenting problem that was long standing and serious. She had brought to the clinical setting a strength and motivation that merely required identification and tapping. Felicia's example shows that even serious problems can be resolved through a search for strengths and exceptions and that when the duration of intervention is brief, the ending process also tends to be brief and formal.

This vignette also shows that in solution-focused therapy the potential for the practitioner (as well as the client) to achieve a sense of gratification is great.

Narrative Theory

Major Concepts and the Nature of Change

Narrative theory asserts that we are all engaged in an ongoing process of constructing a life story, or narrative, that determines our understanding of ourselves and our position in the world (Kelley, 1996; Monk, Winslade, Crocket, & Epston, 1997; White & Epston, 1990). It is the words we use and the stories we learn to tell about ourselves and about others that create our psychological and social realities. Personal experiences are fundamentally ambiguous, and we arrange our lives into stories to give coherence and meaning to them. Our life narratives are naturally coconstructed with significant others in our environments, meaning that their impressions of us have a direct influence on our self-understandings. These stories do not mirror our lives—they shape them! Once we develop a story line, new experiences are either filtered in or out depending on whether they are consistent with our ongoing life narrative.

Any personal narrative includes a process of selective perception. Some story lines are dominant, and others that do not fit the dominant story line are subjugated or suppressed. For example, people with low self-esteem maintain that characteristic because their thoughts and conversations feature themes of self-degradation (perhaps with the language of mental illness). They continue to construct arbitrary life narratives that portray themselves as having certain limitations. These stories tend to be self-perpetuating because of their habits of language and thought and also because of the influence of prevalent cultural values that may impede alternative modes of thinking. For instance, women in American society from certain socioeconomic classes were once, and often still are, expected to be submissive to men. This cultural norm might contribute to the depression of many women (Kelley, 1996).

Narrative practitioners do not help clients to ignore or wish away their very real problems by creating new fictions. Many problems that clients face are quite concrete. But life narratives influence the experiences clients label as challenges and how they address them. Through a process of refocusing, practitioners help clients to construct different life narratives that portray them in a different light. Practitioners place great emphasis on their clients' use of language. They are always alert to the elements of experience that clients choose to express and the language or meaning that is given to experience.

In summary, narrative theory is premised on the idea that people's lives and relationships are shaped by the life stories they share with others in their communities and the ways of life they develop that are associated with those stories (Nichols & Schwartz, 2001). Narrative theorists assume that the self is inherently fluid and malleable. All people are capable of developing new, empowering stories. Clients do not want to have problems and are in fact separate from their problems.

Narrative theory is unique in its attention to the influence of language on one's stories. Even practitioners need to consider that their ability to help others may be hindered when their own language becomes focused on problems and the limiting influence of personal history rather than on client strengths and possibilities.

Problems that bring clients to therapy may be understood as conditions of emotional or material suffering that result from personal narratives that are saturated with negative assumptions and beliefs. Another unique aspect of narrative therapy is its conceptualization of problems as (at least partly) byproducts of cultural practices that are oppressive to the development of functional life narratives. In this sense it can be a therapy of advocacy. The goals of narrative therapy are to:

◆ Awaken the client from a problematic pattern of living (not problem solving)
◆ Liberate the client from externally imposed constraints

◆ Help the client author stories of dignity and competence
◆ Recruit supportive others to serve as audiences to the client's new life story

Assessment and Intervention Principles

Narrative therapy is a process of understanding a client's stories through reflection and then broadening stories through reconstruction. Clients tell and explore their stories, describe a preferred reality, develop goals, develop an alternate story, and in the ending stage evaluate the outcomes of the process. The intervention process may be less structured than in many other clinical approaches. The practitioner and client may meet irregularly and recontract for additional meetings after each session. This relative lack of structure has implications for the ending process.

The assessment stage is brief. Practitioners ask questions about how clients spend their time in an effort to learn how they see themselves. Practitioners ask about strengths, talents, and accomplishments as a means of setting the stage for a constructive emphasis. When asking about problems, the practitioner uses "relative influence" questions to determine how much the client is troubled by them. The practitioner attempts to foster a collaborative atmosphere by inviting the client to ask questions or make comments about the intervention process. There are no diagnostic procedures involved; instead, the practitioner perceives the client as having an individual lived experience to share and build upon. The client is not a victim but a protagonist in his or her life story.

There is a rapid move into the intervention phase. Discussion topics in this process usually include (Monk et al., 1997; White & Epston, 1990):

The client's telling and exploring his or her life story

Externalizing or separating the client from the problem

Opening possibilities with exceptions questions

Identifying values and biases that underlie the client's construction of problems

Asking questions about personal meaning in the client's life

Enabling the client to separate his or her life and relationships from knowledge and stories that he or she judges to be oppressive

Helping the client give up problem-saturated stories that are the result of rigid narratives

Helping the client to "vision" or discuss alternate futures

Encouraging the client to reauthor his or her life story according to alternative and preferred stories of identity

Encouraging the client to consider life perspectives that may be in conflict with the expectations of significant others

Helping the client plan for the future to sustain the new narrative

Endings in Narrative Therapy

The ending of narrative therapy is formulated as a rite of passage, a process in which the client connects with others in a familiar social world and perhaps recruits others in the celebration and acknowledgment of his or her arrival at a new status in life (Epston & White, 1995). This is different than the manner in which endings are approached in other theories, most fundamentally because there has not been a focus on "problems" during the intervention. The intervention has focused on life stories; at its end the participants consider ways to celebrate and substantiate the client's new narrative. Again, this emphasis on inclusion is quite different from the analytic conceptualization of ending as a loss (Epston, White, & "Ben," 1995). Since narrative therapy is less structured than most other clinical interventions, its ending is considered to be a more natural process. Often clients and practitioners do not make a single, definitive decision to end therapy. They may leave the door open for occasional consultations without boundaries on time frames (Freedman & Combs, 1996). Three ending strategies are described in the following sections.

Consultation   In consultation, the practitioner leads the client through reflective conversations and tasks that help the client place the new life narratives into a broad context. Through a series of guided questions during one or several sessions the practitioner helps the client see the continuity of his or her life course and appreciate the new directions taken. The client is helped to recognize the development of strengths and resources and to retrace his or her steps to new knowledge through a review of "historical accounts" such as therapy notes, videotapes, audiotapes, or diaries that were produced during the intervention. The practitioner challenges the client to consider what new directions his or her life may take with this new knowledge. The practitioner also invites the client to indirectly help other clients. That is, the client can share the course of his or her journey and permit the practitioner to use the story as an example in future interventions. Clients are often gratified to know that their own journeys may be helpful to others.

Following is an illustration of narrative therapy with an ending that features a letter from the practitioner that reviewed the client's growth. Notice the language used by the therapist in the letter, as it incorporates metaphors related to the client's journeys prior to and during therapy. The fact that the therapist was a woman with a physical disability is important to the satisfaction she felt at the end of the intervention.

Case Study: The Mountain Climber

Malinda was a twenty-six-year-old married woman who had suffered a skiing accident that left her an incomplete paraplegic. She had recently moved back to the Midwest from her home in Arizona, leaving behind her husband, who had taken her skiing that fateful day. She came to see me on the recommendation of a brother with whom I had previously worked. Malinda was suicidal and remained so during the early part of the intervention.

I worked with Malinda for one year on her depression and poor sense of self. She took the metaphors of her life prior to the accident and created a stronger sense of self to replace the "tumbleweed" image she had during her youth. Malinda got a divorce and moved back permanently to her home area. She got a good job with a research firm where she could use her degree in environmental science to review literature and write abstracts. The hours there were flexible so that she could manage her physical limitations. She had plans to buy her own home. This particular intervention was special to me because I helped someone who was intelligent and gifted to manage a physical disability and create a life beyond that disability. Several years previously I had become able to manage my own disability, purchase a home, and develop a successful career. Many times Malinda's issues were identical to those in my own past. I could guide Malinda on her journey of wellness only as far as I had gone on my own journey.

As part of the ending process I wrote Malinda a letter to solidify her gains and remind her of spiritual challenges that she might face at transition points in her life. I often write letters to my clients as we end our work as a way of encouraging them to continue with their new life narratives.

Dear Malinda,

As I was reflecting over the time I have known you, I reread one of the letters I wrote to your family three months ago. I stated that you needed to redefine yourself, to develop a sense of self out of the emotional, spiritual, and physical parts of you that seemed to be scattered all over the world. That was a mountain you didn't want to climb, and you were willing to die emotionally and physically to avoid it. You lost your body in the sense that you had known it, and you needed to grieve the loss of what you could once do. You will need to struggle with that again and again in your life. The most important thing to remember is that the essential part of yourself is your spiritual being. You are far more than a body.

In the past year, Malinda, you have worked diligently, creatively, and honestly with redefining your "self." You got reinvolved with sports and began dating again. You learned new ways to handle your depression, the most important one being that you need to take one day at a time. You began traveling again to visit friends. It was almost like you were rebirthing yourself. There was safety and security at your mother's house. You learned to respect what you needed from your mother and ask her for it. That took enormous courage. You even became more assertive with your dad, a feat you did not think was possible.

Six months ago you realized how much you needed to set expectations for yourself in relationships. This came with many struggles about respecting yourself and your goals. I want to remind you of what those expectations were: a good support network, travel, wheelchair sports, maintaining interest in ceramics and diving, family relationships, comfort with finances, the ability to say no without guilt, taking care of your body needs, and receiving respect from others. You enjoy developing in many forms—gardening and teaching among them. You enjoy team-work and not competition. You enjoy experimenting with new foods. You respect the environment and its natural beauty. You volunteered at the Children's Home and tutored kids in your own home before finding the job that has the flexibility you need to manage your disability as well as honor your education. You have begun to honor your soul, even though you sometimes doubt that you are spiri-tual. You set out a vision of having comfort with your finances, and your job can provide this.

Lastly, from the time we met you have wanted a home in which you could nest, a home that holds the promise of comfort and renewal. It is exciting to hear that you are targeting areas here in town to buy your own home. It is excit-ing to hear that you have people who can give you support. It is exciting to see your family move closer for support. You have certainly learned how to manage relationships.

Know, Malinda, that it has been a joy for me to watch your family receive healing and to watch you scale your own mountains physically, emotionally, and spiritually. I admire your courage and thirst for meaning in life. Continue to em-brace life with all its joys and sorrows.

Sincerely,
Sheyna

The therapist hopes that the client will save this letter and read it occasionally. It can keep alive the story of their interaction and how the client had the strength to forge a productive life direction.

Personal Declarations   Personal declarations involve the clients' formal circulation of pertinent written information with significant others about their arrival at a new status. Clients have the opportunity to inform others of signifi-cant changes or decisions they have made and perhaps give them an invitation to respond. Clients may choose to write individual letters to certain people for this purpose. Another such news release may include a letter sent to a circle of acquaintances, much like the holiday letters that many of us receive each December.

In the spirit of identifying audiences that bear witness to clients' new self-understanding, clients may join clubs or organizations that will be supportive of their new position in life as the formal intervention ends. Epston and White (1995) cite the example of some clients with "mental illnesses" who choose to affirm their dignity by joining advocacy organizations to combat the public stigmas associated with their medical conditions. Joining activities may also in-volve something so simple as a client who develops an interest in literature (appreciating the stories of others) and becomes a member of a monthly book club.

Celebrations　Celebrations are any special commemorations of a client's development of new life narratives. These can take many forms depending on the client's particular circumstances. They may sometimes include prize giving and awards in ceremonies attended by significant others who may not have been participants in therapy. These commemoratives work especially well with children. The practitioner may or may not be a direct participant in a celebration—his or her role may most prominently include assisting clients to devise suitable celebrations. In chapter 2 we saw an example of this type of ending ("A Spiritual Celebration"). While that celebration did not follow a narrative intervention, the formerly delinquent adolescent client's therapy ending was celebrated with a lengthy ritual at his mother's home where friends and family (including the practitioner) recognized his new, more positive life course. An example of a different kind of narrative celebration follows.

Case Study: Going to Disney World

Martin was a thirty-year-old single white male with a good job in a furniture company sales department. He was referred to me by his probation officer for help with controlling his violent temper. Martin had recently been convicted of assault after fighting with and seriously injuring a neighbor at a holiday barbecue. Martin had in fact been arrested on several occasions for disturbing the peace and fighting in bars. A former girlfriend once took out a restraining order against him for alleged abusive behavior. Martin admitted that he was quick to become upset and resort to fighting rather than using other methods of working out conflicts. He was an effective salesman, but his supervisors had told him that his presentation was sometimes aggressive and intimidating. They had advised him to learn to relax more with customers.

During the year that Martin was on probation we met about fifteen times. He came to see me weekly for the first two months and then came in irregularly. As a narrative therapist I was interested in Martin's telling me the story of his life and where he saw himself at present with regard to his personal goals. I wanted to know how satisfied he was with himself. As he began this process I could see that his identify was tied up with images of the strong, athletic, dominant male. This seemed to have been learned from and patterned after his father (a fisherman) and older brothers, all of whom had a similar perspective on life. Martin realized, however, that he was not satisfied with himself. He was often getting into trouble and losing girlfriends. To help Martin externalize the problem, I asked him to talk about his relationship with anger as if anger were a person. I wondered how anger had become his companion and why he was inclined to let anger accompany him wherever he went. Martin eventually realized that anger was not a necessary component of (or companion in) his life, and he could choose other companions instead. Martin was a reflective man and with my encouragement could see that he might make other life choices and consider broader possibilities for his future than he had been aware of. Martin saw that he was locked into a rigid pattern but that it was changeable.

Over time Martin changed his life narrative from one featuring a strong young man going up against a cold, oppressive world to one of a strong and tender young man who was still in an oppressive world but was seeking connections. I pointed out to Martin that one of the oppressive aspects of his world seemed to be societal expectations of male dominance. This idea confused him at first, but he later came to accept it. Interestingly, Martin chose a new self-image as a "fisherman," his father's career but with a twist. Martin liked to think of himself as carrying imaginary fishing tackle so that he could reel in others ("fish") in a noncombative manner even when they chose to battle with him. His feelings about his father remained strong even as he rejected some of his father's values. During our last six months together we met only monthly, and Martin used those occasions to tell me how his new life story was unfolding. He was calmer, using his skills as a "fisherman" to attract others rather than control them.

Martin was more self-satisfied, and I sensed that he was ready to stop coming to see me. I suggested that he try to think of ways to celebrate his accomplishments and new identity. He gave the issue some thought for a few weeks. I did not suggest anything, because I suspected he would come up with an idea on his own. Finally, he did. He recalled seeing a football player after the Super Bowl walking across the television screen and announcing, "I'm going to Disney World." Martin enjoyed the self-mocking idea of taking on the image of that "macho" athlete and actually taking his parents and two brothers on a trip to Disney World. He thought it would provide him with a pleasant way to enhance his relationship with his family. He also wanted to use the time to let his family get to see his new, calmer self and perhaps share his journey of self-enhancement with them. Sure enough, the family spent a full week at the Florida resort. Martin sent me two postcards from Florida to let me know that they were all enjoying themselves. The postcards were his way of including me in the experience as a kind of thank you. We did not meet again.

Both of these vignettes are examples of rites of passage at the end of narrative therapy focused on opportunities for the changed clients to begin experiencing and sharing themselves with others.

Summary

The solution-focused and narrative therapies represent recent developments in clinical practice. Both of them derive from the social theory of constructionism.

They have much in common in their refusal to make many assumptions about a shared human nature, their perspectives on the self and the nature of change, and their focus on brief assessments, client strengths, and exceptions to problems. In this chapter we reviewed the principles of each intervention approach and how each approach addresses the ending stage of intervention. Solution-focused therapy, being short term, clearly attends to the ending stage from the beginning of the clinical encounter. For this reason there is generally not a prolonged ending process once the client and practitioner decide that their work is finished. In contrast, narrative therapy values celebrations and other rites of passage in the ending phase.

Chapter 7

Family Theory

Clinicians may choose from many practice theories to guide their work with families. Practitioners may select from the theories reviewed earlier in this book (reflective, cognitive, behavioral, and solution focused), as they are not specific to working with individuals. Still, family theories bring the concept of systems much more directly into the practitioner's focus. Working with families (and groups) is qualitatively different than working with individuals. Assessing patterns of interaction and intervening with groups of people adds complexity to the process. Many practice theories specific to family work have been introduced into the literature since the 1950s. We will not review all of them, but in this chapter we will consider two major theories of family practice: family systems and structural family theory. These offer contrasting perspectives on family work and together help us get a sense of the range of available options. As in the earlier chapters we will review the theories and then consider what they recommend or imply about the ending process.

A major difference between the family systems and structural theories is that the former was influenced by psychodynamic concepts and the latter is more cognitive behavioral in its approach. Family systems practitioners are concerned with the emotional attachments among members. As is true with the ego psychology and object relations theories, many of their interventions are reflective in nature. Determining concrete behavioral manifestations of change is not a priority, and thus it may not always be clear to the practitioner when it is time to end the intervention. Family structuralists are concerned with the external "architecture" of the family. They assume that when a family constructs appropriate authority, rules, and boundaries for its members, their emotional lives will be satisfactory. From this approach, decisions about when to end the intervention can be more easily based on concrete cognitive and behavioral indicators. We now turn to a detailed review of each theory.

Family (Emotional) Systems Theory

Family systems theory, sometimes called family emotional systems theory, provides a rich, comprehensive framework for understanding how the emotional ties within families of origin influence us throughout our lives in ways that we often fail to appreciate and tend to minimize (Bowen, 1978; Kerr & Bowen, 1988; Titelman, 1998). Many adolescents and young adults, even when they have positive family relationships, believe that after years of relying on relatives they can become independent people, apart from family influence. This theory asserts, very much to the contrary, that the influence of the nuclear family is always with us. How we as adults manage our relationships, for better or worse, represents a continuation of patterns that we developed in early family life.

Family functioning is considered to be healthy when members can balance a sense of separateness from and togetherness with others and can appropriately control their emotional lives with a developed intellect. Family systems theory is particularly appropriate to guide practice when a family's (or individual's) difficulties are related to unstable relationships within their current family system, resulting in an inability of the members to achieve this balance. The kinds of problems presented by these families in clinical settings include relationships characterized by extreme emotional reactivity and the inability of members to break free from family ties to an extent that they can thrive outside the family unit. The major concepts from family systems theory all have implications for intervention, and many of them can help the practitioner to organize the ending process.

Major Concepts

The Multigenerational Perspective   Individual personalities and patterns of interaction among family members have their origins in previous generations. Further, the influence of extended family relationships might be as important to one's development as the nuclear family. In assessment, an understanding of family member characteristics and interaction patterns over three generations is ideal. The genogram provides an efficient means for completing this task. This is a visual representation on one sheet of paper of a family's composition, structure, member characteristics, and relationships (McGoldrick, Gerson, & Shellenberger, 1999). Information provided on a genogram includes basic facts about family members (dates of birth and death, marriages), their primary characteristics (education, occupation, health status), and their relationship patterns (closeness and conflicts).

Differentiation of Self   Healthy individual functioning is characterized by differentiation, a concept with two meanings. First, it describes a person's capacity to distinguish between, and balance, his or her thinking and feeling selves. Thinking processes represent the ability to look objectively at personal reactions or biases. Emotional reactions provide important information about the significance of situations. Differentiation also refers to one's ability to physically separate from the family of origin in a manner that preserves those emotional ties while not being constrained by them.

Triangles   All intimate relationships are inherently unstable and require the availability of a third party to maintain their stability. The price of intimacy is the experience of occasional conflict, and when in conflict people usually rely on a third person for mediation, ventilation, or problem-solving assistance.

This is a normal and usually healthy process. Serious problems related to one's differentiation may develop, however, when one is drawn into certain triangles within the family. When a weaker (younger or undifferentiated) person is drawn into a triangle in a way that does not facilitate the other two people's resolution of their conflict, that person may be deprived of the opportunity for individual development. The person may, for example, assume the ongoing role of helping the other people avoid facing their problems with each other.

Anxiety and the Family Emotional System   Anxiety is an unpleasant but normal affect that provides us with warning signs for perceived threats (Marks, 1987). An anxiety-producing situation may be perceived as an opportunity for growth or a threat to well-being, and it is problematic only when it interferes with one's capacity for problem solving. Family systems include levels of anxiety, just as individuals do. Four relationship patterns that tend to foster family problems include marital conflict, problematic emotional functioning in one spouse, the emotional impairment of a child, or emotional fusion in which two members distance themselves from each other to reduce the intensity of their relationship. A family system characterized by any of these patterns may develop an atmosphere of anxiety that is shared by all members.

Parental Projection   Psychological defenses are processes by which we protect ourselves from intolerable anxiety by keeping unacceptable impulses out of our awareness (Goldstein, 1995). Projection is a common defense in which one person attributes his or her unacceptable thoughts and feelings to someone else. The "projector" is not aware of having the feelings or thoughts but believes that the person on whom they are projected is experiencing them. Parents often use the defense of projection with their children as targets, because children are vulnerable family members. Within family systems, children may suffer if the parents frequently project negative feelings and ideas onto them. The children may believe that they possess these negative thoughts and feelings and behave as such. They become more emotionally reactive, and the quest for differentiation is compromised.

Fusion   This is the opposite of differentiation. It is a shared state involving two or more people, the result of a triangulation in which one member sacrifices his or her striving toward differentiation in the service of balancing the relationship of two other people. When one person is fused with another, his or her emotional reactivity to the other person becomes strong. He or she does not "think" but "feels" and does so in response to the emotional state of the other person. Neither person is consciously aware of this state, because each lacks the capacity to adequately reason about, or reflect on, the situation. This happens because, for a significant length of time during childhood and adolescence prior to having an opportunity to differentiate, the fused person began to function within a triangle that served the needs of other family members.

Emotional Cutoff   People tend to lack insight into the fact that they are fused, but they experience high levels of emotional reactivity to the other person and may attempt to extricate themselves from the relationship. A common strategy is the emotional cutoff. This term refers to a person's attempts to emotionally distance him- or herself from certain members of the family or from the entire family. Emotional cutoff is the result of a person's inability to directly resolve the anxiety related to fusion, and it prevents the person from forming an identity or satisfying relationships with others. The pattern can continue after she or he leaves home. When physical distance alone is seen as a solution to ongoing family tensions, the person may be disappointed. First-year college students may feel that they can at last take charge of their life when in fact fusion prevents them from investing emotionally with other people.

We next consider how these concepts direct intervention strategies within this theory and then how they can be incorporated into ending-phase activities.

Intervention Approaches

The nature of change in family systems theory involves an opening up of the system. Change requires detriangulation and the building of new alliances among members of the nuclear and extended family. The practitioner attends to the goals of lowering family system anxiety, increasing the reflective capacity of the members, and promoting differentiation by emotionally realigning relationships within the family system. Family systems practitioners do not work with a set of explicit, concrete intervention techniques but rather with intervention strategies. The practitioner is challenged to formulate specific techniques in accordance with a family's particular concerns. Intervention strategies may include a clinical relationship, increasing insight, and detriangulation.

The Clinical Relationship   As a prerequisite to change, family members must experience the clinical setting as safe and comfortable, free of the anxiety that tends to characterize their natural environment. The practitioner strives to be the focus of the family's attention and set a constructive tone for members' interactions. He or she encourages reflective discussion and perhaps provides education about the nature of family patterns. The practitioner must be calm, promote an unheated atmosphere, and maintain professional detachment to avoid emotional reactivity and negative triangulation with family members. The practitioner serves as a model for rational interaction. For these reasons she or he is purposely not highly active within sessions in a social or conversational sense.

Increase Insight   Family systems theory shares with psychodynamic theory a belief that understanding leads to change. Families (and individuals) benefit from understanding that their patterns of interaction have sources in the family's history, and that improving family life may involve revisiting relationships with various nuclear and extended family members. The practitioner facilitates reflective discussions that promote insight, which can be defined simply as the ability to comprehend how one person's behavior affects another person's feelings and behavior in ways that can become permanent. Two techniques that promote insight are person-situation reflection, focused on present interactions, and developmental reflection, focused on the history of the person, family, and the family's patterns (Woods & Hollis, 2000). The practitioner helps members to observe themselves within triangles and to examine their behavior in terms of family themes. This intervention also serves as a normalizing strategy for families that worry that they are uniquely dysfunctional or beyond help.

Detriangulation   This represents any strategy by which the practitioner disrupts one triangle and encourages family members to develop new, more functional alliances or triangles. The practitioner typically encourages reflective discussion and facilitates the working out of conflicts by the members. He or she may supplement these discussions with task assignments, although far less often than would be done in structural practice. For example, if two family members require the assistance of a third party to bring an issue to resolution, the practitioner might encourage them to talk with a certain other family member, one who may or may not be present in the session. The practitioner always encourages the development of attachments that may diminish fusion and reactivity and promote differentiation.

Ending Family Systems Interventions

The major proponents of family systems theory do not address issues related to ending intervention. They emphasize instead the challenges of conducting a thorough assessment and selecting appropriate intervention strategies. There may be two reasons for this lack of attention to the issue. Family systems theory emerged during the 1960s and 1970s, a time when family therapy was conducted primarily by private practitioners not typically faced with time limits. Further, the theory was heavily influenced by psychodynamic thought, which is largely focused on education or insight development rather than problem solving. The absence of guidelines for ending family systems interventions is problematic, because the theory's concepts are highly abstract and provide practitioners with little direction for determining when a family has achieved its goals. We now return to the theory's concepts and identify several that suggest indicators to the practitioner that intervention is moving into the ending stage.

A person's differentiation—her or his development of a balance between rational and emotional functioning and ability to balance states of togetherness with and separateness from others—is the hallmark of healthy functioning. But how does a practitioner or a family member know when these balances have been achieved? And, if they seem to have been achieved, how can one be confident that the changes will persist? These are difficult questions, and answering them is further complicated because differentiation is a relative rather than absolute state. It is likely that few people are "perfectly" differentiated. In fact, perfect differentiation probably cannot be defined. I do not raise these questions as a criticism of the theory but only to argue that the practitioner's determination of a family member's changes in this area must be based on more concrete observations.

Of the many family assessment instruments that are available (Sawin & Harrigan, 1995), several are at least partially suitable as measures of change within family systems theory. It is important to note that no valid and reliable instrument has been developed specifically for use with either family theory in this chapter. The Family Adaptability and Cohesion Evaluation Scale (FACES), however, includes one subscale (out of two) that provides a measure of family cohesion (Franklin, Streeter, & Springer, 2001). Sixteen items related to this variable, scored on a five-point scale, provide data to categorize families as disengaged, separated, connected, or enmeshed. A practitioner could ask families to complete the cohesion scale from the FACES instrument at several times during intervention to help determine whether the family was progressing in its emotional interactions and, consequently, if the intervention was nearing completion.

Another important indicator of movement toward differentiation is family members' abilities to identify problematic triangles and identify new triangles that have the potential to be more constructive. The practitioner can track their abilities to disengage from some triangles and develop new, healthier ones. The genogram provides an appropriate means for tracking changes in three ways. First, it can be redrawn with the family at intervals during the intervention to see if changes are occurring. Second, if different colors are used to represent different points in time, it can depict change without being redrawn. Finally, the family can be asked to draw two genograms—one as they see themselves and the other as they wish to be. The products can be reviewed at times to track progress. It should be a routine aspect of planning for the practitioner and family to determine what new interaction patterns will signify goal achievement. The practitioner can guide members toward closure as these changes occur and persist over some mutually agreed-upon time period. The practitioner can use the genograms during the final few sessions to summarize the family's progress in a visual way.

Case Study: The Family Genograms

The genogram in figure 1 displays a nuclear family in which the father was an alcohol abuser. This "relationship" created several family triangles. During the assessment, the practitioner engaged the family in directing his

Figure 1: Real and Ideal Family Genograms

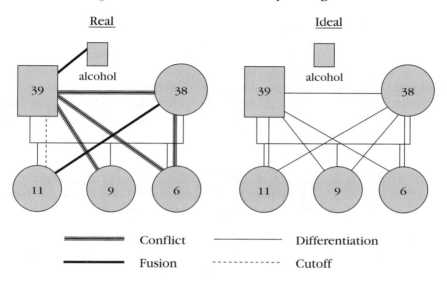

drawing of a genogram, which provided them with a tool to depict family relationships as each family member saw them. The genogram displayed the father's over-involvement with alcohol, the marital conflict, the over-involvement between mother and oldest child, and the disengagement between the father and oldest child. Next, in asking what the hoped-for family picture would look like, practitioner and family produced an "ideal" genogram that indicated sobriety and functional interactions occurring among all members of the family.

At monthly intervals over a six-month period, all family members drew their own genograms of how the family appeared to them at that point in time. Sharing these products helped members see the family situation from multiple perspectives and developed their increased awareness as well as sensitivity to each other. As the intervention goals were met, these individual genograms became more and more similar. Toward the end of intervention, the younger children voiced their awareness that they were all getting closer and the end was in sight. This ongoing process led to a natural and mutually agreed-upon ending.

Lowering system anxiety is a prerequisite for a family's attempts to make changes, because it reduces members' defensiveness and emotional reactivity to one another and facilitates risk taking. Observed anxiety levels can serve as an indicator of positive change if they persist over time in sessions and extend into the family's natural environment. During clinical meetings the practitioner can informally monitor the family's ability to communicate without tension, interruptions, and defensiveness. He or she can also monitor changes in anxiety outside the session by soliciting reports of the tone and content of family interactions. If members are in general agreement about these self-reports, the practitioner can assume their validity and determine whether members are more or less emotionally reactive over time. Consistent changes in a positive direction can help the practitioner determine when the family is functioning well enough to end the intervention. During the final sessions the practitioner can share with the family his or her observations of changes in members' anxiety over time and his or her own experience of anxiety with the family.

Case Study: From Tension to Tranquility

When Tim, age seventeen, was charged with shoplifting, the family court referred his mother and three younger siblings to me for intervention. During the initial assessment I observed that this single mother and her children engaged in frequent and intense arguments as their sole means of communication. The atmosphere was tense, and family members appeared detached from each other, but at the same time they were vigilant in response to the anxiety that was being played out through family conflict. I traced this mode of interaction to the marital discord that led to divorce in the mother's early life, that is, a style that was learned in her family of origin. My intervention focused on increasing the family's insight about intergenerational patterns and the acquisition of more appropriate expression of thoughts and feelings. The family also worked to recognize the anxiety related to the divorce (loss) that was blocking the "release" of Tim, who was striving to differentiate.

Over a period of several months, our sessions led to more peaceful and appropriate interactions that increasingly (and appropriately) excluded me. When these signals of termination became more frequent and consistent, I shared with the family that I was feeling more relaxed and confident after having felt such tension in the early meetings. I invited the family to try to explain my changed feelings and thoughts as a way to test their awareness of changed family-interaction patterns. This personal disclosure ultimately led to a mutual decision that the goals of family therapy had been met.

The concept of emotional cutoff can be operationalized as an indicator of goal achievement more easily than those noted earlier. It represents interpersonal conflicts manifested as physical or emotional distance of family members from each other. Family member differentiation is directly related to members' ability to face each other and interact without emotional reactivity. It is not always easy for the practitioner to determine when cutoff exists between two or more members. Once cutoff has been identified, however, the capacity of the members to become differentiated can be tracked by their extent of inter-action, the content of their interactions, and perhaps their ability to be physi-cally together without reported anxiety or conflict. Changes in the relation-ships can again be tracked on a genogram or by the self-report of members. When the cutoff members are present in the family session, the evolution of their behaviors can be witnessed directly by the practitioner. During the final session the practitioner can review with the family the various relationship changes that have occurred and ask the participants (who are present) to reflect on their emotional experiences in approaching the previously cut-off member. They might also be asked to share their plans for maintaining the relationships.

Because insight is important for lasting change to occur, family members' ability to accurately articulate their relationship patterns, problem areas, and op-tions for creating change is significant. The roles of the practitioner include ed-ucation about family systems dynamics and the facilitation of reflective discus-sion so he or she can monitor the degree to which the members acquire insight during the intervention. If the family members come to a constructive, shared understanding of their system dynamics and they maintain this understanding over time, they are manifesting an important indicator of change. When insight leads to constructive changes in behavior the practitioner may move the inter-vention into the end stage. During the closing sessions the practitioner can ask family members to individually review what they have learned about them-selves and their family.

The following three vignettes describe additional applications of family sys-tems theory and how the practitioner moved into the ending process. In the first two examples, the practitioner was attentive to changes in family member insight, triangulation, and emotional cutoff. The third practitioner attended to triangulation and family system anxiety. Notice that in the second and third cases, outside circumstances caused the interventions to end when they did, even though the practitioners recognized that the families had made significant progress toward their goals.

Case Study: The Empty Nesters

After twenty-six years of marriage and two adult children, Flo could not understand the increasing emotional distance between herself and her hus-band, Jim. Now that both children were independent, Flo was able to take what she called a "firm hand" with her invasive and domineering father. After years of tolerating her father's behavior so that the kids would have their grandfather in their lives, she was calling it quits by telling her father that he was no longer welcome in their home. She wanted her husband to back her up and provide confirmation that her tolerance of her father's be-havior had been important to their family but now could end. In response to this cutoff strategy, Flo experienced unanticipated tension and conflict with her mother. This increased Flo's anger and anxiety, which in turn had a negative impact on her marriage. Jim's increasing withdrawal from Flo reflected his ambivalence about her decision to cut off her father's place in their lives. Jim placed a high value on family interaction.

As their marital counselor, I was initially unable to help Flo and Jim understand these family dynamics. Eventually, Jim was able to verbalize to Flo the underlying anger, dismay, and indirect abandonment he felt in response to her behavior. Amazed by Jim's disclosure, and motivated by her desire to improve the marriage, Flo agreed to explore new ways to restore a relationship with her father. I helped them devise new ways to reconnect, and Jim followed suit in recognizing Flo's feelings and supporting her efforts. While the newly forged reconnection was not ideal, the couple developed a more realistic expectation of an adult child–parent relationship.

To reinforce the insight and changes this couple made in therapy, I used the final two sessions to draw and discuss with them genograms that depicted the family before, during, and after the cutoff and to illustrate the various triangles within this family system. Intrigued by the visual representation of their family dynamics, the couple identified additional relationships that had improved when cutoff was replaced with more functional interactions. At the final session, Flo remarked that initially she had been very skeptical about marital therapy but was pleasantly surprised that it had saved her marriage, restored her relationship with her father, and even enhanced her relationships with her children and brother. She asked to take the genograms home with her so that she could be reminded of her past and current family dynamics.

Case Study: The Zeller Siblings

All three adult siblings from the Zeller family came to see me for help at different times during the same calendar year. They had different presenting problems, but all of them were largely related to unresolved family-of-origin issues. The problematic family themes were rooted in their parents' relationship, especially their ways of managing emotions. The first sibling, Jim, sought my help to learn to control his son's oppositional behaviors. In assessing Jim's current family system I became aware that he and his wife had marital problems. Jim and Patricia had strong disagreements about parenting practices. They had three children, and Jim had become verbally abusive of the oldest son. I also assessed Jim's family-of-origin issues, as I do with all my clients. His father was a minister who was reportedly so fearful of his own father's stern parenting behavior that, in defense, he developed an exaggerated manner of graciousness. This could be so annoying, Jim said, that recipients of his polite manners felt like they were "drowning in a vat of honey." As Jim was growing up, he became able to sense his father's underlying anger, and he experienced an absence of substantive attention from both parents. He felt his mother's detachment when she embarked on a career to help support the family (the family was having money problems at this time). Jim often fought aggressively with his younger brother Amos as an outlet for his frustrations and because he didn't know how to vent feelings appropriately. Their sister Malinda's manner of coping with these fights was to hide in a corner, trying to be nonexistent.

Amos came to the agency several months after Jim for help with changing his tendency to replicate his father's behavior. He was aware of a "false niceness" and an inability to manage anger. Amos was involved at the time in a serious relationship with a woman, and while he wanted to maintain the attachment, he was ambivalent about marriage. He felt that his parents had been deceptive about their disagreements, always hiding their problems from the children. Their divorce had come out of the blue, which made it even more painful for Amos to endure. Consequently, he didn't trust his potential to succeed in marriage. In fact, Amos never seemed able to articulate what he was feeling.

Six months later, younger sister Malinda came to my agency (her individual treatment is a focus of chapter 6 and will not be described in detail here). She had experienced a skiing accident that left her a partial paraplegic. Malinda had left her husband and moved back home. She was very depressed.

I primarily worked with the siblings individually. But, because I noted that all of them exhibited some unhealthy relationship patterns they had developed as children, I arranged for several family sessions. Both of their parents, who had remarried other people, agreed to participate. This was extremely significant to the intervention, in part because the two sons had largely cut themselves off from interacting with the parents. As I had hoped, the experience was helpful to all five family members. I educated them about the power of learned family dynamics and facilitated discussions in which they began to understand each other better. In the sessions I asked each of the children to communicate their feelings about their parents. The parents then described their own emotional experiences as parents. Afterward, I helped various subsystems of the family (the brothers, Malinda and her mother) communicate with each other. The process seemed to clear up many lingering tensions within the family. The children were able to respectfully communicate their anger toward their father. All of them reported at the time and afterward that they had gained a new sense of family, one where forgiveness could take place and old issues could be put to rest.

I felt that my interventions were helpful to the Zellers because of their new insights into relationship dynamics, their willingness to resume identifying with the family unit, and their establishment of healthier communication patterns. They all expressed a desire to maintain contact with each other. My decision to end work with them (at different times) was based on concrete decisions they made that confirmed their progress. Jim and Pat decided to move to another city, where her parents lived. She would feel safe using her own family of origin for support with child care if Jim was feeling overwhelmed. Jim was able to find a good job there, and in fact their financial situation improved. Pat could stay home with the children, and this removed much stress from the family. They continued to have contact with the family of origin. Amos decided to marry the woman he was dating, and to symbolize their partnership they designed a home together.

Case Study: Kathy's Three Parents

Kathy, age fifteen, was referred to me for counseling after a three-week inpatient stay for substance abuse, a problem she had experienced for two years. Her father and stepmother were lawyers, and her mother was an accountant—they were all financially successful. Kathy's mother and step-mother had been good friends prior to the divorce and remarriage. This accounted for a great bitterness between them. There were two other children in the family, both boys without significant behavioral problems. Kathy was the middle child. A major source of Kathy's problems was the lack of quality and consistency in her parenting. This situation had deteriorated after her parents divorced. All three children had learned to manipulate their parents and stepmother to get what they wanted by creating triangles; that is, the animosities and absence of communication among the adults resulted in the children's ability to control what information the adults had. In Kathy's case, this resulted in their leniency in her pursuit of an unstructured, undisciplined lifestyle. She had a history of sneaking out at night, meeting boys, and using drugs. The three involved adults could not agree on limits.

I met with the adults together so that they could understand the negative consequences of their triangle. As a family systems therapist, I focused on their earlier lives to better understand the reasons for their sabotage of each other. I learned that the father had long been a controlling man who often lacked sensitivity to others. He had been his mother's primary care-giver during his teenage years as his father struggled with terminal cancer. He needed to be self-centered and to establish predictability in his life to manage this responsibility without becoming overwhelmed. His father had always wanted him to become an attorney, and he decided that doing so was also a responsible decision. He met his first wife in high school. Her family offered him a stronger sense of secure family at that time, which is partly why he fell in love with her. She was a middle child who learned to survive in her family by being passive, a good listener, and withdrawing during conflicts. She understood her feelings but kept them inside and could not easily verbalize them.

The stepmother had significant losses in her childhood, and Kathy's behavior served to remind her of these losses. She lost a best friend to a drug overdose at age fifteen, her father to alcoholism, and her best friend to an affair. She did not want to have to face similar events as an adult.

I needed to help the three adults interact cooperatively enough to establish appropriate limits and boundaries with Kathy. The major turning point occurred when I was able to facilitate their forgiving one another for past problems. This occurred dramatically in one session. The stepmother demanded an apology from Kathy after she had been highly disrespectful of the adults. Kathy said sarcastically that she did not know how to apologize because she had never seen this done. The adults had been working on this issue together with me, so they were able to do a good job of modeling for Kathy. Father apologized to his first wife for his tendency to be domineering and for betraying his initial marital vows. He was able to thank her for her goodness in their courtship and early marriage. Stepmother apologized to the mother for betraying their friendship, and mother apologized to the couple for teaching her children to disrespect the stepmother. This was a good session, coincidentally accompanied by environmental overtures of a thunderstorm, rain, and sun.

From that time my sessions with the parent subsystem were much calmer and free of the tension that seemed to get in the way of any positive movement. I became aware of my own increased comfort each time I prepared to meet with the family. Further, Kathy was no longer able to manipulate the adults as well. Her problems with substance abuse continued to be serious, however. Eventually, I recommended that the family arrange for Kathy to have additional inpatient treatment. The adults would not initially commit to this. I resorted to confrontation, asking them bluntly, "If you are standing at Kathy's casket when she is nineteen years old, will you be at peace knowing you did everything you could to prevent her drug-related death?" This helped to get through their minimizing of Kathy's substance problem. Our work ended when Kathy entered the residential program, although I did maintain phone contact with them for several weeks. The family demonstrated commitment to change by the need to drive two hours each way for their family education meetings. The improvement in the adult subsystem was most clear to me when I learned that all three parents rode to and from those meetings together. I later felt gratified when, after Kathy completed the program, the family invited me to her graduation ceremony. I decided to attend. I do not typically cross boundaries in this way, but I felt secure that the family and I were finished with each other and that the ceremony would provide a warm closure for me.

Structural Family Theory

Structural family theory was developed by Salvador Minuchin in the 1970s and has continued to evolve through his ongoing work and that of others (Minuchin, 1978; Minuchin, Lee, & Simon, 1996). The focus of this theory is family structure, a concept that refers to the "invisible" and often unspoken rules that organize how members of a family interact. This theory developed in response to a perceived need for intervention methods that could be used with families having multiple problems, such as nontraditional inner-city families dealing with poverty, and other issues contributing to family disruption. The theory was also influenced by the rise in prominence of the social learning, cognitive, and behavior theories and the growing demand for time-limited models of family intervention.

Structural family theory is particularly useful when working with families that are experiencing crisis and disorganization. Its interventions are suited to families plagued by illness, acting-out members, and problems such as drug addiction, crime, single parenthood, and violence. The theory can be used with any type of family. Its major concepts are as follows:

Major Concepts

Roles   Roles are the functions provided within a family by each member. For example, in a traditional family unit, a father may have the role of breadwinner, and the mother may have the role of caregiver. Roles change over time and in different contexts.

Rules   Rules are the behaviors, tasks, and responsibilities to which each family member is expected to adhere. They may be openly articulated or acquired as matters of circumstance or habit.

Subsystems   The family includes subsets of family members who interact in certain contexts that are not equally open to the participation of other members. Subsystems may include parents, adult members, nuclear versus extended family members, siblings, and even subsets of siblings (depending, for example, on age or gender). Subsystems are normal and functional, but they can be problematic when serious conflicts develop between them (parents versus children, for example), or if they exclude certain other members, such as a parent-child subsystem that excludes the other parent. Each family member usually belongs to more than one subsystem.

Alliances   A condition in which two family members or subsystems interact cooperatively is an alliance. Alliances are positive when they contribute to the overall well-being of the persons involved and to the family as a unit. They are negative when they are rigid and exclusionary or otherwise contribute to family problems.

Boundaries   Internal boundaries are the invisible barriers that regulate the amounts of contact that members or subsystems have with each other. It is considered desirable that family members have some balance of access and privacy. Family boundaries may be rigid (members physically or emotionally separated) or fluid (members too close to each other and therefore denied privacy or separateness). External boundaries refer to the separation of the family unit from external systems. It is appropriate for families to keep many of their interactions private from outsiders. The family may also interact as a unit within its community, for example, by attending church activities.

Executive Authority and Power   These are characteristics of the person or persons who are the primary rule and decision makers in the family. It is assumed that responsible adult members should have authority in a family. The persons who have power may shift, however, depending on the context. The power to decide whether to move the family to a new city may reside with the adult members, while the power to decide on a site for the annual vacation may rest with the children (within cost and time parameters set by adults).

Flexibility   The ability of the family to successfully adjust to predictable and unpredictable environmental demands is called flexibility. Family structure implies stability, but a healthy system must be adaptable to change. The family system must also be adaptable to life transitions, including the physical and emotional development of its members and the addition and subtraction of members through marriage, leaving home, birth, and death.

Communication   This concept is universally important in clinical intervention but receives extensive attention in family structural theory. It can be defined as all verbal and nonverbal practices of conveying messages to other persons or subsystems. Understanding family communication provides access to family rules. The two levels of communication include report functions (to convey information) and command functions (to define relationships). Functional family communications are characterized by verbal and nonverbal congruence and consistently observed rules.

Problem Development

Family structural characteristics that may contribute to problem development include power imbalances; disengaged members or subsystems; boundaries that are too rigid or too diffuse; the inability of members to mobilize support from each other when needed; members who rely too much on one other;

member resistance to normal family processes, including the growth and development of others; conflict avoidance; and the failure of the system to realign after a stressful event.

The goals of intervention are to change the existing family structure so that it becomes more functional. This involves various strategies to strengthen, loosen, dissemble, or develop family alliances and subsystems. Change may also involve increasing the available supports for members outside the family system. Understanding the origin of a problem is largely irrelevant to the change process. A principle of structural family intervention is that "action precedes understanding." One or more family members must take action, with the guidance of the practitioner, to change the nature of family interactions. Through restructuring processes that include practicing new ways of interacting and communicating, family members may experience permanent relief from their presenting problems. Insight about the problem situation may occur after the fact, but this is not a necessary aspect of change.

Intervention Approaches

The practitioner acts as a stage director. This is an active posture. The worker does not maintain the detachment suggested in family emotional systems theory but gets highly involved with family processes. Practitioners make an effort to connect interpersonally with each family member, to be perceived as credible and empathetic. This means that practitioners adjust their personal style to fit in with the family's style of interaction. They try to convey an atmosphere of family competence when introducing any of the specific intervention techniques included here:

Teaching stress management skills prior to initiating any anxiety-provoking interactions to enhance the self-control of members

Encouraging the family to track its problem behaviors between sessions so that members can more clearly perceive their structural patterns and get accustomed to working actively in the intervention

Supporting the strengths of the system with compliments about aspects of family functioning that are going well. This includes affirming the dignity of the family with sympathetic responses and nonjudgmental comments about members' behaviors.

Relabeling or normalizing problems so family members do not feel so badly about themselves

Manipulating space in sessions. This is a strategy in which the practitioner asks family members to sit next to, closer to, farther from, or face each other in ways that highlight structural characteristics, such as alliances, subsystems, and boundaries. The technique also demonstrates to families in a physical manner how their structures can be changed. For example, adults who lack power may be asked to sit closely together during sessions to provide support to each other.

Training family members in communication skills, since the source of many family problems is the inability of members to clearly communicate their needs, ideas, and feelings to one another. The practitioner may spend much time instructing families in methods of clear speaking and listening, using space (as described earlier) to facilitate the process. As a part of this technique, the practitioner helps family members redirect the manner in which they process stress, such as withdrawing when communication becomes negatively charged.

Directing simulations (rather than relying entirely on discussions) of actual or possible family situations with role plays as a means of illustrating and changing family interactions. Practicing interacting in new ways helps family members to adjust alliances and other structural characteristics to promote a more functional family system. For example, to enhance their executive authority, spouses may be asked to discuss how they want to respond to the negative behavior of a child in the presence of the children. Detached children in a family may be asked to interact as a means of strengthening that subsystem. In role reversals, members are asked to play the roles of other family members to sensitize them to the feelings of others with whom they may be in conflict.

Assigning tasks, or homework, for members to complete between sessions is a fundamental technique that ensures that family members continuously work toward their goals. Tasks facilitate the implementation of new behaviors in the natural environment, and members can report on their ability to complete these tasks when they return to the practitioner's setting.

A great deal of repetition is necessary in all these interventions, as is true in behavioral theory, before structural changes are likely to be permanent.

Ending Structural Family Interventions

As is true of family systems theory, the major structural theorists provide surprisingly little information about the process of ending interventions. The theory's concepts are rather concrete, however, which helps us to think about strategies for ending. All the following clinical developments can serve as indicators that a family has achieved a more appropriate family structure. Structural theory focuses on behavioral change, and most indicators that intervention is nearing its end can be ascertained by the practitioner through formal change measures, session behaviors, family self-reports of activities between sessions, and the outcomes of assigned tasks.

As noted earlier in this chapter, there is no formal instrument designed specifically for use with this theory. One example of a well-established and partly suitable measure is the Family Assessment Device (Walsh, 1993). This instrument includes six subscales, four of which (problem solving, communication, roles, and behavior control) are consistent with the focus of structural intervention.

These subscales are each composed of ten items that are rated on a scale of 1 to 4. They can be used independently of the other two subscales (affective involvement and affective responsiveness) to capture evidence of structural changes among family members over time that signify goal attainment and a readiness to end. The instrument is brief and practical and has been extensively tested for validity and reliability.

Other scales are also available. The Family Adaptability and Cohesion Scale (FACES-IV) includes one subscale (out of two) that provides a measure of family flexibility (Franklin, Streeter, & Springer, 2001). This concept refers to structural characteristics ranging from *chaotic* to *rigid* and is measured by twelve items scored on a five-point scale. The scale can be completed in five to ten minutes. A practitioner could ask families to complete the flexibility scale from the FACES instrument at regular intervals during the course of intervention to help determine whether they are progressing toward their goals and as a means of selecting an appropriate end point. In the Index of Marital Satisfaction (IMS), twenty-five items are rated on a seven-point scale (Hudson & Faul, 1998). Each partner can complete the IMS initially and repeat the process at set intervals, with agreed-upon target scores to signify a time to end the intervention. While there still may be some marital dissatisfaction at termination, there may be more consensus about areas of concern that can focus the efforts of the practitioner and the couple. Hudson's WALMYR Assessment Scales include other instruments to assess family dynamics of concern to the structural practitioner such as parent-child relations, peer relations, and sibling relations (Hudson & Faul, 1998). Thomlinson (2002) identifies additional formal family measures.

Another tool that can be used to monitor changes in family subsystems and family interactions with outside community resources is the eco-map (Hepworth et al., 2002). This is nothing more than a practitioner's crude drawing of a family's interactions. One version of the eco-map consists of each family member's name scattered on a sheet of paper with a small circle around it. Larger circles can then be drawn around various members, enclosing them to identify family subsystems. Lines can be drawn between members or subsystems to connect family alliances. An eco-map can be drawn as part of the initial family assessment and then redrawn as an ending activity to signify structural changes. A second type of eco-map also includes circles, one of which includes the family as a unit and others that identify relevant community resources (such as neighbors, church, extended family, work peers, institutional memberships, and so on). If a family's goal includes greater community participation, the eco-map can serve as an assessment tool and also as an ending activity to summarize changes in a visual way.

Case Study: Crowded House

The Baileys were self-referred by the mother, who was concerned that her oldest daughter would "get into trouble." Because the mother was unable to be more specific or provide indicators of "trouble," I made a home visit. I assessed the family structure and subsystems in light of individual and family development, communication patters, and resources such as housing. The resulting eco-map (see figure 2) was a composite drawing that I made with input from all members of the family. All of us concluded that the parental, parent-child, and sibling subsystems had developed dysfunctional alliances and that family boundaries were too diffuse. At the second home visit, I drew (again with the family's input) a second eco-map to represent the family goals (see figure 3). I planned to use the second eco-map as an indicator for ending the intervention.

The eco-map was quite illustrative. The Baileys had relocated to a smaller house in a safer community after Mr. Bailey's promotion. Mrs. Bailey continued to take in people who needed a place to stay, resulting in limited family and marital privacy. Mr. Bailey's overtime work increased, the younger teenage daughter forged a strong bond with her brother that provided a cover for the oldest daughter to remain out of the home beyond reasonable limits, and conflict arose among all siblings over privacy issues and personal belongings. The assessment revealed that there had been more family connections prior to the move. Intervention goals were set to support more appropriate authority and boundaries. This included limiting the family residence only to the parents and children, providing footlockers to the older girl in exchange for her keeping curfew and telling her whereabouts when she went out, reinforcing the marital subsystem by

Figure 2: Bailey Family Eco-Map at Intake

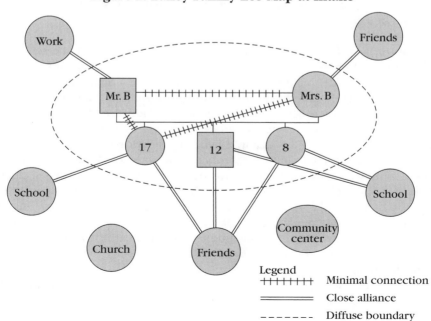

Figure 3: Bailey Family Goals (Used as Indicator for Termination)

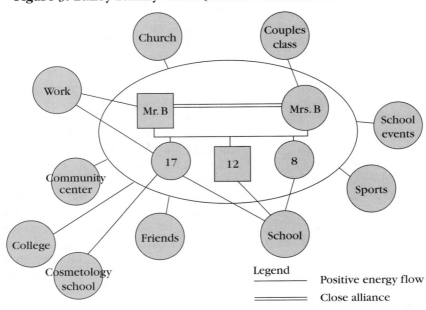

structuring their time alone as a couple, and making the master bedroom off limits to others in the home.

The manner in which the family's termination was organized will be described later.

A major goal (or facilitative condition) for intervention has been achieved when family members show improvement in the amount and quality of their communications. The practitioner, whose teaching of communication skills is often a primary intervention, can monitor how well and how consistently members maintain their new skills. Developing individualized behavior criteria to assess communication changes that occur in sessions and between sessions can do this most directly. For example, family members' responses to the practitioner's questions about how prescribed task activities have been implemented or how certain challenges have been dealt with will always include reports of communication practices. While it is always difficult to evaluate the likelihood of lasting change in this area, directness and a consistent lowering of tension among family members during conversations is one useful indicator. At the end of intervention, the practitioner can summarize for the family as specifically as possible the important adjustments they have made in their abilities to communicate.

The practitioner can also track family movement toward restructuring alliances and subsystems or adjusting internal boundaries. The worker-client process of identifying goals for changes in family structure at the time of assessment is a concrete one. The practitioner and family members determine, for example, that the parental subsystem is too weak or that boundaries between the parent and child subsystems are too rigid. To strengthen executive authority, the practitioner can ask the adult members to document how much time they spend together each week. The practitioner might use time measures to see how this alliance changes over time or may rely on the self-report of family members to monitor this. Toward the goal of developing rules for appropriate boundaries, a child may be asked to monitor how much time he or she is permitted to spend alone in his or her room or out of the house with friends without parental interruption. When adjustments in the desired structures or boundaries have occurred and are being positively reinforced in the natural environment, the practitioner may consider winding down the intervention. The issue of permanence of change can be addressed by evaluating the nature, consistency, and strength of the reinforcements experienced by all members after making changes. At the end of the intervention, the practitioner can summarize, again in concrete terms (time, frequency, and content), how various subsystems have changed in positive ways. The practitioner's or family members' construction of a new eco-map can be an effective way to help families see these changes.

Case Study: Crowded House, Part II

I helped the Baileys create weekly time sheets to document their interactions. Initially Mr. and Mrs. Bailey spent only ten to fifteen minutes interacting alone every few days. By the end of the intervention, their time together averaged several hours per week, usually with an out-of-home activity that did not include others. These time sheets reflected the increase in time that the oldest girl spent at home when she was not in school. As the intervention wound up, I shared the time sheets with the family to highlight their progress. This activity helped to assuage Mr. Bailey's apprehensions about termination.

Toward the goal of strengthening alliances, the practitioner can determine whether mutual support among family members is increasing by their ability to interact more cooperatively within sessions, communicate an understanding of each other's needs, participate in activities that are identified as supportive, and demonstrate through role plays an awareness of each other's points of view. As the intervention nears its end, the practitioner may introduce more hypothetical (versus actual) situations for role-play interactions to evaluate their ability to be mutually supportive in a variety of contexts.

Family structure flexibility may be difficult to measure in the time-limited context of clinical intervention. The point regarding hypothetical role plays after the family has achieved a significant level of stability also applies to monitoring flexibility. Through these role plays (with which the family should be comfortable by now) the practitioner can create scenarios of possible future challenges to family functioning and see how members can adapt their system responses. A wide variety of future-oriented role plays helps members sharpen their coping skills. At the end of intervention the practitioner can help the family generalize from these role plays how else they might be supportive of one another in ways that can benefit many or all of them.

Again, the Baileys provide a useful example in their next-to-last session.

Case Study: Crowded House, Part III

I presented a hypothetical situation where a close family friend asked Mrs. Bailey if she could stay with them for "a little while." Well rehearsed in the use of role play, Mrs. Bailey responded to the request as if the family friend were in the room. She conveyed empathy but based her denial of the request on her responsibility as a parent to protect the family's privacy. She further stated what she believed to be the needs of each person in the household, including herself. Afterward, using a scale of 1 to 10, 10 being the most accurate, I asked each person if his or her viewpoint was represented during the role play. Everyone reported at least an 8.

Structural theorists (and, in fact, all family systems theorists) recognize that the family system requires support from external systems in order to thrive. An increase in community interaction for the family as a whole, or for certain members, is often a goal of intervention. Indicators of change in this area might include family self-reports of new and sustained informal interactions (with friends, neighbors, work peers, and extended family) and formal interactions (with churches and community associations). The practitioner might construct a list with the family of external resources for them to investigate. The eco-map described earlier can be used for this purpose. The family's concrete plans for ongoing community participation serve as indicators that the goal has been achieved. Final sessions can include a review of resources that have been considered and any external supports that the family is using. The practitioner can ask the family members to share their experiences, positive and negative, with various community supports and their plans for maintaining them.

Case Study: Crowded House, Finale

I asked the Baileys to set goals to identify community alternatives for people who might turn to them for housing, as well as other resources for shared family activities, particularly for the younger children with and without the parents. When new resources were discussed in sessions, they were addressed in a context of the family's "goals" eco-map (see figure 3). Each family member's recognition that the eco-map was satisfactory facilitated the end of the intervention.

Finally, endings in structural intervention may include an empowering of the family unit (Wetchler, 1993). Families who achieve their goals can be empowered by the practitioner's moving them toward an egalitarian position. The practitioner not only praises the family for its accomplishments but also affirms that the family has demonstrated good therapeutic judgment in finding solutions to its problems. The practitioner may ask the family members to serve as informal consultants for one or more other families he or she is seeing. The practitioner can describe the other family's circumstances in a general way and ask for recommendations about how the family might address certain issues. If the "consultants" are from a (previously) marginally functioning family, this recognition of their expertise can be a powerful affirmation of their growth.

The vignettes that follow include an intervention that was successful and one that was not. Each illustrates intervention and ending strategies that, however different, were appropriate to the family and clinical setting. The intervention strategies in the first case include a restructuring of executive authority, improving communication skills, rehearsing new behaviors, and assigning tasks. The last of these was key to the success of the ending. The practitioner in the second vignette emphasizes the interventions of education, role-playing, modeling appropriate behavior, and task assignments. He used a fading strategy for the ending and points out that professionals at his agency routinely used this. His disappointing experience shows how lasting change is difficult to secure if interventions related to enhancing the family's outside supports are not successful. This final vignette also provides an example of a "macro" or agency-initiated ending.

Case Study: The Family Drawings

My agency provides in-home intervention services to families identified as at risk for serious child emotional and behavioral problems. These are generally single-parent families living in poverty. Referrals come from a variety of sources, including community physicians. Our clinical practitioners work from a structural intervention model. The families tend to feature a lack of strong authority and consistency in the behavior of parent figures and poor limits on the behavior of the children. One thing that I am always concerned about is whether, at the end of a successful intervention, family members will continue to work on their challenges in constructive ways. For that reason I put a lot of thought into the ending process.

I worked with the Paulson family for sixteen months. The family included Kendra, a twenty-year-old single mother of seven-year-old, five-year-old, and newborn boys. Her mother had moved in with her when the new baby was born, and the two adults were often at each other's throats. Grandmother tried to take on the traditional parent role because Kendra was away working, sometimes at odd hours. Kendra was a strict parent when she was home, but grandmother was permissive and set few limits with the kids. The two women did not get along well in many respects and could not agree on how to manage the kids. Damon, the five-year-old, began to develop behavior problems of aggression in the home, the neighborhood, and at school, partly because he was receiving mixed messages from his two parent figures.

After my assessment I decided to work with Kendra and her mother on improving their relationship. I included the two older children in the process at times, but not often. I felt that if the adults could get along better and agree on appropriate parenting strategies, the children would respond with improved behavior. I met with Kendra and grandmother weekly for about six months and then twice monthly when the situation improved. My intervention strategies included system restructuring so that both adults could assume appropriate roles of authority in the family. I taught them how to communicate clearly, directly, and frequently with each other. I also helped Kendra resolve much of the lingering anger she felt toward her mother. Kendra was still bitter about the lack of supportive parenting she felt she received as a child. The pair was able to learn and practice a process for solving their differences and agreeing on household and child-rearing rules. We practiced these skills frequently during our visits. Occasionally, I would bring in the older boys to talk about what we were doing and to let the adults practice what they had learned with them.

My approach to ending this intervention was powerful, and the idea came to me by accident. One day when I was in the home, long before the intervention ended, the children were behaving in a rambunctious way. I needed to think of a way to occupy them while I spoke to Kendra and grandmother. I suggested that the older boys draw a picture of the family. They did so, and later when I looked at the pictures I saw fascinating portrayals of the family's problems. The pictures indicated where each child saw himself in relation to the others by how large each figure was, expressions on the faces, and where they were positioned. These were crude drawings, of course, done with pens, pencils, and crayons on sheets of typing paper. Because the boys seemed to enjoy drawing, it occurred to me that this might be a good way to monitor the family's changes over time. Every month or so, I asked the boys to draw family pictures. I would then discuss with them and the adults what the drawings showed. As the weeks went by the pictures demonstrated that the family system was stabilizing. The figures of the family members, including the baby, became more equal in size and closer to each other.

When Kendra and her mother became able to problem solve well without my assistance for three months and Damon's behavior improved for the same period of time, it was time to end the intervention. As a closing activity, I asked the four family members (excluding the infant) as a homework assignment to each draw a picture of what they wanted their family to be like. Afterward I used the pictures to review the work we had done together during the previous sixteen months. It was a productive conversation that showed that all of them had made changes that I felt were likely to persist. When we finished I took the pictures and had them mounted together on a mat board. I asked the family what they wanted to do with them, and they all agreed that the mount should hang on the wall of their home. I know that the pictures are still there because the family has occasional contact with another staff member of our agency for linkage services.

I strongly believe that for changes to persist in the types of families we see, the practitioner needs to leave something tangible behind. This reminds the family members regularly how they have grown and that they are capable of managing challenges together. Without something tangible, they are more likely to forget those things when new problems develop.

Case Study: A Mobile Home near the Woods

My agency, Family Preservation Services, provides in-home counseling and case management services that are time intensive and financially expensive. A regional family assessment and prevention team (FAPT) made up of public agency representatives makes referrals to our agency for families whose members exhibit severe behavioral problems. Staff go to the clients' homes three or four times per week, spending a great deal of time with all family members to help them with problems that are serious and long term. An average visit is two or three hours, and the full intervention process can take six months or more.

I worked with the Anderson family for a full year. The mother, her live-in boyfriend, two adolescent sons, and an adolescent daughter came to the attention of several legal and human service agencies because of their physical violence with one another. The mother had filed assault charges against each of her sons, but she also initiated fights with them and with her daughter. They had recently moved from another state into a small, two-bedroom trailer in an isolated rural area. The family members were estranged from each other and disconnected from the nearby community. The FAPT team hoped that we could teach them alternative ways to work out conflicts.

I was in the Anderson home quite a lot. The entire family was ambivalent about my visits, but this is typical of our clients. Sometimes they were happy to see me, and other times I seemed to annoy them. In-home services are highly invasive, so in the best of circumstances families are relieved when we go away. But the Andersons made some very good progress. Through my teaching, conflict mediation, role playing, and modeling, they reduced their use of violence. They seemed to increase their sense of contentment with each other. They were able to step back and think about their behaviors more clearly and became better at controlling their impulses. After six months I initiated a "step-down process," in which I gradually reduced my amount of contact with them. Our agency professionals routinely move into step-down stages to find out if the positive changes we see will be lasting. I move from ten, to six, and then to three hours per week, and I make fewer visits, until ending with a family completely. The process normally takes a few months. Unfortunately, the Andersons' violent behaviors escalated as my time with them decreased. I was surprised and disappointed. So, I resumed seeing them at nearly my previous level of intensity.

After a year had gone by, FAPT decided that despite the family's ongoing difficulties, the in-home program needed to end because of its financial expense. I disagreed with the decision, and my agency tried to work out a compromise with FAPT so that our intervention might continue with some regularity. In the end, this was not to be. My agency supervisor voiced what is an unfortunate reality of public social services—that if the family "crashed" they might later qualify for other types of service. That is precisely what happened. One of the boys was soon removed from the home to a school for adolescents with emotional disabilities, and the girl was removed from the home and placed in foster care.

I understand the realities of public funding, and I was not angry with FAPT, but I felt disappointed with the outcome. I had no sense of closure with the family. I was concerned that they were being left in a vulnerable position, and I was not sure in the end if I had been helpful to them. Their gains had not persisted, and they had always been ambivalent at best about my presence in their lives. I think a big reason for their inability to maintain change is that they never developed any supports outside their family, from the schools or a church or any other organization, that might have provided outlets for stress. They were very distrustful of outsiders of all types. I attempted to process our termination for three weeks before I ended my visits with them, reviewing our work and helping them stay focused on their newer coping behaviors. But they did not seem at all sorry to see me go.

Summary

We learned in this chapter that two well-established family practice theories do not focus on the ending phase of intervention. Still, we can use their major concepts for assessment and intervention to formulate approaches to the ending phase that affirm and summarize a family's gains. In focusing on the family systems and structural family theories we considered several instruments (scales, genograms, and eco-maps) to use during the ending phase. We focused more extensively, however, on a variety of less formal methods to determine when the family has reached its goals and is ready to assume future challenges on its own. These methods also provide the practitioner with discussion topics to bolster the family's confidence during the ending phase. Of course, not all family interventions end successfully, as shown in the final case illustration. Even so, the practitioner's awareness of ending criteria in that situation helped him to understand the family's remaining needs. He could share this with staff from another agency in the event of a later referral or consultation.

Chapter 8

Group Interventions

Group interventions represent a popular and effective type of service delivery in many clinical settings. They may be conducted for convenience (to accommodate large caseloads, for example) or as the intervention of choice for persons with a variety of needs who might benefit from an interpersonal process. In general, treatment groups are organized to meet social, emotional, or educational needs of participating members. There are no practice theories that are specific to group modalities. Any of the theories described in the previous chapters may be adapted for group use. Effective group leadership requires that the practitioner have an understanding of systems, however, because the processes of member interaction are often the most significant aspects of group effectiveness.

Group interventions are fundamentally different than individual and family interventions in other ways as well. One of the most important aspects of groups is the fact that, when effective, they represent a positive community for the members. This community may be more supportive than other natural groups with which the clients are involved. This characteristic makes the process of ending groups challenging for the practitioner who hopes to preserve some of the "community spirit" within departing members.

Types of Treatment Groups

Before considering ending issues in detail, it is important to first consider the types and characteristics of groups. Following are five types of treatment groups (Toseland & Rivas, 2001).

Support groups—promote mutual aid, help members cope with stressful life events, and enhance the general coping skills of members. Examples include single parents sharing the challenges of raising children and children meeting after school to discuss the effects of divorce on their lives.

Educational groups—help members learn new information and the skills needed to use it. Examples include an adolescent sexuality group sponsored by a family planning agency and a prospective foster parents group sponsored by a child welfare agency.

Growth groups—provide opportunities for members to become aware of or change their thoughts, feelings, or behaviors regarding themselves and others. Examples include an adult psychotherapy group focused on general relationship issues and a values clarification group for adolescents.

Therapy groups—help participants make positive adjustments or rehabilitate after experiencing a social or health trauma. Examples include

Alcoholics Anonymous and a first-offenders group in a juvenile diversion program.

Socialization groups—help members develop social skills and new behavior patterns. Examples include a Catholic Youth Organization activity group and a social club for persons with serious mental illness.

Many treatment groups are formal and structured and include sequences of topics and activities that are neatly paced from beginning to end. Other groups are established with only general topics and goals. Their leaders may intend for discussion themes to emerge from the membership. It is often more difficult for practitioners to complete a focused ending in less structured groups because the task is not "built in." In every type of group, however, it is useful for leaders to think of the intervention as including a number of stages. If topical stages cannot always be predicted, there are process stages to monitor. With an awareness of predictable stages, the group leader can be more proactive in attending to the ending stage.

Just as groups are more or less structured, they may also be open or closed to new members after they begin (Toseland & Rivas, 2001). Open groups incorporate the benefits of accommodating more participants, providing immediate support to members, putting less pressure on members for personal disclosure, and tolerating a changing membership well. On the negative side, open groups are less stable and members are slower to trust each other. Closed groups tend to encourage deeper problem exploration, are more stable and cohesive over time, and ensure greater predictability of member behavior. On the negative side, they require long-range commitments from members and are more adversely affected by member dropouts.

Group Leadership across Stages

While there is no single standard outline of group stages, the five-stage model presented here is useful for thinking about group process (Anderson, 1997):

1. The preaffiliation stage is characterized by approach and avoidance behavior among the members, who do not know each other and may feel anxious and ambivalent about the new group.
2. The power and control stage is a transitional one. Members work out issues of status and roles. They may test their authority with other members and the leader and test the leader's boundaries with regard to rules and permissible discussion topics.
3. The intimacy stage is characterized by a productive familial frame of reference. The members work well together on the group's purpose.
4. During the differentiation stage, characterized by a group identity and internal frame of reference, the members begin to see themselves as separate from the total group process and focus more on their individual goals.

5. The separation stage, which unfolds prior to the actual end of the group, is characterized by member awareness of the upcoming end. Members begin to break away physically or emotionally in ways that may be quite different for each member.

Each of these stages features a different set of processes, or patterns of interactions among members. The practitioner is generally quite active in the beginning two stages, before a shared process of member interaction develops. The leader needs to orient members to the group's format and mediate the predictably awkward interchanges that characterize the early meetings. The leader becomes less active during stages three and four. These are considered to be the working stages of the group, where members assume more responsibility for its functioning. The leader becomes more active during the ending stage to ensure that appropriate closure is achieved.

Not all groups progress through the stages described, which represent an ideal type. Some educational groups, for example, may be based on assumptions that the practitioner will be highly active for the duration of the group, and member input will be limited. Further, some client populations may not be expected to move into stages of intimacy and differentiation. Children with behavioral problems, persons with mental retardation, and persons with serious mental illnesses may have limited interpersonal skills or cognitive ability that inhibits their moving beyond the power and control stage. Still, in every group the leader should make sure that there is a connection between the ending activities and the processes that precede them.

Leadership skills and strategies vary depending on the type of group. These can be articulated by considering common leadership tasks across the stages (Hepworth et al., 2002):

Pre-affiliation stage—establish guidelines and objectives, clarify goals and expectations, provide structure, model desired behavior, assure all members the opportunity for participation, encourage discussion of member anxieties and ambivalence, and encourage trust

Power and control stage—minimize changes in membership to ensure stability, encourage balanced member feedback, increase the quality of communication through feedback, and create and model norms for group behavior

Intimacy and differentiation stages—focus on the universality of group themes, support member differentiation, balance time allotments to members, keep the focus on goals and tasks, and become a less dominant presence

The Ending Stage

Certain leadership tasks are associated with the fifth and final group stage. Some of these tasks are similar to those addressed in previous chapters and are listed here but not discussed in detail:

Help members to practice new skills away from the group
Plan with members for possible setbacks
Reinforce awareness of the gains members have made in the group
Identify areas for continued work for each member after leaving the group

The eight additional ending tasks are unique to groups and are described in detail. The second, third, and fourth of these tend to be most pertinent to groups that feature a high level of emotional investment by the members. The other tasks are relevant to all types of groups. It is important to understand that these tasks are not always distinct—there is overlap among them.

Label the Onset of the Ending Stage

The practitioner's focus and level of activity change as a group enters its ending stage. He or she becomes more directive to maximize the possibility of bringing the group to a constructive conclusion. If the ending date of the group is known in advance, the leader can remind the members of that date and begin to initiate the ending activities. The practitioner shifts the intervention focus in two ways:

1. By encouraging members to look toward the future rather than deal exclusively with present-day concerns
2. By considering the group less as a unit and more as a collection of individuals with distinct agendas to complete

Help Members to Grieve

As noted earlier, groups often come to represent supportive communities to their participants. Members and leaders may form close attachments, and an important task for ending is to help members work through the sadness they may feel about the breaking of those ties (Reid, 1997). The principal therapeutic guideline in this four-step process is for the leader to accept and to encourage all expressions of feeling from members about the group.

The first step in this process may be a denial of the group's approaching end or its significance. This is characterized by an avoidance of the topic, so the practitioner must be sure to keep raising the issue as appropriate. Next, some members may attempt to bargain with the leader for an extension of the group. The leader should empathize with this sentiment but not indulge it. The leader must reconfirm in a matter-of-fact way that the group must end in the manner previously articulated. In the next stage of grief, members may feel sadness that the camaraderie of the group may not be replicated in their day-to-day lives. In this stage some members may feel guilty that they have not accomplished enough, or they may regret disclosing certain personal information to the others. Finally, members accept their loss and begin to think positively about their experience and its ongoing significance to their lives. The practitioner attempts to help members reach the stage of acceptance prior to the final session so that positive ending exchanges can highlight that meeting.

The following case study describes a temporary residential program for adolescent runaways. Staff assist adolescents who develop the skills to move into permanent housing through their transition out of the program with a series of ending activities. Many of these activities are intended to give the adolescents an opportunity to work through the sadness they usually feel about leaving treasured friends and staff behind.

Case Study: The Runaway Shelter

I work at a runaway youth shelter. There are always forty to fifty older adolescents who live there while staff work to find them permanent housing and healthy community supports. Most of the kids are in the program for at least three months, and some stay for up to five months. Staff and residents can get very attached to one another in the intimate environment. It is always a special occasion when a resident completes the program and leaves on good terms. It is certainly a positive event, but the staff and residents have mixed feelings when a person leaves. The staff hope that the adolescent will succeed as his or her peer support diminishes. Some residents experience the loss of a friend, and others may feel sad to see a peer move on while they remain dependent on the shelter.

We celebrate a resident's leaving in the form of a going-away luncheon. Everyone is invited, and usually twenty or more residents will attend the event along with a number of staff. During lunch, staff say a few words to the shelter community about the departing resident's achievements while at the shelter, his or her contributions to the life of the community, and the challenges that lie ahead. All members of the community are invited to share their thoughts and feelings with the group as well. We then present the departing resident with some gifts, usually functional items to help with their move, such as apartment supplies. The resident is encouraged to stay in contact with the shelter community and to come back for dinner whenever he or she wishes. Usually, the adolescent visits often during the first few months away, if he or she is living in the area. A final aspect of our ending traditions is that some staff and residents physically assist the person in moving into the new residence. We think that with these practices the adolescents are supported through their transition away from our community, and they are made to feel welcome to remain a part of it.

Address Separation—Individuation Themes

In addition to summarizing general themes that have arisen in the group and discussing how they can be applied in the outside world, the leader may also address topics related to separation and individuation, a theme from object relations theory. This concept pertains to the struggle all of us face to find an identity apart from that of our parent figures, but it is formulated differently in group therapy (Reid, 1997). As the ending nears, the practitioner should give members an opportunity to face and process the ongoing dilemma of how to achieve a life of one's own while maintaining connections to friends, family, and community systems that have been emphasized in the group. The leader should frame the challenge of finding one's identity and purpose in the context of relationships as a healthy one. We hope that the group experience has enhanced the potential for members to acquire and sustain positive relationships.

The group program described in the next vignette includes a series of ending activities for the adolescent members. The leaders did not formally use object relations theory as the basis for organizing the activities, but they nevertheless reflect themes of the individual in the context of larger interpersonal systems. The first activity focuses on the individual group member, the second activity focuses on each member in the context of the group, and the third set of activities focuses on the adolescent in the context of the family and larger community.

Case Study: The Wilderness Group

The wilderness conquest program in which I worked was a forty-two-day group experience in the canyon lands of Utah. Our clients were boys and girls between fourteen and twenty-one years of age. These adolescents and young adults had serious problems with such issues as substance abuse, truancy, violence, and other acting-out behaviors. Wilderness Conquest was an intensive program of hiking, camping, and primitive living for young people who might never have experienced anything of the kind before. They learned to make fires, shelters, animal traps, and maps. It was above all a therapy program. The setting and activities were means to help the participants improve their practical and social skills, gain confidence, learn to be responsible, learn how to address their problems in constructive ways, and set healthier goals.

Outings typically consisted of five adolescents, both male and female, and two staff, also a male and a female. Other support staff participated at times, for example, to make food and supply drops. One of the striking features of the program, and one that made our attention to its ending so important, was that participants were abruptly thrown together into this strange shared experience, and when it was over they would be abruptly returned to their previous environments. They might never see us or each other again. For our part, we would not know if the participants had implemented their plans, maintained their new insights, or been able to sustain support from others. So, in our final two weeks, we incorporated a number of ending rituals. All of them involved themes of independence and reliance on others.

During our fifth week in the desert, each participant was instructed to set up his or her own campsite. The purpose of this activity was to help participants use what they had learned in the program and show themselves that they were competent to survive alone. This began with a five-mile hike alone at night with a fluorescent tube. The participant marked a trail along the way from our base camp and then set up the campsite. The adolescents returned to base camp that evening, but the next morning all of them returned to their own campsites with few supplies and spent three days alone. They set up "mail boxes" amid piles of rocks at the edge of their camps so that staff could check in with them daily while not interrupting their solitude. After the third day the participants returned to base camp in silence. That evening we all sat around a fire and, finally breaking the silence, shared our experiences.

Next, we implemented a series of rituals involving the entire group based on Native American traditions. During a fire ceremony, each person wrote down a negative life pattern that he or she wanted to leave behind in the desert. These were thrown into the fire and burned. The next day we built a "sweat lodge" of hot rocks placed in a hole surrounded by a shelter, like a sauna. Before entering the sauna each person lit bands of sagebrush, and the smoke was intended to release a person's negative energy before he or she entered the lodge. This experience symbolized a cleansing of the old self and the rebirth of a new self. Even the process of walking backward into and out of the lodge, as a fetus would exit the womb, was part of this symbolism of rebirth. The rituals were all part of a summing up of what each adolescent had accomplished in the desert and prepared each person to carry positive aspects of the experience into their "normal" lives. Participants were reminded of their debts to the other members of the group, as they had clearly relied on each other's support to succeed in the demanding program. On the last day, support staff brought a feast to our campsite in the desert, and we celebrated the end of our six-week journey with a sumptuous meal.

The desert adventure was not the entirety of the adolescents' therapeutic experience. We went directly from the desert to a bed and breakfast in a small town, where we were met by the adolescents' families and initiated a three-day workshop. The families had been involved with our staff by mail and brought completed workbooks for this closing experience. During the three days the kids and their families set goals, owned up to their previous negative behaviors, got all of their secrets out, made amends, and arranged linkages with follow-up agencies in their home areas. This was a highly structured workshop. The adolescents could talk among themselves informally during breaks and for short times in the evening, and many of them exchanged addresses and phone numbers. Our final program activity was a graduation ceremony. It was much like a high school commencement, including a speaker, but with far fewer people. From there, the families scattered to all areas of the county.

Process One Member's Departure

It is rare, even in closed, time-limited groups, for an entire membership to begin and end together. Some members leave, with or without notice, along the way. This is not usually disruptive early in a group's life or if the group has open membership policies. But once a group has developed cohesion, a member's departure is significant to those who remain (Yalom, 1995). They may miss the personality and contributions of the member. They may feel guilty that they said something to drive the person away or did not work hard enough to create a positive atmosphere for that member. They may also feel envy, based on the ambivalence that many therapy group members feel about participation. Many group interventions require a significant commitment and are often emotionally difficult. Even motivated members may vacillate between their desires to learn and grow and their desire to avoid the stresses associated with growth.

Group leaders often struggle with deciding what to do about a member who drops out. Should the member be pursued or left alone? It is usually best to respect the value of self-determination and recognize that dropping out is the client's choice (assuming that the group is voluntary). It may be appropriate for the leader to call the member to discuss the decision and perhaps invite him or her back to explain the reasons for leaving. Beyond this, nothing else should be done to pursue the departing member. Of course, any formal rules about dealing with members who leave the group should be developed during the orientation stage.

It is always important, however, to process the event with the remaining members and encourage them to voice their reactions. Sometimes a remaining member will volunteer to call the absent member, but the leader should always reflect on the rules established earlier when considering this action. The leader should also look at the big picture when a member leaves. That is, the leader should assess what may be happening in the group to discourage members from continuing. When clients leave a group because they have met their goals for participation, the leader should conduct any of the structured ending activities described in this chapter that are appropriate to the occasion, focusing only on the departing members.

What follows is the account of a therapy group coleader's actions following the dramatic walkout of a long-term member. The leader had a testy relationship with the member for many months. After the client left, never to return, the leader tried to contact her to process the event. Both leaders processed the episode with the remaining members the following week and framed her walkout as therapeutic.

Case Study: "I'm Outta Here!"

I am the coleader of a private practice psychodynamic therapy group that consists of six members, three males and three females. The other coleader is a man of approximately my age (thirty). Ours is an open-ended, free-format group that focuses on the here-and-now concerns of members related to their management of interpersonal relationships. We meet weekly for ninety minutes. Members can remain in the group as long as they feel they are making progress toward their goals.

The client with whom I had a striking ending experience was Vicki, a thirty-year-old single Caucasian female. She was referred to the group after several years of individual therapy with a psychiatrist, who came to feel that her problems were primarily interpersonal. Vicki had an avoidant personality style, desiring relationships (particularly with men) but not being able to sustain them. It was apparent to me that she carried a great deal of anger toward her mother, whom she felt had always been critical of her. She expressed this anger indirectly to others.

Vicki was in the group for over a year. She insisted all along that she had little in common with the other members because most of them were married. I saw this as an excuse for her minimal participation in our discussions. The other members tolerated her behavior but encouraged her to talk more often. When she did talk Vicki tended to monopolize the group, focusing on her own needs and feelings and ignoring those of other members. Vicki had strong negative transference reactions to me. While I was close to her age, she acted toward me as a mother figure, and as such she became easily upset with me. She reacted negatively to my interventions and believed that I did not like her. My coleader was supportive of my efforts to work this through with the client.

During one session in which she was being quiet I attempted to engage Vicki in the conversation, again challenging her avoidance. To my surprise, she angrily and abruptly got out of her chair and shouted that she was "outta here." She ran out of the room screaming at me. Interestingly, just the week before she had made a significant step toward overcoming her interpersonal distance by participating more genuinely in our discussion. Apparently that event proved threatening to her, as she seemed to be looking for a reason to leave. I followed Vicki out of the room and asked her to wait, but she continued running down the hallway screaming, "I never want to see you again!"

To see if Vicki was serious, I waited until she did not come to group the next week before attempting to contact her by phone. She did not answer. I left a long message on the answering machine congratulating her on being assertive rather than passive in her behavior toward me during that final group session. Vicki did not call me back but called my coleader shortly afterward, and in that conversation she asked him to thank me for that feedback. She never returned to the group.

Was this a successful end for the client? In our prescreenings for the group, we encourage potential members to allow for a four-week closure process. The purpose of this structure is for us to set aside designated closure time each week for a departing member. Other members are given a chance to share their reactions over that period of time. Although Vicki did not follow our recommendation, I believe this was the only way she was capable of ending. Granted, the ending could have been more beneficial to Vicki if she returned at least once more to get feedback from the entire group.

My coleader and I had a difficult time processing the event with the group members the following week. They viewed the experience as a disaster. I presented my interpretation of what had happened first and then invited the members to comment. They seemed to agree that Vicki had been difficult to engage in the group since the beginning. Many of them agreed that perhaps Vicki was better off not continuing in the group, but still they felt badly that her leaving was not more cordial. Most of them felt that they could have been more nurturing of her. I explained that some people cannot bring themselves to process an ending directly, because it means they have to honestly face feelings that they prefer to hide. It took several weeks before we completely moved away from the topic of Vicki's departure. The best part of this difficult process is that it helped the remaining members reflect in some depth about their own reasons for participating in the group. Several of them admitted to occasional ambivalence, and we helped them accept those feelings as normal.

Process One Practitioner's Departure

Just as one member's leaving can have a significant impact on a group's functioning, so may the departure of one coleader have such an effect. Regardless of theoretical orientation, practitioners should be aware that in co-led groups some members will come to identify with or feel closer to one of the coleaders. Additionally, the relationship between the two leaders may provide a positive atmosphere or balance to the group's processes. Much is written in the psychodynamic literature about the importance of selecting coleaders to promote therapeutic transferences from members (Schermer & Klein, 1996). For example, in mixed therapy groups focused on helping members develop interpersonal skills, male and female coleaders may help members learn to relate comfortably to both men and women.

When one leader departs, even with appropriate notice, group dynamics will change. Not all members will react the same way, but common negative results include a decline in attendance and in overall group cohesion (Wexler & Steele, 1978). Members who react negatively to the change in leadership also tend to, at least temporarily, pull back from shared group issues and become more focused on themselves. Nothing can be done to prevent the negative dynamics that result from a change in leadership, but the effects can be minimized with proactive planning. When one coleader leaves the group, he or she should follow the established protocols (if these exist) that apply to any members who leave. At a minimum the coleader should announce his or her leaving with appropriate notice and share the reasons for leaving and his or her positive experiences as a participant with the group. The other coleader should also reflect with the group on the shared leadership experiences; present any plans to replace the departing coleader, if applicable; or share ideas on how the group might manage the loss. The leaders' directness with these issues will facilitate group members' eventual return to their primary purposes.

Resolve Unfinished Business Prior to the Final Meeting

The practitioner should try to make sure that all or most of the materials or activities related to the formal purposes of the group are completed before the final session (Walsh, Hewitt, & Londeree, 1996). The last meeting of any treatment group should be highly structured, and a significant portion of the session should be devoted to ending activities. The leader may reserve some time at the beginning of the session to allow for the introduction or processing of new material, but this should be relatively brief. There is a tendency among participants who want a group to continue to bring up new issues for discussion at the final meeting. These members may hope that the group will be able to continue past its stated end date, or their action may represent a denial of the fact that the group is ending. It is important that practitioners not get sidetracked and explore the specific issues that the members raise in this way (unless, of course, a genuine crisis has occurred). It can be productive, however, to explore the meaning of a member's raising of such issues, that is, to recognize this as a reaction to the group's ending.

Case Study: The Family Education and Support Group

My family education and support group was a nine-session, nine-week program for adult family members of persons with serious mental illnesses like schizophrenia. The purposes of the group were to provide families with education about their ill relative's disorder and to provide a setting in which they could support and problem solve with each other. I conducted the group twenty times over a seven-year period. I paid careful attention to the ending of the group, because I wanted the members to feel encouraged to seek additional education and support for themselves in other forums. As part of this process I tried to complete our coverage of educational material at the second-to-last meeting.

I contacted each referred family prior to its acceptance into the group. I sent each family a short letter describing the course and followed up one week later with a phone call. During the conversation, I answered questions the family member had about the program and, if the person decided to join, I conducted a brief survey to solicit input into the group's content. This information helped me plan sessions in accordance with member needs. I asked the family to make a commitment to attend at least three sessions.

I provided a structure for the group in the early sessions but tried to become less directive and more facilitative as the weeks passed. At the first meeting I introduced myself, reviewed the goals of the group, and summarized the input given by members during the phone survey. I then asked the families to introduce themselves. Many participants were reluctant to say much about their struggles, being unaccustomed to doing so and feeling anxious in the new setting.

The group topics were sequenced in an effort to gradually build member cohesion. At the second session we covered the topic of community resources. This always stimulated much sharing and was not so sensitive that it intimidated member participation. The group process was significantly enhanced during this session. The emerging group norm of interaction continued through the coming weeks. The third meeting consisted of my presenting information on the topic of psychiatric diagnosis. The following week's meeting, however, featured an open-ended discussion of issues related to having a family member with mental illness. It was the first session devoted to mutual support rather than education. It established a pattern of our meetings being alternately devoted to formal presentations and informal discussions. I encouraged the family members to rely less on me and to focus more on sharing their knowledge and experiences with each other. During the fifth session I made a formal presentation on psychotropic medications, and this was followed one week later by another open-ended discussion. The seventh meeting included another presentation, this time about the nature of roles provided by various professions in the health care system.

During the eighth week, our second-to-last meeting, I began attending to the ending process. Group members were self-directed by this time, and I offered two options for the evening's agenda. I could help the group organize a discussion about a new topic in which they had expressed interest, or we could devote the meeting to additional sharing and open discussion. I kept in mind that there was only one session remaining and tried to bring recurrent group themes to closure. In preparing for this meeting I reviewed the group's evolution and identified topics about which there had been particular interest and that might require additional attention. I was more directive this week than I had been for awhile.

The final meeting, then, was structured but did not include a great deal of formal content. My responsibilities included introducing a speaker from a local family organization, directing an ending discussion, and collecting evaluation forms. The meeting began with my encouraging members to address any unfinished business from previous sessions. Following this, we heard a thirty-minute presentation by a representative from a consumer group (such as the Mental Health Association or Alliance for the Mentally Ill). I wanted to provide a direct and personal link to another family organization for those group members who might like to join. The speaker provided an overview of the organization's mission and activities and highlighted ways in which family members could participate in that organization.

In the second half of the meeting I asked the members to share their impressions of the group experience. I reviewed the nine-week course, including its goals, what emerged as significant themes, what information was presented, and what members had shared with each other. I then asked members to respond to the following questions:

What did you learn that was important to you?

How comfortable did you feel about sharing personal concerns with the group?

How can you apply your learning to situations outside the group?

How can you generate support systems for yourself outside the group?

How do you feel about termination?

Finally, I asked the members to complete and return the evaluation forms.

I reserved thirty minutes of social time at the end of the meeting and provided light refreshments, so the members could chat informally and say goodbye to each other.

Structure the Final Session

In most groups, the possibility for closure is enhanced when prominent themes are addressed in a structured final session. The session often includes member reflection activities (Forsyth, 2002). As one example, the leader can ask members to address, one at a time:

How they perceived themselves in the group

The major issues they have dealt with

Their achievements, conflicts, and turning points

Their ongoing challenges for continued growth after the group ends

Anything they would like to say to the group as a parting comment

The amount of time each member spends on this task will vary depending on the size of the group but should rarely exceed five minutes or so. It should not provide an opportunity for members to emote in detail and perhaps dominate what is intended to be a shared, balanced activity. The leader should follow up each member's summary with a request that the rest of the members share their observations about the individual's contributions to the group. The giving and receiving of feedback is a regular part of any group, but this summation is often what the members carry with them long after the group has ended. The practitioner should make sure that this process is upbeat and constructive.

This activity represents an opportunity for members to deal with the process of separation and to bring to a conclusion the relationships they have developed in the group. Comments often deal with how another member served as an important model or an inspiration to try something new. Often members recall advice that was helpful, and they describe specific critical incidents in the group's life, such as an experience of confrontation or anger that was worked through. The leader participates in these conversations but avoids making specific comments about each member, as this may invite unnecessary comparative evaluations. It is also useful for the leader to be physically in a position at the end of the session to share a final goodbye to each member as he or she departs, perhaps with a handshake or a hug.

Many of the illustrations in this chapter have included examples of structured final sessions. We will now review an example of an open-ended group in which the leader maintained enough structure that each departing member got a positive send-off.

Case Study: The Art Therapy Group

There are several ending activities that I use in my art therapy work at a short-term, inpatient substance abuse treatment facility. The average stay in the setting is about seven days, just enough time for clients to become medically stabilized. My art therapy groups focus on the three goals of emotional expression, interpersonal connection (client to client, staff to client, and client to outside resources), and beginning-level behavioral change, such as relapse prevention and coping responses based on understanding environmental cues. I try to generate several sources of therapeutic support for clients, utilizing community supports to broaden their repertoire of helping relationships. Toward this end, the power of the group can be amazing, and art experiences can be a wonderful forum for identifying and developing supportive relationships.

A challenge in this setting is managing a client's profound sense of loss that comes with becoming intimate, even in a short amount of time, with the group and then leaving, often abruptly, as discharge is sometimes sudden. The clients who remain also experience a sense of loss. One ending ritual that supports the client's appreciation of the power of community involvement is our goodbye ceremony. The client who is leaving sits in the middle of the group, and each member reflects on his or her relationship with the client, directly to the client. Afterward, the client communicates his or her feelings back to the group. This is a constructive process, as members always emphasize strengths and remind the departing client of challenges that he or she must face as a recovering substance abuser. This activity is affirming not only for the departing client but also for those who remain, as they witness over and over again the significance of the community.

One of my favorite activities, which activates clients' emotions related to loss and transition, involves clients' artistic illustrations of what they need to leave at the treatment facility and what they need to take with them from treatment. Examples of things to be left behind include panic, isolation, chaos, anger, fear, clinging to pain, depression, sadness, emptiness, negativity, betrayal, and resentments. Things to be cultivated from treatment often include serenity, peace, happiness, appreciation, gratitude, hope, a positive attitude, support, willingness, and courage.

One young male client, when asked to complete this activity, chose themes of chaos and serenity. He used a blue marker in his picture to symbolize both of these concepts, using a distinctive line quality to represent the seemingly disparate feeling states. Serenity was illustrated as a smooth, clear line, untangled from the web of chaos drawn on the paper's opposite side. Our group discussion focused on the parallels that exist between the two ideas, proposing that serenity can, in fact, be found in and arise out of chaos. We continued to dialogue about the line organization within the picture. It suggested the client's awareness of his own responsibility for emotional transformation and the existence of hope in the midst of addiction chaos. The group decided that active personal responsibility coupled with a developing sense of faith in the recovery process would contribute to the chaos-serenity transformation visually represented in the client's artwork.

Another directed arts activity that helps clients identify needed changes and promote supportive social networking is the recovery-related gift exchange. Clients are paired and asked to create a recovery-related gift for the partner based on what they think the partner needs. Clients are directed to remain present focused. Examples of drawn gifts include candles that represent spirituality and wisdom, groups of family and friends that represent needed support structures and community connection, toolboxes that represent learned coping strategies, and clocks that represent a slowing down and increased mindfulness of purposeful daily activity. One client created a three-dimensional oyster with a "pearl of wisdom" inside, sharing with his partner his need to look inside himself for the power and strength to guide his recovery. Clients often find humor and comfort in such interpersonal exchanges, benefiting from both the giving of themselves and the accepting of the gifts of others.

Celebrate the Group's Significance

Some intervention groups include celebratory rituals as final activities to mark the significance of the overall experience (Gutheil, 1993). These ending activities are similar to those described in the previous section but are more symbolic in nature. Rituals can be understood as activities that symbolize stability and the significance of personal bonds while helping group members to accept change. There are many possibilities for such celebrations depending on the size, purpose, and client population of a group as well as the creativity of the leader and members.

Several of the case illustrations in this chapter include rituals of various types ("The Runaway Shelter," "The Wilderness Group," and "The Art Therapy Group"). Chapter 11 includes additional examples. Described next is an intensive weekend retreat that includes good examples of rituals that are intended to help members understand the importance of the retreat and encourage them to carry on with what they have learned after they leave.

Case Study: The Multiple-Family Weekend Retreat

I conduct multiple-family weekend retreats for families with children who are homeless. The families are in the process of moving into permanent housing and are referred by the housing agencies with which they are involved. The goals of this intervention are to strengthen families by providing training in communication, stress management, and decision-making practices. Having parents and their children meet together to address common concerns is an effective means of providing family mental health services. A major assumption of the modality is that family growth can be promoted more fully when peers rather than professionals are included in the intervention. I find the weekend retreat format to be preferable to traditional agency-based weekly groups, because they are more intensive and promote greater cohesion. Attendance at weekly agency groups is often problematic as well. The family retreats include about ten families with their young children, and about thirty to forty people in all. I recruit ten or twelve students to help implement the intervention. Thus far, I have conducted five weekend retreats.

The group retreats are held on Friday evenings from 5:30 to 8:00, and then on Saturday from 9:00 until 4:00. The retreats are held at parks or camps, and the families spend the night. The weekend focuses on two themes, "Strengthening Families" and "Families Have Fun Together." There are four formal group sessions on building trust, effective communication, managing stress, and decision-making practices. During the didactic portion of each session, parents are presented with information to help enhance their parenting skills. Between the sessions are various activities geared to having fun and also adding meaning to the session content.

The weekend retreat is intense, and families can become attached to one another. They may not be accustomed to this much supportive contact with other families. I pay careful attention to the closing ceremonies so that families can feel energized and affirmed as they go back to their normal lives. The ceremonies are also intended to encourage the families to continue the work they have begun at the retreat. There is a closing ceremony at the end of each day.

On Friday evening, after the families have been together for only a few hours and participated in one of the four scheduled groups, there is a "positive statements" activity. Each family is asked to sit in front of the other families. One member is given a candle and holds it while making a positive comment about each member of his or her family. When that person is finished, the candle is passed to another member of the same family, who does the same thing. Once the entire family finishes, the candle is passed to the next family, who continues the same process. If any member cannot think of a positive comment (this is not unusual with young children), the other participants offer honest suggestions. The passing of the candle adds solemnity to the activity and also symbolizes the connections of the families with each other.

The final two hours of the second day are used to focus on the ending of the retreat. There is a "Family Olympics" for forty-five minutes, with recreational activities that are intended to relax the participants after the final group intervention session. Next, each family works together to create a banner—a collage created on linen sheets using drawings and magazine pictures—on which they depict their family strengths. An alternative activity is the creation of scrapbooks about the weekend in which families can include photographs of themselves at the retreat (I always take a camera along). Finally, after a short period of completing the formal evaluations, the families take turns sharing their banners with the rest of the participants. Other people can comment about the family's strengths. Families keep their banners, and I always hope that they will display them on a wall at their new home as a reminder of their work during the weekend. This closing ceremony seems to be successful. The families are tired and eager to get home, but they usually express gratitude about the experience and linger for awhile to say goodbye.

Summary

Because groups are small "communities," their endings sometimes merit a different type of attention than endings with either individuals or families. The practitioner needs to consider not only the needs of individual members but also their attachment to the dissolving community of supportive others. When groups have been successful, members have formed ties that may not be easily replicated in the outside society. In this chapter we reviewed five types of groups and the stages, leadership strategies, and ending strategies that are common among them. We considered eight particular strategies that can assist practitioners to bring treatment groups to positive closure.

This chapter also brings us to the end of part 2 of the book. At this point we have completed our review of ending strategies associated with various theoretical perspectives on clinical intervention. In part 3 we again turn to ending processes in a general sense and review the range of thoughts, feelings, and behaviors that both clients and practitioners may experience during them. These reactions are based on personal characteristics of the client and practitioner as well as on other circumstances of the intervention that are not associated with a formal theory.

Part 3

Endings across
Service Settings

Chapter 9

Client Reactions to Endings

Although we have covered much ground in our study of clinical endings, we have not yet considered in sufficient detail the range of reactions that clients and practitioners experience in the process of ending. These reactions include the thoughts and feelings that the participants experience and the behaviors that they demonstrate. It is important for practitioners to understand how these reactions affect clients' abilities to move through the ending process and what the experience means to them afterward. As we shall see, clients' reactions do not have to be positive in order to be beneficial, but clients should be monitored and processed to maximize their chances for satisfactory closure. In this chapter we consider the range of positive and negative reactions that clients have to the ending process and the personal and clinical factors that influence those reactions.

Positive Reactions

Pride in Accomplishments and Increased Sense of Competence

The ending of a productive intervention symbolizes for clients that they have achieved certain goals and accomplished what they set out to do. The end is a marker of success, and clients can feel good about many if not all of the results. This may be particularly true when the process has been challenging. If you think back, for example, to college courses that were difficult but also interesting and important, you can understand the feelings of not only relief but also pride in an accomplishment that did not come easily. You gained knowledge and skills that were indicators of your increased competence in some area relevant to your career or personal life. This is the feeling associated with the end of a positive clinical experience. Even when the ending does not occur under optimal circumstances, the process may demonstrate to the client that she or he has greater competence for managing the loss than previously imagined (Levin, 1998).

Increased "Real-World" Activity

Considering that interventions help clients deal with their life challenges in largely "unnatural" settings, it makes sense that they should apply what is learned in the clinical setting to circumstances in their natural environments. The client who seeks help with overcoming passivity will attempt to use assertion skills on the job or with friends. The depressed client will incorporate new activities into daily life to combat the experience of low energy. The client who seeks greater self-knowledge will apply new perspectives to interpersonal activities. As the intervention ends, the client may naturally, or with encouragement, increasingly apply these skills to everyday life. This is a process of weaning away from dependence on the practitioner that should be encouraged. The practitioner should encourage the client to trust his or her own judgment.

A New Capacity for Other Attachments

When a person has sought clinical assistance with interpersonal problems, a positive reaction to the ending is a renewed desire to develop or nurture interpersonal attachments. Even when the person has sought help for problems that do not involve relationships, he or she still may learn how to use others for support more appropriately. The client may connect with new persons or reconnect with existing associates in a different way. The client with family problems may interact differently with those relatives or may begin to occasionally seek advice from a trusted friend.

Sadness

Sadness is a normal human emotion that may be quite healthy to experience and express. It does not necessarily have a connection with negative outcomes. Sadness can be understood as having or expressing sorrow. It can range from a mild, momentary unhappiness to a feeling of intense grief. Clinical practitioners tend to see certain negative emotions as warning signs of significant problems in the client's coping capacity. When a client shares sadness at the fact that the relationship is ending but does not become emotional, we tend to be appreciative. When a client expresses this sadness with a strong affect, we tend to feel alarmed. But people express the same emotions differently, and we need not be concerned that an emotional expression of sadness is an indictor that the client is regressing. Sadness indicates regret that the valued relationship will not continue, and it is normally an indicator that the experience was a positive one. It is usually best for the practitioner to allow the client's expression of sadness without reframing or interruption and to accept it as part of the difficult process of saying goodbye.

Relief

The reaction of relief can be understood in several ways. It may represent the client's excitement about the fact that he or she does not have to continue with an intervention that wasn't wanted in the first place. This is certainly true of involuntary clients—those who have been mandated or in some way coerced into the intervention. The client who is mandated to receive a psychological evaluation for alcoholism after receiving a DUI citation and does not see the need for intervention will be quite relieved after the necessary intervention is complete. Clients who have benefited from and enjoyed the clinical experience may also feel relieved that the experience is over. They may view clinical intervention as something that they should not need because it indicates personal weakness. The client who requires housing services may utilize the resource but at the same time regret needing the assistance. When this client completes the intervention, he or she may feel relieved to be able to rely on him- or herself again. In either example the sense of relief represents a positive reaction.

We conclude the review of positive reactions to endings with the story of Jamie. She began her therapy with great pessimism about her future but had a positive clinical experience and felt much better at the end. She was proud of her achievements, felt competent to manage her life without counseling, and had developed a capacity for satisfying relationships. Her practitioner tells the story.

Case Study: No Time for Sadness

Jamie was an eighteen-year-old college freshman when we met. She had not lived away from home before. Jamie had more adjustment problems than the average new student because of serious emotional problems that dated back to her childhood. She described her mother as emotionally absent and her father as abusive and a sexual molester, not of her but of other children in the neighborhood. Jamie had a lifelong history of anxiety, panic attacks, fears of being alone, and fears of sexual intimacy. She had been in and out of therapy since age nine and had taken medications at times. Jamie also had many strengths. She was intelligent, insightful, and articulate. She was motivated to confront her problems.

Jamie and I met about fifty times over two years, with many breaks during holidays and two summers. I worked from an ego psychology perspective, using our relationship as a basis for encouraging Jamie to work on her problems. I was about the same age as Jamie's mother and became a surrogate parent for her. I encouraged Jamie to reflect on her feelings in new ways and to gradually confront anxiety-provoking situations. I encouraged her to keep a journal as a way to explore her thoughts and feelings, especially as they pertained to mixed feelings about her father. She tried medications, but they were not effective and were discontinued.

I began to think about ending with Jamie six months before we made the decision. She had been doing well academically for several semesters, was involved in a healthy relationship with a young man, was no longer having panic attacks, and was able to internalize that her father's actions were not her fault. She described what I interpreted as termination dreams on several occasions. In these dreams she was sent to the principal's office in high school after getting into trouble, but I came to the office to defend her. Eventually, I felt that Jamie wanted to end but was reluctant to raise the topic, so I suggested that we end. She immediately agreed. Our formal ending occurred in one session with one booster session scheduled for a month later.

Jamie was thrilled because of what the ending meant to her. It made her happy to look back on her therapy experience, to compare herself now to the person who had come to college two years before. We reflected on the fact that Jamie was now able to let go of the bad feelings about herself related to her father. She said that she now had what she needed to love herself and that she felt worthy of being loved. Jamie added that she could now talk to her family, friends, and boyfriend about her feelings without becoming overwhelmed. She used the word *empowered* to summarize her progress. Despite our closeness, Jamie did not show any sadness about our relationship ending. This was a good thing in her case. Jamie had been sad for so much of her life, and she said it felt good not to be sad about this experience.

Problematic Reactions

Avoidance of the Topic

When faced with a difficult termination, some clients choose to ignore it. This may represent a learned behavior that characterizes many endings in a client's life. It is important to understand that clients who behave in this way may not be aware of their own emotional responses—they may be hiding the reaction from themselves as well as other persons. This is why Goldstein (1995) encourages practitioners to explore a client's lack of evident reaction to an ending. It is possible that the client does not really have strong feelings about the ending. If the client does have feelings and is ignoring them, they should be explored, as this may represent a maladaptive way of dealing with loss. But a balance needs to be observed here. The practitioner should not assume that the client is avoiding or minimizing the topic or project his or her own needs or feelings onto the client. The practitioner can ask probing but neutral questions to explore the issue, such as: "I notice that you have not said anything about this being our last meeting. Can I ask if you have given it any thought?" or "You seem to be taking this process very calmly. Am I reading you correctly?"

While it is customary in many settings to have some type of farewell ceremony or observance at the end of an intervention, these activities can reinforce the client's avoidance. We saw in chapter 4 that the client who brought champagne to her final session of analysis was doing so more as an avoidance technique than a celebration. Because the practitioner recognized this possibility, she said nothing to the client about the gesture, and the client eventually and thankfully decided to talk about her feelings related to the ending.

Case Study: Where's Jeannette?

For my graduate school field placement, I was an in-home counselor working with families who had a child identified as at risk for out-of-home placement by the courts or schools. I was a twenty-four-year-old single Caucasian woman, engaged to be married later that year. Our agency provided parenting skills training and also counseling and case management services for the identified at-risk family member. In this particular case, I worked with Jeannette, a thirteen-year-old African American female who had demonstrated aggressive behavior and received multiple school suspensions. I planned to work with Jeannette on her anger control, family relationships, peer relationships, coping skills, and depression. I also felt that Jeannette needed a female role model. I worked with the mother and father on their own parenting skills. I spent about seven hours weekly with the family over a period of four months, which was customary at my agency.

It took me a long time to develop a good relationship with Jeannette. She was mistrustful and quiet by nature and often said nothing to me at all. I became frustrated by her refusal to talk with me at her home, so I decided to take her out for community activities. I always asked Jeannette to suggest how we might spend our time together, but she never would. After talking with my supervisor, I decided to take her out on some of my own errands, trying all the while to engage her in conversation. For example, I once took her to a bridal shop to give me advice about wedding gowns. This worked well. We developed a very good relationship, and her body language became much more positive, even though she never became highly verbal. I could see that this shy girl had become quite attached to me.

The academic year was ending, and I needed to leave my field placement agency. Again, with the advice of my supervisor, I told Jeannette a month in advance of my leaving. She said nothing about this. Finally, the time came for me to leave. I had planned to introduce her to the new counselor on a Wednesday. I reminded Jeannette of this meeting on several occasions. The new counselor and I arrived at the home at 4:30, when Jeannette always arrived home from school. After we had waited for about forty-five minutes, Jeannette called and told her mother that the bus had broken down, so she had walked to a friend's house from school. Her mother reminded Jeannette that we were waiting for her, and I'm sure she knew this, but she claimed to have forgotten the meeting was today. The other counselor had to leave for another appointment, so we arranged to meet Jeannette the next day. My client's mother and I went to pick Jeannette up from her friend's house. She said nothing all the way home. As I dropped her off, I reminded her of the appointment the next day with her new counselor and myself.

The next day when I went to the home, the entire family was present. We carried out a family activity that consisted of each family member writing down positive comments about the others, then we put them in an envelope and read them out loud. All the family members, including Jeannette, seemed to enjoy this activity, although she stayed in the background and did not actively participate. I then gave everyone a copy of a family picture I had taken and said my goodbyes. I also took one more family picture and promised to mail them a copy. Just as I finished, the other counselor arrived, but during the commotion in the home I hadn't realized Jeannette had run into the bathroom. Once I noticed this, my client's mother and brother and I all knocked on the door to tell Jeannette that she need to come back out into the family room to meet her new counselor. She refused to do so until I left, so I did. I later learned that Jeannette interacted rather well with the new counselor, but I felt badly that I didn't get a proper goodbye.

Denial of the Topic's Significance

The client may not avoid processing the topic of ending but may deny its significance. The intervention may not have been productive for the client. If so, the practitioner's failure to explore the issue might reinforce the client's inability to see significance in other supportive relationships in the future. In chapter 4, John insisted that his practitioner's move would not be a problem for him. This was coming from a man who had no other relationships of substance and who was desperate for such a relationship. John's recurrent life problems were directly related to denying the significance of interpersonal contact. Allowing John to deny the therapeutic work without comment would have facilitated his persistent self-defeating attitude.

In the following vignette, both the client and social worker seem to have denied the significance of the ending process, even though the intervention had been positive.

Case Study: The Man in the Basement

Richard was almost fifty years old and had a long history of paranoid schizophrenia. I had worked with him for more than a year. He had been an easy client—happy, pleasant, and reliable about keeping his appointments at the mental health center, and he always took his medications as prescribed by our physician. On the other hand, he had no goals or ambitions and wanted only to be left alone in his small basement apartment at a neighborhood boarding home. He stayed home all day, usually in his dimly lit room. He occasionally went outside for walks, but he believed that whenever he was outdoors his brother-in-law followed him in a helicopter and shot "negative radar" into his heart. Richard got along well with the other six residents at the home but had superficial relationships with them. I liked him a lot. He came to the agency every two weeks, let me know that he was doing well, and asked how I was doing, always with a big smile on his face and a loud, gruff laugh. He got along well with the doctor, too. I wished he did more with his life. I encouraged him to consider some changes in his lifestyle, but he was very firm about being happy as he was.

When I was leaving the agency, I was concerned about how to end with some of my clients, but not Richard. I figured he would be able to work with anyone, considering that he was friendly and comfortable with his isolation and did not require much contact. I let him know two months in advance of my leaving, and we had a congenial but uneventful final meeting. But I found out two months later that Richard had not been back to the agency. He was not taking his medications and was making physical threats against other people at the house, who he thought were conspiring against him. My former supervisor called me to see if I would return just one time and try to get Richard back on track with his agency routine. This was an unusual request, considering that Richard had a new caseworker. I went out to his house and talked to Richard through the basement bedroom door, but he refused to come out. I was surprised and disturbed. It seemed that our termination affected him more than I had realized. But how was I to know? He seemed so agreeable about it all.

In retrospect, I was mistaken about Richard. He appeared to cope well with the end of our relationship. Despite his outward appearance, however, he was not able either to identify or express his feelings regarding the termination. His relationship with me may have been his only source of support. He did not realize what the end of that relationship would mean to him, and neither did I. Richard's concrete thought processes and superficial demeanor were an obstacle to his ability to understand or express the consequences of this ending.

An Extreme Sense of Loss

The loss of the clinical relationship is often significant, but the client may react in an extreme manner. This may manifest itself in requests for additional contact that are deemed inappropriate by the practitioner. The ending may evoke the pain of previous separations for the client (St. Clair, 1999). Significant loss reactions are more common with open-ended approaches, as these tend to be longer term and permit the client to reflect on a wider variety of life concerns. The loss reaction may be viewed as a positive response if the client is an involuntary one. The following vignette describes a client who was emotionally devastated by the loss of her practitioner.

Case Study: The Anxious New Mother

Tammy and I had a great relationship. When we first met at the mental health center she was in crisis. She was in the last trimester of pregnancy and experienced an increase in her symptoms of schizophrenia. She was not able to take medications because of her physical condition. Tammy had frightening paranoid delusions of other people trying to harm her. I spent a lot of time with Tammy during those first months to help contain her distress, and we became comfortable with each other. Her husband was also supportive, but he traveled a lot with his job. After her child was safely delivered, Tammy resumed taking medication and experienced some relief from her symptoms, but she was still anxious and afraid to be alone. She would not go shopping or take her daughter for a walk by herself. We worked together on strategies to reduce her anxiety, and her husband and parents participated in this process. Tammy could not tolerate being alone, however, and she began calling me at the office five times a day or more. The receptionists became annoyed with Tammy. They were in an uproar over the monopolization of their time, and we had to devote a general staff meeting to developing plans to reduce Tammy's calls and lengthy messages.

Our relationship continued to be good, but six months after her child was born I took another job and needed to transfer my clients. Tammy was upset, as I expected, and she resisted a transfer. She begged me to continue seeing her. Her anxiety increased, and her calls became even more frequent. Her paranoia resurfaced, and she wondered if I had planned all along to gain her trust and then leave her. I spoke with my supervisor often about this problem. Despite our efforts to accept Tammy's feelings about my leaving and our offer to introduce her to a new worker before I left, she refused to continue with the agency. I never heard how Tammy was doing after that. I didn't think I had necessarily done anything wrong, but I felt terrible.

In Tammy's case I utilized clinical and peer supervision to process the ending and identify strategies to help her manage the transfer. I attempted to prepare Tammy for the ending by discussing it with her as early as possible, setting appropriate boundaries, and offering to introduce her to a new worker. Unfortunately, her past experiences with loss were so great that she could not tolerate the end of another relationship.

A Recurrence of Old Problems—an Introduction of New Problems

Clients who anticipate an ending and are not sure they are prepared to function adequately afterward may begin to reexperience the presenting problem or experience new problems. This upsurge in problems may be a manifestation of anxiety about the idea of losing the practitioner's support. It is possible of course that a client will have an actual upsurge in environmental stresses that coincidentally corresponds with the end stage of the intervention. Usually these problems are not serious enough to require an extension of the intervention. If clients have made progress in therapy, they should have the resources to deal with the problem. The practitioner can lower the possibility of "doorknob confessions" (the unexpected sharing of new problems as the client is on the way out the door) by proactively addressing the client's anxieties about ending. The practitioner can normalize the client's anxiety, evaluating the significance of the reported new problems, reviewing his or her progress, affirming the client's competence, and identifying areas for further work.

A Request for Additional Help

Clients may request additional sessions if they are reluctant to end the clinical relationship. They may feel anxious about the absence of professional assistance regarding the presenting problems or want help with unrelated life concerns. This may occur even if the client recognizes the achievement of personal goals. Next is an example of a client who viewed the practitioner as an ongoing "consultant."

Case Study: The Practitioner as Consultant

Jane came for help at the university counseling center because she was so anxious that she could not study or complete her assignments. She was intimidated by her younger student peers and the faculty, because she was an older student and lacked self-confidence. Jane was bright and motivated, and within several weeks I was able to help her manage her stress through relaxation and time management strategies. She felt better and was so impressed with her progress that she asked for my help with other issues in her life, including conflicts with her husband, her desire to be more free of her mother's influence, and ways of coping with her acting-out adolescent son. I was flattered by Jane's attention toward me, but her requests went beyond the functions of the center, which always had a waiting list. I must admit I did see Jane for several more weeks because I liked her and always had an enjoyable hour with her. Eventually, I had to limit her use of my time. Jane was pretty angry with me when I did this, partly because I had prolonged her stay beyond the initial purpose of her visits.

Notice that the practitioner did allow the client to receive some additional sessions, against his better judgment. This made the eventual ending more negatively charged than it should have been.

A Request for a Dual Relationship

A dual relationship is one in which the practitioner interacts with the client in more than one context, whether professional, social, or business related. The practitioner who serves as the client's landlord, personal friend, business associate, or even romantic partner would have a dual relationship. These are almost always considered to be unethical because of the possibility of exploiting the client (see, for example, the National Association of Social Workers' *Code of Ethics*, 1996). Sometimes, however, particularly in rural areas, dual relationships cannot be avoided. The practitioner may need to take his or her car to the client's repair shop because it is the only one in town. The practitioner may need to provide case management services to the minister's son because he or she is the only social worker in town. If the dual relationship is unavoidable, the practitioner should secure informed consent, seek ongoing supervision, and document all activities to minimize the risk of conflict of interest charges (Herlihy & Corey, 1997).

Dual relationships may occur while the practitioner and client are working together or after the intervention is over. Sometimes a client will take the initiative to form a dual relationship with the practitioner after the clinical relationship ends because of an inappropriate dependence. In extreme cases, the client may want to become the practitioner's friend or, more commonly, maintain occasional contact through informal visits, phone calls, and lunches. If the client is a community businessperson he or she may want the practitioner to use his or her services. The client who has been sexually attracted to the practitioner may want to pursue a relationship now that the intervention is over. These relationships represent the client's desire to inappropriately hang on to the relationship, and the potential for the practitioner exploiting the client (even unintentionally) is great. The practitioner who is tempted to pursue a dual relationship that can be avoided should consider this as evidence of some unmet needs in his or her personal life and address those needs in another way (Malmquist & Notman, 2001).

Missing Sessions or Abruptly Dropping Out

As the end approaches, the client may begin to miss some sessions or stop coming in altogether. For some clients this is a reaction to negative feelings, of not wanting to go through a process of ending that might be emotionally difficult. For others it might represent an indirect decision to test how they will function without the clinical relationship. This is usually frustrating to the worker. Even when confronted, some clients do not want to or cannot share the reasons behind this behavior. Sometimes it is best for the practitioner to accept the client's behavior as a coping skill for managing the end of relationships.

Expressions of Anger

A client who is angry about ending an intervention may or may not express the feeling openly to the practitioner. There is nothing wrong with feeling angry—it is a normal, healthy emotion that is probably too often suppressed in relationships. However, it can be a highly charged emotion and thus not always acceptable to the client (or practitioner) who experiences it. This may indicate a client's general pattern of indirect communication or discomfort with emotions. Anger can be indirectly expressed in a variety of ways. The client may accuse the worker of selfishness, argue with the worker about the need to end, accuse the worker of ineffectiveness, refuse to pay a bill, and schedule and fail to keep appointments. Feelings of anger may reflect clients' belief that the practitioner is rejecting them.

Case Study: Battling Barbara

In my early twenties I worked as a ward attendant at a psychiatric hospital with young adult and adolescent clients. One of these was Barbara, who was fifteen years old. I was her designated one-to-one staff member. All patients were assigned to a staff member who was responsible for meeting with them on a regular basis to see how they were getting along on the unit. Barbara became attached to me, and this created a big problem when she left. She called me into her room the night before being discharged to her parents and asked me to take her home with me. Well, of course I could not do this and said so. First she cried and hugged me, but then she started beating on me with her fists. I thought she was teasing and laughed, but the blows became more forceful. She was a big girl and was hurting me. I couldn't get out of the room because she was standing in front of the door. In her rage she kept hitting me on the arms and back until I was on the ground calling for help. It was quite a scene, as a few other attendants had to come in and settle Barbara down. Things calmed down quickly, but the rest of the evening was quite awkward for us. I tried to talk with her about what her leaving meant to her, but she refused. When I came to work the next afternoon, she was gone. It was a terrible way to end our relationship, and I have to think she felt even worse about it. I'm not sure how I could have prevented that angry scene, except perhaps by talking to Barbara more often during her last week about her leaving. I don't know if even that would have helped, though, because the adolescents on my unit often expressed their feelings more with their actions than their words.

Aggressive Acting Out

The term "acting out" refers to inappropriate behavior in response to a feeling rather than a direct expression of the feeling or an appropriate behavior. It is usually associated with negative emotions such as anger and is often seen with clients who do not have the ability to understand their emotions or express them directly. It is common with children, adolescents, and populations with limited reflective capacity, such as persons with mental retardation. In the following vignette a client with mental retardation acts out her emotional reactions when the case manager leaves.

Case Study: The Relief Counselor

I worked for several years as a relief counselor in a program for persons with mental retardation, visiting clients and families in their homes. My job was to teach and reinforce the practice of basic living skills so that my clients might eventually move into supported living apartments. April, just fifteen, was a particularly challenging client. I only worked with her for two and a half weeks. I was "on loan" to her family by my agency while their primary provider hired a full-time case manager. April had mild mental retardation and also had Prader-Willi syndrome, a condition in which the person eats compulsively and is unable to experience satiation. Thus, April was extremely obese. Her treatment plan involved a strict schedule of daily activities while she gradually developed a capacity to tolerate change in her schedule. Whenever April experienced a deviation in her activity schedule she became upset and aggressive. I was warned that she might physically strike out at those times. Because of her size this could be dangerous for the person with her.

I visited April every day for several hours. Her mother went out to run errands when I was there. We watched television, played games, ate reasonable amounts of nutritious food, and read books. I tried to develop a good relationship with her, be a positive model (I was only five years older than she), and consult with her mother about ways to help her become better prepared for independent living. April also had a positive relationship with her mother's boyfriend.

April knew all along that I was a temporary counselor, and I knew when my last day with her would be. I reminded her of the upcoming change every day during my final week with her. I said that this was a chance for April to show that she could tolerate change. April did not reveal her thoughts or feelings during these conversations. I did notice on my second-to-last visit with her that she was more preoccupied.

This all changed during our last day. April was slow to engage in her routine. She was quiet and tense. We got behind schedule and were not going to have much time to play Monopoly, her favorite game. When she refused to do her reading, I suggested we both take a five-minute time out to sit quietly and take deep breaths before proceeding. I tried to help April say what she was feeling and to complete her activities, but this was difficult for her. Late in the afternoon, during our Monopoly game, April began to damage the cards. When I asked her to be careful about this, she became angry. She tore up the cards and play money then threw it around the room. Now I was anxious. I asked April again to talk out her feelings. She could not say anything but still appeared to be angry. I suggested that we take another time out.

While we were sitting in the small room, April said, "We're not going to tell mom about this, are we?" Well, I had an obligation to document a client's behavior and report it to the caregiver, but I suggested to April that she could tell her mother what had happened. At that point April jumped out of her chair and grabbed the charting folder in my hand. When I resisted, she scratched my arms and took the documents from me. She tore them up just as she had the Monopoly money. I was frightened now, for myself as much as for her. At that moment her mother's boyfriend came home. When he walked in the house, April calmed down. Still shaken, I left a few minutes later.

I thought that I had done something wrong, that I had mishandled the circumstances of our last meeting. April's mother had been critical of our agency at times, and I expected that she would call our director to complain. To my surprise, April's mother called to thank me for my work. She said that April would have acted out her anger in that way no matter what I did. April was upset at having to endure another change, and she did not want me to leave because she liked me. The mother explained that the more she liked someone, the more disruptive she became when the person needed to leave. April simply did not know how to express negative emotions.

I did go back the following week to say hello to April. She was calm and pleasant. What I learned from this incident is that I need to read a client's chart more carefully when accepting a transfer so that I might better predict the client's behavior in certain situations. I need to ask staff who have previously worked with a client about their experiences. I should also have included the family in a plan for my ending, so that we could all have input into making it a constructive experience for April.

Testing the New Worker

In cases of transfer from one practitioner to another the client often "tests" the competence and attitudes of the new worker. Can the new worker be even close to as good as the last one? Will he or she know as much? Be as empathetic? It is natural for clients to wonder about these things and to want to withhold full participation in the process until they have a chance to test it out. The new practitioner can be proactive in managing this process by following certain guidelines. A practitioner should acknowledge the significance of the change, encourage discussion of the previous practitioner, be sensitive to any loss content in the client's communications, communicate willingness to work with the client, and be self-aware of any feelings of competition. It is also common for the practitioners to make the mistake of setting out to prove that they will be as good as the former professional. They may try too hard to make the client like them, set goals with the client that are overly ambitious, or try to achieve goals too quickly in this attempt to prove themselves.

Factors Influencing Client Reactions

Degree of Success or Satisfaction with the Intervention

Clients generally experience more positive than negative reactions to the ending stage if they perceive that the intervention has been successful. Still, their emotional reactions may be mixed even in these situations. Analytic thinkers tend to be sensitive to the complexities of clients' emotional reactions to endings, and they are careful to monitor them regardless of the overall course of the intervention (Kramer, 1990; Kupers, 1988). In recent years, however, as other theories have grown in prominence, practitioners are focusing less specifically on the problematic aspects of ending and more readily acknowledge its positive aspects. Fortune (1987) states that there has been an overemphasis on problems associated with ending clinical intervention. She conducted a study of the clients of social workers who practiced from a variety of theoretical perspectives and found that clients reported positive feelings about the relationship far more often than negative feelings after the intervention ended.

In the two illustrations that follow we can see both sides of this issue. Both involve the same practitioner and two clients seen simultaneously.

Case Study: Keeping the Customer Satisfied

I met Lois after her brief psychiatric hospitalization for suicidal threats. She was referred to my mental health center for follow-up counseling. About forty years old, Lois had just moved to our city with her husband, who informed her almost immediately that he was involved with another woman and wanted a divorce. He left Lois with their two middle-school girls. She seemed angry with me when we first met, and I could not blame her for being angry with all men. But we arranged to meet on a weekly basis, and I arranged for a medication evaluation with our agency physician.

Lois and I met regularly over a period of ten weeks and talked by phone on a few occasions. I encouraged her to ventilate, listened actively, affirmed her worth and good judgment, and helped solve her practical problems. I was her only personal support at the time, so I also referred her to a time-limited therapy group for women. She steadily worked through her adjustment reaction. When her moods were low she became frustrated with me, but in general we got along well. Lois enjoyed her therapy group and also benefited from the medications. She did not want to become therapy dependent, however, and she initiated the end of our work before I would have. We organized a four-week plan of tapering off both our sessions and her use of the antidepressant medications. Lois was proud of herself for surviving her crisis. She decided to divorce her husband and eventually return to her native state. She couldn't thank me enough for my help, but she understood that it was time to move on, and she never looked back.

Things went differently with Barbara. She was the same age as Lois but was a divorced mother dealing with issues of alcoholism in her family. She wanted short-term counseling for help in giving up her "enabler" practices with her alcohol-abusing adolescent kids. She was studying to become a hospital chaplain and was eager to get her own family problems under control. This turned out to be a difficult intervention for me. In my view, Barbara's enabling behaviors were only one aspect of the problems in her family. I encouraged her to scrutinize her family patterns. She tended to view this as criticism despite my frequent acknowledgment of her strengths.

Barbara was quick to identify reasons why she could not change her behaviors. This frustrated me, and I suggested to Barbara that perhaps some longer-term work might help her to achieve her goals more thoroughly. She politely stated that she did not want to make such a commitment, and she decided to take a break from counseling. We had met six times, and Barbara said that she felt some relief from her problems. She was pleasant during our last session, so I was surprised to learn that she sent a letter to my director soon afterward complaining of my poor work. She felt that I was unqualified for my job and uninterested in her, yawned through our sessions, and failed to provide her with useful input. She said she would never return to the agency and would not recommend any of her friends to come.

The practitioner in these vignettes remarked that he was often surprised by his clients' reactions to the end of their interventions. He could never be sure if his own evaluations of the interventions' effectiveness matched the clients', even when they discussed the matter. Some clients who are not satisfied are reluctant to admit this while the intervention is in process.

Context of Brief versus Long-Term Intervention

As a general rule, the range of reactions that people have to the ending of any relationship correlates with the length and depth of the relationship. The longer we know someone, the more feelings and history we share with that person. The intensity of a relationship also makes the ending more complex. When other people have been a part of our lives in some significant way, we will miss them. This principle also applies to clinical relationships. The client and practitioner may not get attached to each another in a short-term clinical relationship. After a lengthier relationship, one in which the client has shared more sensitive personal material with the practitioner, the end might signify more of a loss and evoke painful responses from the client. This principle even seems to be true of analytic intervention. In one follow-up study of a small number of clients after analysis, it was learned that the client still reflected on the therapy and the therapist (Epstein, 1989). The nature and extent of this reflection depended, however, on the amount and length of the therapy, the time since it ended, its perceived benefit, and the perceived quality of the clinical relationship.

At times clients can develop strong attachments to the practitioner during short-term interventions, as shown in the following vignette, although they may not persist for long.

Case Study: The Hot Chocolate Man

I worked for a crisis intervention hotline on the night shift, taking phone calls from frantic, depressed, and anxious people. Some of these people were contemplating suicide because of circumstances that left them feeling alone and hopeless. I might spend an hour with such callers, providing them with support and active listening. Often they felt better after the call. They decided to live, to address their problem in some new way, or to seek ongoing assistance from a mental health clinic. At the end of some of these calls it was gratifying to hear how grateful the callers were for my help. Many times they thanked me for saving their lives. They might go on and on about how they wanted to repay me in some way. I appreciated their sentiments but always suggested that the best thing they could do, since it was the middle of the night, was to make some hot chocolate and then go to bed. Most of them liked the idea. They'd rarely call back.

Previous Experiences with Loss

The client's history of managing relationship losses has an impact on the nature of her or his reactions to the clinical ending. While the end of the clinical relationship may be significant, some clients manage loss well. They see the clinical relationship as an instrumental rather than primary one. They are not overwhelmed with grief and do not feel so alone that they are unable to continue functioning effectively in their various life roles. Other clients, particularly those who have always had few reliable supports in their lives or who have not experienced loss as frequently, do not manage loss as well. They feel a greater void in their lives and experience a grief process that may be difficult to work through. Their feelings may result in requests to continue, expressions of anger, or acting-out behaviors. The practitioner should assess the client's ability to cope with relationship losses in advance and focus the ending process accordingly, so that the client's gains are not undone.

Following is an example of a practitioner who was surprised at how upset the client became when their ending date approached. The practitioner recovered well, however, and organized a positive ending process for them both.

Case Study: The Business Cards

How do I end a nine-month relationship with a client who never missed an appointment? I remember asking myself. While I enjoyed all my clients, Delores was special. She was my first client at the mental health clinic staffed by graduate students in social work and psychology. This fifty-four-year-old African American woman was a regular at the clinic, having worked with two other practitioners during the past two years. As a person with schizoaffective disorder, she presented numerous challenges for me throughout our relationship—from assessing her needs and cognitive abilities to tailoring intervention techniques to address her chronic problems.

My work with Delores was challenging due to the vagueness of her thoughts and feelings. Delores often communicated with facial expressions and gestures, assuming they were sufficient. She also suffered from episodes where she would "lose time" after the "voices in her head" over-whelmed her. Panic attacks were common, yet Delores was unable to iden-tify events surrounding the attacks. Deep breathing, progressive relax-ation, and visualization exercises proved beneficial to her. I also employed solution-focused techniques to help Delores identify her strengths and ways to mobilize herself into action.

Because her affect was so erratic and her thought processes often un-clear, I began the ending process three months before our last session. In each session I reviewed our work together and acknowledged Delores's achievements. She did not act surprised when I reminded her of the date of our last meeting, but I was not convinced that she understood our rela-tionship would, in fact, end. I continued to devote time each session to ex-ploring where Delores had been at the beginning of our work and how she had changed since then. As the number of our remaining sessions de-creased, I provided more of a balance between what Delores had achieved and what she needed to work on in the future. Exactly one month from our last meeting, I started off a session commenting about how much time we had left. Delores burst into tears and was unable to communicate for most of the hour. Despite our weekly termination discussions, Delores said that she didn't truly think it would happen. I could only remind her that our re-lationship would end, as badly as she seemed to feel about the fact. Our re-maining sessions were devoted to processing Delores's strengths.

I wanted to do something special for our last meeting. I felt it should be a celebration in honor of Delores's hard work. We walked to a nearby park and talked about the progress Delores made and the strengths she could rely on to get her through difficult situations in the future. As a me-mento of our time together, I had a set of business cards made for Delores to carry in her purse and place around her house. On one side of the card were our names and the dates we'd worked together. On the other side was a list of Delores's strengths. I suggested that she read these cards from time to time. Not only did she seem to appreciate the cards then, but a week later I received a note from Delores including one of the cards and a message that she hoped I'd hold it dear to my heart.

Current Life Situation

The clinical experience represents only one activity in a client's activities of daily living. It occupies a small portion of the client's time. Most clients are also involved in jobs, schooling, relationships, and social activities. For this rea-son, the client's reaction to the end of the clinical relationship is greatly influ-enced by what else is happening in his or her life. Does the client have other people to rely on for positive interaction? Can the client seek out help from oth-ers when needed? Is the client involved in other productive life activities? Is the client optimistic about the immediate future? If so, his or her reactions to the end may not be remarkable. Is the client lonely? Does the client have little to do during the day? Are the client's primary relationships conflicted? Is he or she discouraged about the immediate future? If so, his or her reactions to the ending may be problematic.

School social workers often remark that ending work with their young clients is difficult because this occurs in a context of other endings (Morse, Bartolotta, Cushman, & Rubin, 1982). For many students the end of the school year is a time of exhilaration. For students with family problems who have found support among professionals in the school system, however, this time of year may be frightening. They must end relationships with psychologists, social workers, nurses, teachers, and friends all at the same time. The effect can be devastating. Tori, a social worker, expressed this dilemma eloquently.

Case Study: The End-of-the-School-Year Blues

Often our experiences of closure with clients happen abruptly or not at all, that is, when a child moves away with no notice. This is difficult for me, and often for the children, especially if the family is transient and the school doesn't know where they've gone. I worry about the kids in those situations. If they have been responsive to our work I am concerned that they feel abandoned. One difficult ending occurred for me when three boys I had gotten to know well in an elementary school were removed from their foster home after one of them allegedly molested another boy sexually. They were gone, just like that! It was difficult for the entire school staff, but I want to emphasize the difficulty for those children.

A different type of problematic ending occurred for Joan, a prison social worker. Prison inmates are separated from all of their loved ones. When they develop an attachment to a clinical practitioner, it can be very difficult for them to let go.

Case Study: Miss Jeffers

As a young, single, female social worker in a men's prison, I occasionally have to deal with strong attachments that some inmates form with me. My work with Chris provides an example. Chris was twenty-nine when I met him, and he had served twelve years of a fifty-year sentence for the murder of a young woman. During his childhood Chris had been physically and sexually abused by his father, and as an older adolescent he could not relate comfortably to women. One day, after a girlfriend abruptly broke up with him, Chris became angry and then got drunk. He killed a woman who happened to be passing through the park where he was resting.

My prison facility specialized in providing interventions for persons with mental health problems. One of my responsibilities was to conduct a time-limited "stress and coping" group. Chris was a member of that group, along with five other prisoners. I did not have a coleader. We met ten times and discussed a variety of stress and anger management strategies. Among the techniques I introduced were poetry, journaling, and other forms of self-expression as ways to reflect on feelings. Chris began to write poetry, and he enjoyed sharing it with the group. I supported Chris's new interest. Eventually, it came time for the group to end. I conducted a standard ending process, talking with the members on the last day about what they had accomplished and how they might continue to use what they had learned. In retrospect I should have reminded the members about prison policies that would restrict their future interactions with me. Formality is a hallmark of prison life. For example, I was always "Miss Jeffers" to my clients.

Chris was transferred to another prison a month later. After two months I received a friendly letter from him, including some poetry. This presented a policy issue that I immediately took up with my supervisor. In the prison setting an inmate must get permission from a superior to contact any staff member for a nonroutine purpose. The process is intended to preserve clear boundaries in staff-inmate relationships. My supervisor advised me to write back, acknowledge reading the letter, remind Chris that we were not to have further contact, and refer him to appropriate resource persons at his own facility. I did so, but he wrote back two months later, again including some poetry. In fact he wrote to me five times during the coming year. My supervisor advised me to respond the same way each time, but after the fifth letter she told me to let Chris know that I would not write again.

But the letters kept coming, every three months or so. I became more concerned when two of the letters had both romantic and threatening tones, as if he would be upset if I did not reciprocate. Of course, he had no way of knowing if I was receiving his letters or even worked at the prison anymore. But there were clinical, policy, and risk issues involved. I cared about Chris's quality of life but needed to take care of myself. My supervisor and I decided that she would get a message to Chris that further efforts to reach me would be considered policy violations and be reported as such. We also decided that I would not read his letters if they continued to come. Fortunately, no letters came afterward.

There is often a tension between my desire as a social worker to help prisoners develop as people and the desire of the institution's staff to maintain a formal, safe environment. Prisoners often have few pleasant and supportive relationships in their lives. They can become quickly and deeply attached to staff who are responsive to them. For that reason I did not want to report Chris for disciplinary action after he started writing to me, but eventually I had to set a clear limit.

Meaning of the Clinical Relationship

What does it mean to a client to have a relationship with a clinical practitioner? At one end of the spectrum, the relationship might be the most important aspect of the client's life, one without which the client might feel that he or she could not go on living. At the other end, it can be a terrible intrusion, a perceived waste of time, and a violation of freedom, comparable in pleasure to a trip to the dentist! Clearly, this perception will have a great impact on the client's reaction to its end. Knowledge of the client's attitude about the meaning of the relationship is essential for the practitioner in planning for its ending. It is important to understand that the meaning may not be evident from a client's external behaviors. The "surprise" aspect of this issue is evident in the following two vignettes.

Case Study: The Life That Might Have Been

Several years ago I worked as a member of a palliative oncology care team in Vermont. We provided counseling and social services for patients with life-threatening cancer. The team was based in an agency that had received a three-year grant for the program. Many clients were on our caseloads for years without interruption, because we were able to follow them whether they were living in the community or in the hospital. I worked with the team for two and a half years, but before the grant ended I enrolled in graduate school in Boston and had to leave. I accepted my admission to the program several months before needing to move. I began sharing the news with my clients a few months before I left.

I was a young practitioner then, probably more anxious about announcing my departure to clients than I would be today. In that program I was accustomed to ending with clients when they passed away—the fact that I was the one leaving was ironic. I can remember thinking how much better it would be from a clinical standpoint if my clients died before I left, so I would not have to leave them. But I had known Rose, a widow in her mid-seventies, for more than one year, and despite her cancer she was getting along well and might survive for another year or more. We had a good relationship. She was in the hospital for a series of chemotherapy treatments when I told her about my leaving.

I expected that Rose would be upset and view my departure as a blow to her limited support system, but she surprised me! When I told her of my plans, her first reaction was to be excited. She thought it was wonderful that I was moving on with my life and career. She asked about the details of my move to Boston and my career plans. Rose had spent her entire life in rural Vermont. She had had a good life and a great family, but I realized that day that a part of her always wondered how her life might have been different if she had left home and seen more of the world.

Professionals who work with older adults know that facilitating a life review is an important intervention. At the end of one's life a person's sense of identity and meaning is affirmed by telling the story of his or her life. Rose undertook a different kind of life review that day. She talked with me for a half-hour about what her life might have been like if she had moved away from Vermont. It occurred to me that she saw me as having the kind of life she might have had if she had been born fifty years later. It meant a lot to her that I was leaving, as if a part of her would be going with me.

Rose and I met once more after that. Her feelings were mixed this time about my leaving. We had a nice visit and summarized our work and relationship. I talked with her about the person who would be taking my place. There was an unspoken issue in the air that day, one that I often sense in working with dying clients. It was the big question, What will the end be like? That is so private and difficult for clients to confront. I did write a letter to Rose after I got settled in Boston, letting her know where I was living and how my new life as a graduate student in the big city was getting underway. I knew that it would be important for her to get that news from me. I later learned that Rose lived another six months before passing away.

I learned several important clinical lessons from my ending with Rose. I learned not to be afraid of engaging a dying client in life review sooner rather than later. Also, it had never occurred to me that a professional's departure from an agency might be positive for a client who was staying behind. I usually expect when an intervention has been working well that the client will be sad. Rose identified with me in a way that made her genuinely happy that I was undertaking a new life adventure.

Case Study: The Drone of Apathy

Several years ago, while a trainee at a counseling center, I was assigned to work with Craig, a twenty-three-year-old depressed man. He was classified as an "advanced case," meaning that he should receive intensive therapy and careful monitoring because of a recent suicide attempt. I saw Craig twice weekly over a period of about twelve weeks. My supervisor instructed me to focus the therapy on our relationship. This was because Craig felt unloved and unworthy of anyone caring about him. My supervisor helped me plan for our sessions and kept me focused on the theme of relationships. Therapy was rather existential in that we often considered such basic issues as the meaning of life and whether there were good reasons for living. We routinely discussed his feelings about being in therapy and whether he thought I cared for him. Craig always came to our meetings but never seemed to move beyond his characteristic apathy and sense of unworthiness. This was frustrating for me despite my supervisor's affirmation of my efforts. Once while seeing me he was briefly hospitalized after another suicide attempt. This was related to a letter he wrote me that revealed some personal information that he later regretted disclosing. I visited him at the hospital, but he still didn't say much.

Our therapy ended at the close of the academic term. As part of the ending process I asked him again to reflect on the meaning of our work together. He denied its significance. I always thought that our relationship meant something positive to Craig, and I felt good about that. On the other hand, I never had any sense of reward for my time with him. Never before had I worked with a client who left so much the same as when he first came to me.

Eighteen months later, out of the blue, I got a card from Craig in the mail. It was quite upbeat in tone. He indicated that he knew I had cared for him and that our therapy had been important to him but that he had never been able to say so. He assured me that he was "still alive." The card transformed how I felt about my work with Craig. I was able to experience a sense of reward long after the fact. What I learned from this experience is that my not knowing about a client's feelings and attitudes about our work should not be the critical yardstick for measuring whether it was significant.

Cultural Traditions

The practitioner should always develop an awareness of a client's cultural traditions, particularly if the client is a member of a racial or ethnic group very different from that of the practitioner. The professional should assess the client's attitudes about seeking help, attitudes about professionals, verbal and nonverbal behaviors, and preferences for types of interventions. The worker should also learn the client's traditions with regard to ending relationships. Sensitivity to this issue can promote a positive ending experience, while a lack of awareness can compromise an otherwise successful intervention. Following are examples of both types of endings.

Case Study: The Chef

I work at a university counseling center. My client William was a twenty-nine-year-old single, Burmese male with posttraumatic stress disorder. He had been a soldier in a war in his home country, and his symptoms were related to fears about being victimized by crime in our city. William was terrified of homeless panhandlers and believed that they might kill him, even though he knew on a rational level that they lacked the means or intent to do so. His anxieties were compounded by his experience of being a minority in America and his observations of how minorities are mistreated. William was concerned about his limited ability to speak English and his social isolation.

During our sessions I attempted to work within William's cultural frame. This included affirming his fears rather than labeling them as paranoia and helping him learn to make reality checks when he was upset. For example, I let him take my lamp apart during one session because he was afraid there might be a bomb in it. He also requested that he not be videotaped (which was routinely done at the agency), because he was fearful of what would happen if other people learned about things he had done as a soldier. I also affirmed William's culture when I accepted a place of honor in his life. William always wanted to keep his head lower than mine and to avoid eye contact with me as demonstrations of respect. It was hard for me to understand all the important practices in his culture. For example, one day he complained abruptly that we should stop working together. When I explored the reasons for this, he said that I had crossed my legs during the session—a sign of disrespect in his culture. We resolved that issue, and our relationship continued. I sat with my legs uncrossed, and both of us avoided eye contact.

William overcame many of his fears, and our sessions began to include less volatile content, such as his desire to cook Burmese food. Being able to fix Burmese food was important to William, representing a healthy desire to stay connected with his culture. He was reluctant to do so, because his roommate did not like its smell, so we worked on ways he could negotiate with his roommate to be able to do this.

After ten sessions, William was experiencing few irrational thoughts, was able to identify his stress triggers, and was looking forward to graduating from the university. As we ended our work he invited me to his house for a thank-you dinner. I declined the invitation, however, citing my professional code of ethics injunction to not accept gifts from clients. William was very hurt by this. Looking back, I believe that my declining the invitation undid some of the positive work that he and I had done to honor his culture. It also made our ending more awkward than celebratory. I feel now that I sent William a conflicting message. With the dinner invitation William had been acting in ways I had encouraged with respect to his roommate.

Although I still would probably not go to his house, I think I would now negotiate a way to accept William's cultural ways of saying thank you and goodbye. I would invite him to bring food to the office, where he and I could share a meal and maintain the setting of therapy.

Case Study: The Apache Tear

Occasionally, a client will want to conduct his or her own ceremony to celebrate the ending of a clinical relationship. This may be especially important to clients from certain cultural backgrounds. The practitioner should welcome such a ceremony if it stays within reasonable limits of time and expense. I shared a very moving ending of this type with Rebecca, a Native American client.

Rebecca, forty years old, came to my mental health agency to get help with anxiety and depression. She was a recovered cocaine abuser but experienced so much anxiety that she was physically ill, feeling light headed and nauseous every day. Rebecca was tormented with worries about the physical and emotional welfare of her adoptive father and brother and her ability to stay free of drugs. Her anxiety seemed to be rooted in a fear that she was going to lose control of her life. To prevent this she tried to be perfect, in complete control, because she had been so out of control several years earlier.

Rebecca was born on an Indian reservation in the western United States. She was given up for adoption by her parents at age seven. Her adoptive parents were Caucasian, but they encouraged Rebecca to stay involved with her Indian culture. She visited her natural father every year on the reservation and interacted with Native American groups in her current area of residence. I wondered if it would be difficult for Rebecca to work with me, a Caucasian female, but the racial difference did not appear to be a barrier. We worked together for four months, about ten sessions, to control her anxiety through a variety of cognitive and behavioral activities. Rebecca made excellent progress, and we agreed that the time had come to end our work.

When we met for the last time, Rebecca presented me with a polished gemstone, a smooth, dark stone that she called an "Apache tear." The stone was dark but became transparent when held up to light, and a small "tear" could be seen in its center. The stone had been given to her by a friend many years before, and now she wanted to pass it on to me. She explained that the Apache tear symbolized both struggle and one's hopes for a better future. She said that she had been struggling for years, but now she could look ahead with confidence and self-acceptance. She wanted to give me the stone as a thank you. She added that she had had the stone blessed by a tribal healer before bringing it to me.

We spent a fair amount of time during our final session talking about the Apache tear. I thought that it was a wonderful gesture. It was very important to my client to give me the gift and also to explain its history and significance. Agency policies often prohibit or discourage clinical staff from accepting gifts from clients. Sometimes, though, it is important for the client to give a gift, and refusing it would be destructive to the relationship. I will treasure that stone forever.

Usual Coping Style

Personality can be understood as the sum total of emotional and behavioral traits apparent in a person's life that are usually stable and predictable (American Psychiatric Association, 2001). One's personality style is a major determinant in negotiating all life situations, including the manner of ending relationships. Several authors have written about the impact of personality type on the course of clinical intervention. Alexander and Abeles (1968) identified four types of "normal" client dependency traits and how they may influence the clinical encounter. These include dependency on the family, social network, the practitioner, and the human service system. These authors found that as intervention proceeds, a client's system dependency and social dependency tend to decrease, while therapist and family dependency change unpredictably. They concluded that clients' development of dependent relationships with the practitioner early in therapy leads them to make increasing demands on the practitioner. When this occurs the relationship may become conflicted, and its end may be unsatisfying for the client. Practitioners are thus urged to monitor their clients' dependency over time so as to keep it within reasonable limits.

Holmes (1997) asserts that the interaction between the practitioner's and client's personality styles may affect both the appropriateness and timing of the end of the relationship. His scheme focuses on clients who are either ambivalent about ending or who avoid the issue and practitioners who tend by nature to be controlling and structured or overempathetic. The structured and controlling practitioner may incorrectly assume that an avoidant client (who will not openly express a desire to continue) is ready to end and possibly implement the process on the basis of some external schedule. The structured practitioner will, however, be more likely to make an appropriate decision to end for the ambivalent client (who may never decide for him- or herself). The overempathetic practitioner may be reluctant to introduce the issue of ending with an ambivalent client and instead wait too long for the client to make that decision. On the other hand, the empathetic practitioner may accurately sense the avoidant client's struggle with that issue.

The importance of Holmes's work is in bringing attention to the interaction of worker and client personality characteristics, which probably influences processes in other stages of intervention as well. What follows is an illustration of how one client's personality style communicated to the practitioner that he was managing the ending well, when in fact the client was affected adversely.

Case Study: Structured Worker, Avoidant Client

I worked with Rod for two years. He was twenty-five when we met and had paranoid schizophrenia. He was a loner, trying to minimize the outside stimulation that prompted his hallucinations. He was bright and well read but often irritable. Rod never seemed to like me—I seemed to be an outlet for his frustrations. He routinely degraded me, and while I tried not to be defensive, he did get on my nerves at times. I felt that I was working hard with him, and I usually get along well with clients who have schizophrenia. I couldn't understand Rob's negative attitudes, but I kept trying to keep him engaged in the treatment process. We worked together on stabilizing his mood, minimizing his symptoms, improving his social life, and getting him into job training so he could eventually work and have his own apartment. Through my case management, other professionals became involved in his care. We reached a point where he was ready to be transferred to a case management team, where he would have a primary case manager, vocational specialist, and housing specialist working with him. He had almost completed his job-training program and was ready to begin a job as a computer programmer.

Rod was excited about his progress, although he still experienced the symptoms of his disorder, and he was eager to move on. He viewed his transfer as a sign of progress and, because he was often angry with me, he shared no regrets about the transfer. I was probably relieved myself, as I had been disappointed with the nature of our relationship. Thus, it was a surprise to me that within one month of the transfer Rod despaired about his difficulties with a new job and attempted suicide. He survived the overdose but complained to his primary case manager while in the hospital that he felt very much alone. He said he did not feel close to his new staff and believed I had abandoned him. I visited Rod, and he seemed sincere about these feelings. It upset me to realize that I had taken for granted that he was pleased to be finished with me and that I had perhaps allowed him to move on too quickly. In retrospect, I can see that Rod was more attached to me than I thought and that my frustration with him resulted in my readiness to transfer him when the opportunity arose. There was apparently some point in my work with him that I decided, without being aware of it, that I didn't want to invest more energy into his care.

I also understand now, in retrospect, that I became quite task focused with Rod and measured his progress strictly in terms of his movement through the case management system. Because our relationship was difficult, I didn't put as much of my energy into monitoring how well we were working together. Had I been more sensitive to his way of managing relationships, I might have considered that we needed to maintain ours for a longer period. But he avoided sharing his feelings with me, and I could not make a strong connection with him.

Summary

In earlier chapters different types of endings, common ending tasks, and ending strategies from the perspectives of various clinical practice theories were presented. The manner in which a practitioner addresses a clinical ending is also dependent, however, on the individual client's reactions to the intervention and its approaching end. In this chapter we have looked at many possible client reactions to the ending process. We considered positive reactions, such as pride, an increased sense of competence, and an increased enthusiasm for life activity and attachments. We also considered clients' negative reactions to ending, such as avoidance, denial, a felt recurrence of old problems, and anger. In describing the factors that influence a client's reactions to ending I have attempted to articulate issues to help practitioners minimize the negative reactions. Of course, the practitioner's own feelings have an effect on the ending process as well. That is the topic of the next chapter.

Chapter 10

Practitioner Reactions to Endings

In chapter 9, we focused on clients. Now we consider the range of reactions that practitioners experience as they end clinical relationships. All practitioners should develop habits of monitoring their reactions, both positive and negative. Doing so will maximize their chances to facilitate satisfactory closure for themselves and their clients and to build careers that feature professional satisfaction. Both personal and clinical factors influence practitioner reactions to endings.

Positive Reactions

An Enhanced Sense of Competence

All practitioners are concerned with developing the skills and knowledge that will help their clients resolve problems and achieve goals. They want their clinical effectiveness reinforced and their self-esteem enhanced. In one cross-cultural study the practitioner's need to feel competent was identified as central to the help-giving process (Frank & Frank, 1993). Practitioners can evaluate their effectiveness with single-subject research designs, satisfaction surveys, the reports of clients and their significant others, observations of client behaviors, and peer and supervisory feedback. When this feedback is positive, the practitioner's effectiveness is validated, and he or she is motivated to undertake new clinical challenges. Frank and Frank suggest that this sense of competence raises the likelihood of future effectiveness.

Pride in the Client's Achievements

When a clinical encounter includes a positive ending, the practitioner feels personally rewarded. This feeling may reflect a basic human need for generativity (Erikson, 1968), self-actualization (Maslow, 1968), cognitive consistency (McClelland, 1985), or existential fulfillment (Yalom, 1980), among others. Still, this feeling of pride is not always complete or unmixed. The following vignette describes a situation in which a practitioner felt good about what the client gained from their work only months after the intervention ended.

Case Study: Ambivalence in the Relationship

I once worked in a mental health clinic program for persons who were HIV positive. My client, Ben, had worked with many clinicians over the years, which compounded his difficulty in trusting others. When we met, he was a thirty-three-year-old, Caucasian, divorced, gay man who worked as a nurse. He had been HIV positive for six years. His mental health problems included depression and substance abuse. Ben frequently relapsed with his substance use, and on a few occasions he was involuntarily committed to inpatient facilities. Ben was also socially isolated and pursued anonymous sex rather than lasting relationships. He had experienced childhood sexual abuse and saw himself as unworthy of anything good or lasting in life.

I had up to twelve months to work with Ben (the remaining time my program would be funded). My intervention approaches included cognitive-behavioral interventions for relapse prevention and psychodynamic, insight-oriented work to reduce his depression and enhance his ability to develop relationships. We agreed to meet weekly, but his participation was often erratic. Ben seemed to connect with me at times and then pull back, wondering if I really cared about him. Once he was briefly hospitalized for suicidal ideation, and I visited him at the hospital. I think my visit helped Ben accept that I was concerned about him.

Eventually, we began working well together. I suspected our ending would be difficult for Ben because of his relationship problems, so I began processing it with him six months in advance. I affirmed his improved motivation and ability to seek intimate relationships rather than anonymous sex and reviewed the process by which he had become able to trust me. Still, these conversations were difficult. They reminded Ben that our relationship was temporary.

It seemed to me that our last meeting was disappointing for both of us. We again reviewed and summarized our relationship and his accomplishments, but the conversation felt rather flat and mechanical. If our therapy could be framed as the writing of a novel, we merely scanned the dust jacket that day. Ben asked about continuing contact with me. I told him it would be inappropriate, and he didn't push this. That was it! I wasn't able to introduce Ben to his new counselor, because that person would not be available for a few weeks.

Two months later, I was wondering about Ben and gave in to an urge to call him. Incredibly, he had been discharged that same day from a hospital. He had spent five days there for a drug overdose and suicide attempt. He told me that he missed me, got depressed after we ended, and started drinking again. He was seeing his new therapist and things were going okay with that person, but he missed our sessions.

I had mixed feelings about this phone call. For one, I felt guilty. Was it my fault that Ben had not been able to manage the end of our relationship differently? Did I do something wrong as his therapist? But I also felt some gratification that I had this chance to talk with Ben. Some therapists might say that I should not have called him. This was not something I usually did, but I believe that my need to hear from him reflected my investment in the clinical relationship. I also think that hearing from me helped Ben affirm that his significant "object" was still there. This episode reminded me of the importance of the client having time to solidify new alliances before older ones disappear. I congratulated Ben for surviving his recent experience, but I never called him again.

Sadness

In the previous chapter it was noted that sadness is a normal human emotion that should be freely experienced, if not always expressed, in the clinical setting. Practitioners often feel sadness when a clinical relationship ends if they have enjoyed the experience and become fond of the client. Sadness is a positive reaction to the ending, because it indicates regret that a valued relationship will not continue. When the feeling is appropriately expressed it may enhance the client's positive outcomes as well. It is an important indicator to the client that the experience was a positive one for the practitioner and that the client was significant to him or her. Practitioners who work with children often struggle with letting go, having mixed feelings much as parents do when their children grow up (Lanyado, 1999).

Practitioners need to decide whether and, if so, how to share their sadness about ending an intervention with the client. It is always risky to share personal feelings with a client, because a practitioner does not want the client to assume any responsibility for the practitioner's feelings or well-being (L. Shulman, 1999). The decision for whether and how to do so should be based on the practitioner's general style of interaction with the client and sense that doing so will enhance the client's feelings of self-worth rather than be upsetting. If practitioners decide to share their sadness or any other personal feelings, this should be done during or near the final meeting so that it will not interfere with interventions still taking place. It should be done briefly, with a modest amount of emotional expression, as the practitioner's sharing of feelings will probably be very different from the manner in which the clinical relationship has developed.

Practitioners may experience relief rather than sadness if they are pleased about ending the intervention. The experience may have been stressful and unrewarding. While practitioners should not deny these feelings, neither should they share them with clients. Further, practitioners should be careful to avoid nonverbal communication of such reactions to clients (such as an eagerness to finish the session).

Case Study: The Hospice Family

When I introduce hospice care to families, I tell them that the services are for people who have an illness for which aggressive treatment is not expected to be beneficial, and the goals of care shift from cure to comfort. I introduce myself as a hospice social worker, a part of a team, and let people know that my role is to help connect them to community resources, support them as the disease progresses, and guide them through the process. From that point on, I allow people to talk to me in whatever way is comfortable for them.

I met Ellen, seventy-four years old, and her family the first day she was in our hospice program. I provided them with the basic information about hospice, including our philosophy of care, goals, and who from our team would meet their various needs. During our first meeting, Ellen was sitting in her recliner in the living room. She could walk around her house without assistance but had a nursing assistant to help her with bathing. Eleanor, one of her four children who lived in the area, was identified as the family member who could handle the emotional tidal wave of day-to-day hospice life. She had taken a reduction in her work hours to be available to her mother. All her siblings worked full-time and had families. Ellen had lived alone since her husband's death many years before.

Ellen did not ask many questions about what to expect as her disease progressed. She had already taken care of funeral arrangements and legal matters. What we talked about during most of my weekly visits was her children. She told stories of raising her children, what struggles they were facing, and how proud she was of them. And they were good to her. They came to stay with Ellen in shifts. They tended to her needs and were compassionate and patient. They kept her spirits high and communicated with the hospice team about their mother's needs.

On a Friday, the nurse reported that Ellen was not doing well and might not live through the weekend. I had grown close to this patient and family, and it was important to me to see her one more time. I arrived at the house at the end of my workday. Eleanor took me into the kitchen, a habit we had developed when she had to tell me something she did not want her mother to hear. She told me that her mother was very anxious. She was moving restlessly in bed and would not close her eyes. Eleanor assured me that all the medications had been given as scheduled, so she did not attribute the restlessness to pain. I said, "Maybe she's got something on her mind. Why don't I talk to her for a few minutes?" Eleanor seemed unsure of how to respond. She said, "Please don't upset her." I told Eleanor that I would speak gently and do my best not to upset her mother.

When we walked into Ellen's bedroom, she gazed at us with frightened eyes. I sat in a chair by the head of her bed, and Eleanor sat at her feet, caressing her legs. I asked her some questions to which she did not respond.

She only looked at me. I stroked her cheek and said, "You know, I have loved coming to see you. I have enjoyed our talks and getting to know your family. All your children love you so much. You have been such a good mother. You have taught them to love one another and depend on each another. No matter what happens, they are going to stick together, and they'll be okay. They will miss you, but they will remember you always." Ellen closed her eyes and stopped breathing. Eleanor asked, "Is this it?" I nodded. I believe I had offered Ellen the reassurance she needed to let go of life. She had lived six weeks since being admitted to our care.

I stayed with the family as they waited for the arrival of Ellen's son, the nurse, and the funeral-home worker. Each child spent some time saying goodbye to mother. The family looked to me for guidance and structure. I gathered everyone together in the living room and asked what would help them—telling stories, saying a prayer, or just being quiet. The family agreed that prayer would comfort them. We joined hands and I waited for someone to begin. When no one said anything, I prayed with the family. I prayed for what I had told Ellen her family would do—comfort one another and keep the memory of Ellen alive in their hearts—and for God to comfort them during their days of sorrow.

I attended the funeral and met with the family one more time. We sat outside the home of Elizabeth, Ellen's other daughter, on a warm spring evening, drinking iced tea while Elizabeth's children played around us. We talked about how everyone was coping. Church, returning to work, and time with family provided each of Ellen's children strength and comfort. They all felt that they would remember their mother lovingly and that they would continue to adjust well. They also reported that their children appeared to be coping well. I gave them some information about signs to look for indicating difficulty in adjusting to the loss of their grandmother. I invited them to contact me again for additional support, but I did not hear from any of them.

In hospice work it is difficult to separate from a family with whom we've spent such an intense time of life. But the family ultimately needs to be left alone, and when successful, we take satisfaction from what we have provided them.

Problematic Reactions

A Diminished Sense of Competence

Positive clinical outcomes enhance practitioners' sense of professional competence. Likewise, an ending that is disappointing to practitioners, particularly when they attribute this to their own actions, can have the opposite effect. Practitioners often tend to struggle with the need for perfection in their work (Noy-Sharav, 1998). The degree to which this affects the worker's confidence with future clients depends on its frequency, the practitioner's personal coping style, and the nature of the challenge faced in the clinical relationship. Even when practitioners feel that they should have been more effective with a client, that disappointment need not diminish their sense of competence. They may maintain a positive attitude and focus on what can be learned from any perceived mistakes. Further, some practitioners work with difficult clients (for example, those who lack motivation, are long-term substance abusers, or have personality disorders). They may come to accept a low probability of impact or learn to feel satisfied with small increments of change. Negative reactions to a poor clinical outcome are most significant among new practitioners, who have a relatively short history of clinical practice and cannot easily put an incident into perspective (Blask, 1998).

Guilt

Clinical practice is a complex endeavor even for the most experienced professionals. During assessment the clinician attempts to learn everything that is relevant to the client's presenting issue, but this is rarely possible (exceptions may include situations where the task is, for example, determining concrete resource eligibility). The best a practitioner can generally hope for is to ascertain a solid outline of the client's life circumstances that can serve as a basis for organizing interventions (Rauch, 1993). Disciplined practitioners develop theoretical frameworks and models of practice to help guide their work with clients. Even so, the intervention process touches on more variables than the practitioner can ever comprehend in advance. Working with incomplete information and ambiguity is a professional way of life!

Because of these issues, it is likely that after a practitioner finishes working with a client, he or she will always be able to identify things that could have been done differently to produce a better outcome. This can happen whether the actual outcomes were primarily positive or negative. This review is healthy, as doing so ensures that the practitioner will develop new knowledge, skills, and talents for future situations. A negative reaction that the practitioner may have at the end of the intervention, however, is guilt, a remorseful perception of having done something wrong or self-reproach for supposed inadequacy. In some cases practitioners can make mistakes that significantly affect the client in an adverse way. But as I often tell clients, guilt is not a productive emotion unless it is translated into constructive action. Confidential relationships with peers and supervisors can help to ensure that practitioners do not dwell on guilty feelings or become incapacitated in their ability to invest in future clinical work.

The Agency's Role in Dealing with Client Suicides

When a client commits suicide, the practitioner may experience a range of emotions similar to those felt by the client's family and friends, including grief, sadness, loss, shame, guilt, anxiety, and anger (Farberow, 2005). On a professional level, the practitioner may experience feelings of a failure of responsibility, loss of self-esteem, disturbed relationships with colleagues, doubts about his or her skills and competence, and fears of retribution and judgment from supervisors. Strategies for supervisors to help practitioners work through these emotions include providing information and education about the possibility of client suicide, establishing policies and procedures to follow so that the practitioner can feel supported, and arranging for "psychological autopsies," or shared staff discussions about the event so that all agency practitioners can learn from the event.

What follows is an example of a practitioner who experienced tremendous guilt about a client's suicide. He looked to his professional peers to help process his feelings, but organizational circumstances made this difficult. This example should make practitioners and supervisors aware of the need to be ready to intervene immediately with the clinician whose client commits suicide. The practitioner is likely to feel so guilt ridden and generally upset that good clinical judgment cannot be used for a period of time.

Case Study: The Suicide

I once worked at a mental health agency that was well known in the region for its sensitivity to clinicians' development, training, and support. At least it was for awhile. The organization went through a series of changes during a ten-year span that involved cutbacks in funding and staff. As a result, what was once a highly professional agency that provided extensive clinical supervision devolved into one experiencing strained relationships between administration and staff and less collegial relationships among clinical staff, who were consistently being asked to do more with fewer resources. The way in which the agency handled suicides (which were fortunately quite rare) was adversely affected by these changes.

The first month I worked there, a client of one of my colleagues, Mike, committed suicide. The client was a single mother of two young children and had struggled with depression for several years. Mike received a phone call from the client's estranged husband one day informing him that the client had shot herself while alone at home. The husband said that the suicide was an act the client had evidently been contemplating for some time.

Mike was devastated, of course. Our agency policies mandated that in the case of client death, the clinical director was to be notified immediately, day or night, and would arrange to meet with the practitioner to review the event. In this case Mike met with our clinical supervisor, Frank, at the office. Frank asked Mike to review the intervention that had preceded the suicide, and then they processed possible reasons why the event happened in the context of the therapy. Frank was by nature an empathic, supportive man, and he consoled Mike, reassuring him after their conversation that he had not been negligent in the client's death. Following this meeting, Mike and Frank both met with the executive director for another review of the incident and to process what steps Mike or the agency should take with the family. Mike went to a memorial service for the client but did not approach the client's family, leaving them the option of making contact with him if they so desired.

The clinical director encouraged Mike to process the event with the full clinical staff at one of our regularly scheduled peer consultation meetings. The purpose of these presentations was to educate staff about the possibility of client suicide, to brainstorm together how to respond to such incidents, and to provide support to the staff member. It was left to the discretion of the practitioner and clinical supervisor how soon after the death this presentation should be made. Mike wanted time to adjust to the incident and waited three weeks before presenting the case. At the staff meeting he became tearful as he described his hurt and his anger at the client for taking her life, but the support he received reassured him of his clinical competence. I noticed that the staff seemed to become closer as a result of discussing these delicate topics. Afterward Mike was reluctant to talk about the suicide, but he admitted that the support he received from the agency had helped him with his grief and self-doubt.

Dale was my client for two years at the community mental health center. He had schizoaffective disorder. At the time we were both in our late twenties. Dale experienced slow and sometimes confused thought processes, auditory hallucinations, and bouts of depression. He retained insight into the fact that he had a mental illness, and this made him feel hopeless at times. We worked together pretty well, I thought, although Dale was rather withdrawn and preoccupied. I liked him, but he was not one of my favorite clients. Neither was he demanding in terms of the time and effort we spent together. We worked toward his vocational and social goals with a variety of psychosocial rehabilitation activities. Dale was particularly interested in making friends, as he felt lonely, although he worked part-time. He took medication prescribed by our agency physician. Dale had mixed feelings about taking medicine, but he agreed to do so with no more or less enthusiasm than he did the other interventions.

Incredibly, I had another client at this time whom I thought was at high risk for committing suicide. This may sound terrible, but I took particular care to thoroughly document all my interactions with her, so that if she killed herself my efforts to minimize that risk would be evident. But the office secretary called one afternoon to let me know that it was Dale who had hung himself at his home. His mother had found him. He didn't leave a note, but his mother learned that just the day before Dale's new girlfriend had broken up with him. I didn't know that he had a girlfriend, but I did know that he had a great fear of being alone in the world.

Looking back, I think I went into shock. I was overwhelmed with guilt, fear, and anxiety, all at once and relentlessly, for days afterward. Had I overlooked something in Dale's behavior that might have prevented his death? Was my casual attitude about his program an indicator of disinterest? Why didn't I know about this girlfriend? He had missed an appointment with the physician recently—did he have enough medication that week? How should I act now? Should I contact his mother, whom I knew? Should I attend the funeral? Would I be sued? Would I be in trouble at the agency?

I needed someone to talk to. A few years prior to this incident, when clinical supervision was provided twice weekly, both individually and in a group, I would have had many such people available. But things had changed. We had expanded in staff size and number of departments. Caseload sizes had risen, staff development activities had diminished, paperwork had increased, and clinical supervision was provided selectively. Our clinical director left the agency, and a replacement had not yet started. There were only three people with whom I felt comfortable. I consulted with them, reviewing all the questions I had asked myself and trying to come to terms with Dale's suicide and convince myself that I was not to blame.

My executive director talked with me the day after the suicide. He was warm and supportive, but before long he spoke of administrative procedures. I had to fill out a report, and our supervising county board sent a pair of staff out for an investigation of the clinical circumstances of the suicide. I knew this was necessary, but it made me feel like a criminal suspect. I did not go to the funeral service, because it was for family only. I don't think I could have gone anyway, feeling so guilty. And I never called Dale's mother. Some staff warned me against doing so, in part because she might become litigious. In retrospect, I hate that legal issues were raised so often. Within a week life went back to normal for others at the agency. I was able to work, but my anxiety persisted for a good month afterward.

Avoidance or Delay

There are five reasons why a practitioner who recognizes the importance of clinical endings may avoid the topic or delay its processing with a client:

◆ If the practitioner tends to be affected emotionally by an ending but has difficulty facing or sharing these feelings, he or she may reserve little time for that stage in clinical practice. This practitioner may or may not be aware of his or her emotional responses and may be hiding the feelings from him- or herself as well as the client.

◆ The practitioner may delay processing the topic out of a concern that the client may take the opportunity to inappropriately bargain for additional intervention.

◆ The practitioner may be concerned that the client will use the ending as a reason to prematurely stop investing in the intervention.

◆ In short-term interventions, the practitioner may delay any ending tasks to make more time for active intervention.

◆ The practitioner's avoidance behavior may also represent an institutional coping style for a type of ending that is frequent and always difficult.

Regarding the final point, consider this example from Amy, a young social worker in her first professional job.

Case Study: Death at the Nursing Home

I work at a nursing home, the final residence for the men and women who reside there. The facility only has fifty beds, so staff get to know all the residents well. Most of the residents have organic and physical impairments and require a great deal of hands-on care. They die regularly, sad as it is. I was surprised when I first started working there to learn that when a resident died, the staff didn't do anything to mark the occasion. They helped the family with funeral arrangements but only in a formal way. The residents' deaths bothered me a lot, but since nobody else talked much about them, I figured that it just wasn't appropriate. I decided on my own to go to the funerals of the first few residents I knew who died. It was helpful to me, a way to achieve closure with them. Otherwise, I just felt it was odd that when someone died the staff didn't respond on a feeling level. I thought that the staff just got used to it happening and didn't think much of it. I eventually stopped going to the funerals myself. I guess I got used to residents dying, too. But it still seems odd that no one even talks about it.

An alternative example of how to manage these issues is seen in staff coping practices at a dementia day-care agency (Hasselkus & LaBelle, 1998). Staff experience stress routinely as clients decline and move toward death or to a nursing home. They strive for what can be called a "good death," however, with careful attention to the needs of the resident and family. They also schedule regular informal support meetings and celebrations of various types to preserve a sense of family at the agency for themselves.

The major problem in all these circumstances is that through avoidance and delays the practitioner risks overlooking those common ending tasks that are important to the client. Clearly, there is no reason that the ending stage needs to be protracted. From some theoretical perspectives and in some agency settings that feature short-term or even single-session intervention, the process may be quite brief. Nevertheless, if the end of the relationship is not addressed, the client may feel devalued or be less prepared to embark on life after the intervention.

Offering Additional Contact Inappropriately

A major ending task is to discuss with the client any circumstances under which he or she may have additional contact with the practitioner. There are situations such as those involving optional booster sessions where such contact may be appropriate. Sometimes, however, when the practitioner has mixed feelings about ending the relationship or when the client requests (or pleads) for more assistance, an additional contact offer may not be appropriate. For example, the practitioner may invite the client to call with updates, write letters, or stop by the agency to say hello. The practitioner who is leaving an agency may promise to come back to visit the client. These arrangements may be considered a type of denial or avoidance of the ending, and often the promised follow-up visits do not take place. One study found, for example, that when student practitioners leave agencies and promise to come back to visit clients, they do so only 15 percent of the time (Brill & Nahamani, 1993)! This is distressing to those clients and may undo some of the good that the intervention has achieved.

Factors Affecting Practitioner Reactions

The Practitioner's Theory Base

In part 2, we reviewed a variety of theoretical bases for clinical intervention and considered their different perspectives on endings. One determinant of the practitioner's reaction is the degree of theoretical congruence between the desired and the actual process of ending. This is an important issue, because as Fortune (1985, 1994) found, there is often a lack of congruence between what practitioners describe as their preferred means of ending and what actually occurs. Two other studies have shown that practitioners who work from short-term theoretical perspectives experience more planned endings than those who work from long-term approaches (Everson, 1999; L. Shulman, 1999). If practitioners end an intervention in a theoretically desired manner, they will feel more satisfied. They may feel dissatisfied if circumstances prevent appropriate attention to an ending process or if they see a client for a time period beyond what the client typically considers appropriate. The latter issue arose in the following vignette.

Case Study: A Couple in Conflict

A colleague referred Don and Kathy Brower to me for couples therapy. They had been married for five years. Don was a forty-five-year-old attorney and Kathy, thirty-two, worked in the home. They had a two-year-old daughter named Sarah, and Kathy was eight-months pregnant with their second child. Don had a thirteen-year-old son, Frank, from a previous marriage who lived with them. Kathy had also been married before. The couple sought help because they had serious disagreements about parenting. Don thought Kathy was too strict with Frank and too involved with Sarah. Kathy felt that Don did not help enough around the house, was irritable with the children, and sabotaged her attempts to discipline Frank. Their goals included forgetting past resentments, learning to communicate and compromise, and reengaging as a couple.

We met over a period of two years, and I intervened from a structural family perspective. Kathy's pattern was to vent angrily at Don and bring up her past resentments. When their new daughter was born, her frustration with Don only increased. Don's style of relating was to withdraw when confronted and communicate in a highly intellectual manner, denying strong feelings. I included homework assignments as a major part of the intervention. For example, I asked Don to take responsibility for certain household tasks and to monitor his tone of voice with the children. I instructed Kathy to spend specific amounts of time with Don after putting the girls to bed. They also had an assignment to spend time together outside the home once per week, taking turns planning the activity. Unfortunately, there appeared to be little progress. Kathy continued to complain that Don wasn't trying to change. Don said that no matter how hard he tried it didn't seem to make a difference to Kathy.

I eventually confronted their stagnation. I challenged them to articulate why they were trying to save the marriage and shared my belief that each of them seemed to be waiting for the other to end it. I noted that they were being poor role models for their children. Regarding the clinical ending process, I said that they needed to decide if they really wanted to stay together, and if so they would have to find another therapist with different skills. That is, my skills in structural family intervention had not been effective. They implored me to continue working with them, saying that they sincerely did not want to give up. I agreed to do so, however reluctantly, but still no progress occurred. Finally, with the support of my clinical supervision group, I followed through with my decision to end working with them. I felt certain by then that I could do no more to help them mend their relationship.

In retrospect, I held on too long with this couple and should have ended months sooner. They were initially a likable couple, and I identified with their struggle to stabilize a blended family, as I too had divorced and remarried. But I now realize that the couple had avoided important issues around money, sex, and values from the beginning. Don got his emotional needs met by spending time with his son, and Kathy likewise maintained her involvement with their daughters. I think that what kept them together was a desire not to fail at marriage a second time and an awareness that their upper-middle-class lifestyle would be compromised if they divorced.

Whenever I question the desire of my clients to commit to a change process, I give them the benefit of the doubt, possibly for too long. I certainly did so in this case. I stayed with the Browers against my better judgment simply because they kept saying that they wanted to change. This was one of the few couples I worked with for this length of time without helping them to meet some of their goals. It was quite frustrating for me, and my feelings interfered with my ability to finish on a constructive note.

Ability to Plan for the End

When the practitioner has an end point in mind for the intervention, she or he can plan ahead to maximize the possibility of achieving closure. When a clinical relationship ends abruptly and unexpectedly there is less opportunity for the practitioner to complete the end phase. Abrupt endings can be due to client dropout or various circumstances in the participants' lives that require a change in their routine, such as illness in the client's family or the practitioner's program reassignment. These unforeseen events increase the possibility that the practitioner will experience negative reactions to the abbreviated ending process. For some practitioners, including school social workers, abrupt endings are a way of professional life due to school system policies related to rotating school assignments, unanticipated client moves, and other changes brought on by the end of the school year. Those professionals do the best they can to cope with these occupational hazards, but the process can be difficult.

Case Study: An Annual Dilemma

School social workers have to get used to frequent transfers and abrupt endings. I provide services to three middle schools each year, and at the end of a school year I may be transferred from one or two of them, depending on our system's staffing needs. Although I have worked at six schools in the past four years, that doesn't mean that I should neglect attending to the endings of relationships with students and their families.

I recently had an experience with a twelve-year-old girl named Stephanie that was difficult for me because I had not sufficiently planned for the possibility of our ending. Stephanie was referred to me in her seventh-grade year because of truancy problems. I worked with her for four months. As in all such cases an assessment meeting was conducted with Stephanie, her mother (the father was absent), the school guidance counselor, and myself. I had a hard time contacting Stephanie's mother by phone, so I made a home visit. What I found there shocked me! The living conditions were awful! Her mother was living in a small two-bedroom house with her five children, a friend, an aunt, and the aunt's child. Mom was not at all defensive about the crowded furnishings—she knew she needed help. I quickly arranged a meeting of our school system's care coordination team, a group that includes several social service agency representatives, to put together a comprehensive family intervention plan.

Progress was unusually rapid in this case. Mom had to go to court, and her neglect of the children was legally established. But with the help of county social services, child protective services, and family counseling, the family situation improved greatly. Mom attended parenting classes and proved to be an eager learner. As a result, Stephanie, who was the oldest child, no longer had to take on so much domestic responsibility. Her school attendance improved, her grades improved, she got involved in some school activities, and she made plans to attend summer school. The school attendance of the other children also improved. The family's house received some major repairs, and the children all got new beds. I met with Stephanie weekly at first and then every other week to support her strengths and teach her how to be a successful student. I had daily contact with her mother for awhile, but my calls tapered off gradually as the other team members became more involved. I felt gratified with the family's progress.

Eventually, the school year ended. I had expected to continue working with Stephanie and her family when the new school year began in the fall, but I was transferred! I was not expecting this, but then again, school assignments can always change unpredictably. I was surprised at how much it bothered me not to be able to keep seeing this family, because my work had gone so well with them. School social workers all experience a kind of "automatic termination" with their clients at the end of a school year. We do not often have "clean" endings with them. On the other hand, we are often able to check up on our clients if they are later followed by other social workers in our school system.

I did see Stephanie's mother at court one day the following year. She was there for a reason unrelated to Stephanie, and it was nice to talk with her. I felt good when she said that the family had enjoyed working with me. But I never got to talk with Stephanie again, and I always regretted that. What I learned from the experience is that I should try harder to make contact and have some type of closure with all my clients at the end of each school year, whether or not I expect to see them again. The lack of closure with this family was difficult for me.

The Practitioner's Attachment Needs

Practitioners are not always eager to admit that they get some personal needs met through their work. Most of us believe that the welfare of the client should be paramount, and a focus on our own needs may make us seem self-centered. This concern is generally unfounded, as most practitioners choose their career in large part because of the nonmonetary satisfactions it will provide. Of course, it is possible that one's practice can be influenced inappropriately by the extent to which clients help to meet one's personal needs. This is one reason why clinical supervision is so important. The quality of practitioners' personal attachments, for example, has been shown to affect their approach to clinical endings. In one survey of 118 therapists, practitioners with secure attachments were found to experience less anxiety and sadness during termination, and those with more anxious attachment styles experienced more of those feelings (S. R. Shulman, 1999). Practitioners with the more anxious attachment styles were also more active with clients in summarizing and reviewing the intervention process, which is a positive behavior.

The following list of common personal needs may have an effect on the practitioner's reaction to the end of intervention, some for better and some for worse (Hepworth et al., 2002; Kocan, 1988; Schoenwolf, 1993):

- ◆ The need to be needed by others (which may make letting clients go difficult)
- ◆ The need to be liked
- ◆ The need to feel like an expert
- ◆ The need to be in control of relationships
- ◆ The need to rescue clients (particularly those whose problems are similar to those of the practitioner)
- ◆ The need to help clients become independent (this is common among young professionals who are in the process of separating from parent figures)
- ◆ The need for clients to become perfect

When we notice ourselves having an unusually strong reaction to the end of a relationship with certain clients, either positive or negative, it is worth exploring the reasons for that reaction so that we may develop greater self-awareness.

Case Study: Fried Chicken and Warts

I met Pete when I worked in a residential program at a mental health center. Pete was in his fifties and lived in a government-subsidized apartment near the center. My job was to be a support for him—take him to the store and to the doctor, help with his household duties, link him to community services, and monitor his symptoms of schizophrenia. We spent a lot of time together and had an easy rapport. He gave me, among other things, the secret to good fried chicken (cook it until all the blood comes out) and a remedy for getting rid of warts (rub them with a dirty dish towel that you then bury under the back steps). In addition to my practical functions, I provided Pete with companionship. He frequently told me stories of his mental illness, as if he were trying to make sense of what had happened to him.

Pete felt the medications helped him, but not because he had a mental illness. He said it made the demons that plagued him become quieter. Many of our talks started with a status report about his demons. Pete always struggled with the demons, except for the few times he excitedly told me that God had "taken them out of" him. He described the physical sensations that occurred as they were removed. Unfortunately, they always came back, and Pete would wonder what he had done to make God keep him in this condition.

Pete and I worked together for a year and a half and saw each other at least twice a week until I took a job at an inpatient psychiatric unit. When I said goodbye to Pete, I remember feeling sad at how accustomed he was to the process of professionals coming into and leaving his life. It seemed harder for me to say goodbye than it was for him. I kept up with him through a friend who worked at the center until she, too, left for another job. I always worried that Pete's case managers were not giving him the same time and attention that I had.

One day I was on the hospital unit when Pete was brought in on an involuntary detainment order. He was disheveled and yelling, and I noticed that his dentures were gone. I had never seen him angry with anyone besides his demons. He was sicker than I had ever seen him. Immediately I got on the phone with his residential counselor and demanded to know how he could get this bad before someone noticed. I felt sad and disappointed in the system. I felt even worse when I learned that he had recently lost his apartment.

Pete was later discharged to a group home and then moved to North Carolina to be with his daughter. He called me at the hospital one day to say he was back in a state facility. The last time I heard from him was on a Christmas Eve. He called to thank me for a carton of cigarettes I had sent him for the holiday. I had sent them against my better judgment when I remembered how he used to complain about the smoking restrictions in hospitals. I could have stayed in touch with Pete after that last phone call, but keeping the relationship going meant having to think about where he had started and where he was now. I didn't make a conscious decision not to call him again, but I never did. I'm not sure it was the right thing to do, just as I'm not sure I handled the ending with him in the best way.

I learned a lot from the experience. I learned that the more you care about clients, the harder it is to see them move on, especially to lesser circumstances. I learned that ending is harder when you maintain some contact with clients but have no control over the care they get. I made the ending harder for myself by believing that no one else could care for Pete as well as I did. It was naive of me to believe that his stability over two years was because of my work and that his sickness now wasn't just the symptoms of schizophrenia recurring, as they probably always would.

Part of what I carried away from my experience with Pete is that endings usually include ambivalence on both sides. Thinking about the relationship gets confusing when you commit your heart to the process. But I have come to believe that a certain amount of pain when someone is hurt or leaves is worth learning the secrets of great fried chicken and the cure for warts.

How the Practitioner Manages Loss

Coming to terms with the loss of people close to us is one of the ongoing and difficult challenges of our lives. With few exceptions people come and go, and all of us manage this fact and its consequences differently. The theory of self psychology asserts that the important people in our lives become parts of who we are, and when they leave, a part of us dies, in a sense (St. Clair, 1999). Practitioners should not consider their clients to be friends, of course, but they do develop attachments to many clients, and leaving them can represent a loss. In a study of 131 counselors it was found that the intensity of practitioners' grief reactions related to past losses correlated with their anxiety during clinical terminations (Pietro, 1998). Those counselors who had a general pattern of internalizing grief tended to process clinical endings less thoroughly, and those who externalized their grief (processed it openly) achieved positive closure more often.

The following vignette provides a striking example of how a practitioner may not fully appreciate the extent of her attachment to a client and experience a loss reaction until long after the contact ends.

Case Study: The Funeral

A recent experience made me understand that we don't always know when the clinical relationship ends or whether we have achieved closure. My story is about an adolescent client named Chester. I began seeing him when he was ten years old and his parents were divorcing. Chester was an only child, an extremely bright boy, and he took his parents' conflicts hard. They were fighting over him, over custody and visitation, and he wanted to make all those decisions for himself! My goal was to help Chester get through the crisis, help him learn how to communicate his feelings to his parents, and help him make decisions about how he wanted to live with his parents after their divorce. He was an eager, involved client, and his parents wanted the best for him as well. I did not provide family therapy, but I got to know both parents and had regular conversations with them. One of them always accompanied Chester to my office and would occasionally participate in a session.

I saw Chester for two years, and his therapy progressed well. We met weekly for one year, every two weeks for six months and monthly for the last six months. His parents completed their divorce proceedings and structured their new lives to include their son in ways that were loving and considerate. Chester, who continued to be an outstanding middle-school student, learned how to set appropriate boundaries with his parents and how to assert himself with them. I felt very good about the work I had done with Chester and his parents. I did not close the case at that time, however, because I still received occasional phone calls from his parents. They called every few months to ask questions about such practical matters as how to arrange visitation schedules and how to deal with their adolescent son's changing needs and lifestyle. I did not see Chester at all during those few years.

One day, out of the blue, Mrs. Arnold called to tell me that Chester was dead! He had died from an allergic reaction to a bee sting! I was shocked and cried with his mother on the telephone. This was so unexpected! Mrs. Arnold asked me to come to Chester's funeral. It was important to her that I come, because I had a special relationship with the family, but it was equally important to me. I felt strongly that I needed to go. I had never gone to a client's funeral before, even though the opportunity had presented itself. Why did I feel so strongly this time? I'm not entirely sure. I knew that attending the funeral would help me achieve closure with the family, as I would probably not have further contact with them. It would be a chance for me to say goodbye to them and to Chester. I don't think that the Arnolds needed me there—about a thousand people came!

What this experience taught me is that the end of a clinical relationship is not always marked by the final session. We connect with some clients in a way that seems to transcend the professional relationship, even though we observe reasonable boundaries with them. Clinical practice can be emotionally taxing, and it is not always possible to separate our personal and professional selves. I think it was appropriate for me to attend Chester's funeral, so that I could experience the closure that helped me to move on.

The Quality of the Client's Life

A common practitioner task during the end stage is to help the client outline strategies for the maintenance of gains. Even when the intervention has been successful, the client's postintervention life may include challenges that put the client at risk for new problems or the resurgence of presenting problems. Practitioners may have mixed feelings about ending in these situations, wishing that they could do more to preserve clinical gains. The client may face stresses that the practitioner can do nothing about, such as poverty, unemployment, discrimination, limited social and material supports, serious interpersonal conflict, or physical or mental deficits. The school social worker featured in the following vignette expresses sadness about her client's difficult home situation even as she recognizes her positive role in the client's life.

Case Study: The Diabetic Adolescent

I worked with Samantha for two and a half years while she was a student at my middle school. She was labeled as an emotionally disturbed student and also had severe diabetes. Samantha lived with her mother, who also had diabetes and was debilitated to the point of being blind. I began school-based counseling with Samantha because of her difficulties in the school environment, which included a lack of ability to get along with her peers, follow teacher instructions, and watch her diet in the cafeteria. She was a feisty child, but we developed a positive connection. We met every few weeks. I also intervened on occasions when, for example, Samantha had an angry confrontation with a peer and she threw a tantrum in the clinic because the nurse would not let her go home after she claimed to be sick. Samantha often feigned illness to try to get out of school.

My ending with Samantha occurred as she neared the end of eighth grade. We had worked together on and off since she was a sixth grader, and she actually had a pretty good eighth-grade year. She had made a number of changes that helped her do better in classes and with her peers. I was quite sentimental about her leaving. I had worked with her for so long and watched her become more mature. We talked more than usual in those last few weeks about her expectations for high school, her goals for herself, and what she had accomplished in middle school. It felt good to be able to enjoy Samantha as she was preparing to move on. It was a longer ending than I tend to experience as a school social worker. Samantha expressed sadness that she would not see me anymore. On the last day of school, I gave her a card with a poem about believing in herself.

I called Samantha once after that, in August, to talk about her readiness for high school. I told her that we probably would not talk again but that I would check on how she was doing with the social worker at her high school. I talked with that social worker about Samantha's school and family history to orient him to her needs. Samantha's family environment was getting worse at that time. Her mother's health was deteriorating, and her fifteen-year-old sister had a new baby in the home. I knew that Samantha would probably continue having difficulties with school in the context of the changes in her life. So, this ending experience was both difficult and gratifying. I hate to let students go when I know they will continue in the same school system, and I had become unusually fond of Samantha. But I know that I helped her make some useful changes.

The Quality of the Practitioner's Personal Life

One's professional career occurs in the context of one's personal life. As is true for everyone, life's ups and downs will affect work, including a practitioner's approach to clinical endings. If the practitioner is dealing with his or her personal conflicts, for example, there may be less willingness to tolerate conflict with clients, and endings may be viewed as a welcome relief. With a recent loss of a significant personal relationship, a practitioner may be inclined to hold onto those clients with whom she or he feels close. The practitioner's capacity to manage an ending may even be affected by envy of a client (Noy-Sharav, 1998). This may occur when the practitioner is frustrated with his or her life course at the same time a client is making major strides. The practitioner may become angry that he or she is not receiving the same support as the client. In another scenario, the pregnant practitioner is likely to be emotionally stirred up by this major life transition and its physical changes (Chiaramonte, 1986). She may become more emotionally reactive and, to the client's detriment, more vulnerable to self-absorption. This could result in less attention to the ending process.

The Practitioner's Job Satisfaction

High job satisfaction facilitates effective clinical ending processes (Resnick & Dziegielewski, 1996). Practitioners' positive feelings about the work setting help them feel relaxed and supported in their clinical activities. This contributes in turn to an ability to attend to clinical interventions in a deliberate, unhurried manner. These researchers also found that effective ending practices lead to increased positive feedback from clients, families, and administrators, contributing to practitioners' job satisfaction! High job satisfaction also correlates with low levels of work isolation and high levels of interdisciplinary contact.

Unfortunately, we all know about, and may have worked in, agencies where clinical staff are exhausted and even angry about adverse working conditions. Factors contributing to these conditions may include high caseloads, paperwork demands, and the absence of quality clinical supervision and staff development opportunities. Practitioners may feel deprived of some of the satisfactions that motivated their pursuit of a clinical career. The negative attitudes that derive from these conditions can affect practitioners' attitudes toward clients (Bassett & Lloyd, 2001; Kilburg & Nathan, 1986). Staff may be pleased when some clients leave the agency, not because their goals have been met but because it temporarily reduces the caseload and provides a reprieve from related job demands. They may feel intimidated rather than challenged by a difficult client when regular supervision is not available. The practitioner may lose emotional energy to invest in clients and respond to them in detached, dehumanizing ways.

These issues relate to the organizational influences on endings mentioned in chapter 4. The range of practitioner reactions to these adverse factors includes capitulation (giving in to the system), advocating for changes, finding a comfortable niche, and burning out (Netting, Kettner, & McMurtry, 1998). Individual strategies for preserving the quality of clinical services include:

Continuously building one's clinical knowledge base
Maintaining realistic goals for oneself and for clients
Understanding personal limitations
Seeking regular feedback about performance
Building a support system at work
Placing boundaries on work
Establishing relaxation habits and outlets for tension

Organizational change strategies include:
Staff development programs
Supportive agency policies
Clarity of job descriptions
Facilitating formal and informal agency support systems
Administrative balancing of caseloads and providing opportunities for variety

In the vignette titled "The Suicide" that appeared earlier in this chapter, the practitioner noted some issues related to job satisfaction that affected his ability to come to terms with a difficult ending. Both practitioners and their agency administrators share responsibility for ensuring that staff maintain enthusiasm about their important work.

Confidence in Clinical Judgment

The practitioner's reaction to an intervention that ends negatively for a client—that is, when goals are not achieved or the client's presenting situation becomes worse—is based in part on how confident the practitioner feels about the appropriateness of the intervention activities. Clinical intervention requires a series of decisions that must be made in light of incomplete information at many steps along the way. The practitioner never knows for sure what will result from an intervention task. If a clinical worker believes in retrospect that she or he acted responsibly and competently with the client, particularly if the worker received outside support from a supervisor, the worker will not be as adversely affected by a negative outcome. If the practitioner has doubts about decisions he or she made, the ending will be more difficult.

The vignette that follows dramatically illustrates a practitioner's mixed feelings about making a clinical decision that resulted in an abrupt, premature ending with her client. She did an excellent job of processing her dilemma with peers, however, and then felt much better about the outcome of her intervention.

Case Study: The Violent Wife

I provided in-home counseling to a family of four that had been identified as at risk for serious emotional and behavioral problems. I interacted primarily with Latoya, a twenty-eight-year-old newly married biracial mother of two children (a seven-year-old girl and one-year-old boy). Latoya had a history of psychiatric treatment, including hospitalizations for obsessive compulsive disorder. She was rigid, controlling, impulsive, and easily angered. She also had a history of violence, including a felony conviction, and this fact was central to my later dilemma with her. Latoya's new husband, the father of the younger child, lived in the home but did not initially participate in counseling. He worked two jobs, partly, I think, to escape the highly charged home situation. The couple argued often and almost violently, and the seven-year-old was aligned with Latoya against her stepfather.

The intervention went well. I initiated a structural family intervention. Latoya's husband soon joined us for counseling, and I helped the three older members assume more appropriate roles in the system. I also supported the development of a positive parental alliance. The family began to get along better, and the husband began to stay home more often. But then, after twelve weeks of progress, Latoya's husband informed her that he was having an affair. She became angry and threatened him with physical harm. He moved out of the house, and Latoya's behavior became more erratic. She was obsessed with punishing him for the affair. Latoya informed me during one of my visits that she planned to kill him. She shared with me a plan for doing so. Now, this was a woman with a prior conviction for assault. She had never tried to kill anyone, but the situation was explosive, and I felt that she might follow through. This is where my role changed, and our relationship abruptly ended.

I informed Latoya that there were limits to our confidentiality and that I needed to inform her husband that his life was in danger. I tried to explain my reasons as thoroughly and calmly as I could. Latoya became furious and demanded that I leave the house immediately and never contact her again. I felt terrible, but I left and attended to my duty to warn. I spoke to her husband and then called the local community mental health agency to request an evaluation of Latoya for possible hospitalization. Despite my efforts, they chose not to investigate. Fortunately, Latoya did not act on her impulses, but her husband did stay away. I tried to maintain contact with her in the coming weeks, but she refused to speak to me. She wouldn't talk on the phone. I sent her a letter to again explain my actions and request additional contact, but she didn't respond.

This was one of the most troubling and abrupt endings I ever encountered, as Latoya had been progressing so well. I felt that I had done the right thing, but with so many other mixed feelings involved, I sought supervisory help in reviewing the incident. I spoke to my agency supervisor and also called a community professional with whom I sometimes consulted. They both supported my actions, and eventually I felt good about my decision. In fact, I wondered if Latoya had meant for me to warn her husband as an indirect way of controlling herself.

To my surprise, Latoya called me nine months later. She had reconciled her anger with her husband, and they were expecting another child. She said we needed to talk but that it was about her daughter's behavior, not herself. During my first visit I again reviewed the issue of our last session. Latoya listened quietly but did not want to dwell on it. Though my visits continued, they were always focused on her daughter. But that was fine, because Latoya had resumed her use of medications and gained some insight into her problematic behavior patterns.

Unlike the previous illustration, the following one concerns a practitioner who was unsure about how to manage the dilemma of wanting to end work with a client when others felt that the intervention should continue. The ultimate outcome, which was also related to the practitioner's lack of confidence in his interventions, was disappointing to him, particularly in retrospect.

Case Study: The Little Princess

One family with whom I was eager to end working included a four-year-old African American girl named Sierra. I worked in adoption services at a child guidance clinic but had no prior experience with kids that young. Sierra had been given up at birth and was placed with a foster couple who later decided to adopt her. The couple was concerned, however, that she might become a difficult child because she had temper tantrums and sometimes stole items from neighbors' homes. My job was to help make Sierra ready for adoption with regard to her behavior. I requested and was given Medicaid authorization for thirteen individual and thirteen family sessions over the course of one year. I thought I might connect well with the family because I was married myself and had three children.

Things went badly from the start. Most troubling was the fact that the foster mother wanted me to attend to her needs that had nothing to do with the adoption situation. She complained often, for example, about her husband's lack of responsiveness to her, and she wanted me to help her deal with that. She also called me frequently between appointments to report minor problems, for example, to tell me that Sierra was not feeling well. I admit that I was also annoyed that both foster parents seemed to indulge Sierra with attention and gifts but were never quite happy with her. They seemed to be looking for a perfect child. Having said all this, I add that they were considered by myself and other staff to be suitable adoptive parents.

I also had trouble working individually with Sierra, although in retrospect it was mostly because of my own limitations. At her age, we could only engage in play therapy, and I never seemed to connect with her. We seemed to go through the same quiet, aimless motions every time we met. My frustration was complicated by the fact that Sierra was a big favorite of the other clinical and support staff at the agency. She was an attractive child, always perfectly dressed and groomed. Other staff called her "little princess." I saw no evidence of serious problems in Sierra, and it occurred to me that her problem behaviors might be in response to the attitudes of her foster parents. I worked with the family, or tried to, on behavioral management issues and how they could better reinforce Sierra's positive behaviors.

After the twenty-six sessions, I felt that the family situation regarding Sierra had improved and it was time to end. The foster mother begged me to continue working with them, however, and my supervisor, who also knew the family, supported her request. I disagreed but went along with the plan. I got authorization for twenty-six more sessions, another full year's worth, with no real conviction that they were necessary for the goal of preparing the family for adoption. I did my best, but more than ever the mom was asking me for help with her own concerns. By not confronting her inability to use our time appropriately, and the fact that their own marital problems seemed to perpetuate Sierra's occasional tantrums, I wasted time.

After the second year I insisted to the parents that we end. During the last two months I got at least two calls weekly from the mother complaining of trouble with Sierra and with her marriage. But Sierra was clearly ready for permanent placement, so in that sense I can say the intervention was successful. But I regret that I developed resentment toward Sierra and bitterness toward the mother because of her nagging behaviors. Unlike with many of my other clients, I planned no special celebrations for the final session. We met and reviewed the service plan, and I again explained that there was no need for us to continue. I then did something I had never done before—I walked to the lobby and opened the door for the mother so she could walk out. She called the agency one week later to request additional services. I told the receptionist to tell her that she would need to start the intake process all over again: filling out forms, going on the waiting list, and probably getting assigned to a new counselor. Mom did not call back.

With hindsight I can see that I should have directed our movement into the ending phase much sooner. The family was in the working phase, while I had moved on mentally into the end phase, and the disjuncture frustrated me. I should have negotiated specific goals and a timeline with Sierra's parents and my supervisor at the end of that first year. I should have also gotten more assistance with organizing a play therapy intervention.

Summary

This chapter described the variety of reactions, both positive and negative, that practitioners may experience during the end stage of clinical intervention. These reactions may be based on personal, agency, client, and theoretical factors. All these factors can affect the quality of the ending and the outcome of the intervention for the client and the practitioner. By understanding this range of reactions, practitioners can better prepare for the many circumstances that influence their manner of ending interventions with clients.

Chapter 11

Additional Ending Activities

Thinking back over my process of writing this book, I am most grateful to the many practitioners who offered their stories, sometimes quite personal, of noteworthy clinical ending experiences. I accumulated more examples of clinical endings than I could neatly fit within the body of the book. Still, many of these examples provide useful ideas for ending activities from a variety of practice perspectives. My own "ending activity" consists of presenting some of these additional ending activities.

The chapter begins with an overview of the topic of ending rituals. A variety of examples are then presented, each one organized as follows:

1. The objective of the activity
2. The theoretical perspective(s) from which it is drawn
3. The relationship of the activity to the intervention goals
4. The activity itself

Rituals

A ritual is any formal activity that is appropriate to a special occasion. It endows those events with a sense of being special (Gutheil, 1993). Rituals are best implemented during times of change that produce a sense of uncertainty in the participants. Rituals symbolize continuity, stability, and the significance of personal bonds while helping people accept the inevitable change. Rituals can provide effective ending experiences for all clients, particularly those who have difficulty managing their emotions. The structure of rituals provides a safe framework for clients in which to express their thoughts and feelings. During endings with clients, rituals affirm the importance of closure and imply that gains from the intervention can continue. They enhance clients' and workers' abilities to communicate by bringing structure to their final interactions. Following are several types of rituals that practitioners might utilize in their clinical practices.

Formal Service Evaluations

Standard agency evaluation forms can serve as simple rituals with excellent potential to process clinical endings (Gutheil, 1993). Looking at and filling out a routine agency (or practitioner developed) form can provide distance and objectivity that contribute to the review of the clinical work. This detachment can paradoxically facilitate expressions of feeling—it gives the client "official" permission to respond to such questions as what it felt like to ask for help, what he or she liked most and least about the process, and how he or she is planning for the future. Practitioners and researchers are often critical of these evaluation forms, because they are not perceived as capturing the essence of a complex interpersonal process (Pekarik & Guidry, 1999; Perkins, 2001; Stallard, 1996). Still, the structure of such forms helps some clients organize their reflections about an intervention, whereas an open-ended invitation to look back might be threatening to inarticulate, cognitively impaired, or nonassertive clients.

Case Study: Can We Talk?

I once conducted a time-limited and voluntary parenting skills group for several years at my community services agency. I always distributed evaluation forms at the second-to-last meeting so participants could return them during our final session. The form consisted of about fifteen questions, each of which required a "strongly disagree" to "strongly agree" response. I'll never forget the beginning of the final session of my second group experience when a member raised her hand. She said, quite assertively, "I don't know what kind of information you think you're going to get from these questions, but it would be more useful for us to talk about them rather than make checkmarks." We proceeded to have a discussion of the forms that was, in fact, more revealing about the members' experiences than the forms alone would have been. From that time on I still distributed the evaluation forms and asked members to complete them. But I began the final session by inviting members to give their verbal reactions to the questions. That way, members had the option of openly discussing items on the form. Most of them did so, and it became a wonderful ending process for the members and for me. They seemed to feel good about the possibility that their ideas and suggestions might make a contribution to future parents who would attend the group.

Expressive Tasks

Art forms such as painting, drawing, cutouts, music, poems, and stories promote clients' articulation of their thoughts and feelings. These activities tend to lower anxiety, move the client past inclinations toward intellectualization, and stimulate emotional processing (Dallen, 1986). As ending rituals they are particularly useful with clients who are not verbally articulate. Themes on which the practitioner might focus an expressive activity include:

"Goodbye to the old and hello to the new"
Best and worst memories about the intervention
What the client will miss the most and least
How the client is experiencing the transition

Expectations about what lies ahead

Sharing picture books with messages about the importance of relationships (especially with young children and lower-functioning clients)

The practitioner's participation in expressive activities creates a parallel process, as he or she is also likely to experience feelings about the ending more fully (Wadeson, 1989).

The following vignette describes a painting project that helped a group of adults with serious mental illness feel bonded at the end of their treatment experience.

Case Study: The Museum

I am an art therapist and once led a social skills development group for persons with schizophrenia at a psychiatric hospital. These groups were always small, with four to six members. The clients could not always organize their thoughts, let alone communicate well, so I conducted many activities that did not rely on verbal skills. When it was time for a group to disband, my tradition was to lead the members through a process of creating an acrylic painting on a large canvas. This was a popular final activity, because we permanently mounted the painting on a wall of the inpatient unit in a small reading room affectionately called "the museum."

We began the activity with a discussion of the subject of the painting. For example, we once decided to paint an underwater scene that included fish, rocks, plants, and the seafloor. I made a brief sketch on the canvas as a guide to where the various elements should go, and then we began. My job was to encourage everyone to participate and make sure that no one dominated the process, including myself. The entire activity took ninety minutes to complete and was capped the next day with a brief and informal hanging ceremony. Most group members seemed to feel special that something they had created would be on permanent display.

Status Elevation Ceremonies

Ritual strategies for clients experiencing life transitions can include status elevation ceremonies (Rouse, 1996). For example, discharges from hospitals or residential facilities can be understood as transitional crises, times in which clients' relationships and sense of self are in flux. For clients who have experienced a loss of status due to confinement in an inpatient facility, it may be important for the practitioner to help initiate the process of status "elevation" prior to discharge (Ramon, 1989–90). The practitioner may organize a formal celebration such as a party with significant others to celebrate a rite of passage. The practitioner may also link the client with new agencies and social situations so the client can begin to develop those new relationships while maintaining the relationship with the practitioner. In these ways the practitioner provides the client with a safe place to process reactions to these new developments prior to the ending.

Case Study: Going Home

The ending strategy described next was developed in a psychiatric hospital environment but could apply to any setting in which a client has been removed from his or her natural environment for a significant period of time (Brabender & Fallon, 1996). It is based on cognitive-behavioral theory and is compatible with individual or group interventions emphasizing skill acquisition. The essence of the activity is a review and application of ways the client can apply new skills to the postfacility environment. The client is helped to manage the discharge transition by refining skills that will be necessary for success. Ideally, this technique is done in a graduated fashion and begins several sessions before the client leaves.

The strategy can be illustrated with the example of an adolescent female who had problems with oppositional behavior and was preparing to return home to her family after living in a residential facility. The girl learned new coping, communication, and conflict-management skills while in the facility. To help the client make a successful transition, the practitioner and other members in the client's group role-played significant figures in her life with whom she anticipated using the new skills. These role plays included potentially difficult situations so that their mastery could increase the client's confidence. The practitioner also gave the young woman homework assignments to apply these skills, first with facility residents and staff and then with her visitors who lived outside the facility. That is, the adolescent practiced her skills with increasingly demanding audiences. As the client implemented these tasks, the practitioner and group members processed their outcomes and helped the client problem solve in areas of difficulty prior to her leaving.

We now turn to a variety of other ending activities that might be practical for clinical use. These are organized by their applicability to individuals, families, and groups.

Additional Ending Activities for Individuals

Story Time

The objective of the first activity, story time, is to affirm the child's strengths. The theoretical perspective is play therapy, but it could be used with any intervention with young children. This activity focuses on the child's competence, strengths, and sense of worth.

A standard ending technique in play therapy is sharing a written story with the client. Children, particularly young ones, do not often respond to purely verbal interventions. The general theory behind play therapy is that children are capable of expressing and working through their concerns through the media of play, including art and storytelling. As a final activity it is helpful for the practitioner to compose a story that includes symbols of the child's strengths and resources for dealing with challenging situations. These stories need not be very long—a page or two is usually sufficient. There is in fact an entire book of stories that can be adapted to fit many intervention themes (Davis, 1990). The practitioner writes the story prior to the final session, perhaps including a picture with it. He or she reads the story to the child and, in the tradition of play therapy, talks to the child afterward about whatever topic the child raises. The child is given the story to keep at the end of the session.

A Walk in the Park

The objective of this activity is to allow the client to organize the format and content of the final session in a way that will be significant to him or her. The activity is compatible with ego psychology, cognitive theory, behavior theory, structural family theory, and narrative theory. The client's taking control of the process demonstrates to the practitioner that his or her goals have been achieved.

I once stumbled on a simple idea for an ending activity that might work well in a variety of agencies. I was finishing up six months of counseling with Kathy, a domestic violence victim. She had come a long way, working through a substance abuse problem and coming to terms with a history of sexual abuse. My supervisor felt that preparing a client for the ending was always important, so I talked with Kathy during our last month together about her accomplishments and plans.

At the end of our second-to-last session, I asked Kathy if there was anything special she wanted to plan for our last meeting. I said it was up to her. She quickly suggested that we go to a nearby coffee shop for lunch and then take a leisurely walk outdoors. Kathy had spent much time recently in an inpatient substance abuse facility and often said that she wanted to get outside more often. So that is what we did, and it was a pleasant final meeting. We talked about a variety of topics, only some of them directly related to her work in the program. I later realized that giving Kathy control over how we ended gave her a chance to celebrate. Seeing her get excited about the outing helped me to realize that our relationship had been special to her. It was a clear mark that she had reached a transition point in her recovery.

I wouldn't make this offer to any client. Looking back, I think I knew what Kathy was likely to select—some form of getting outside and enjoying the spring weather. If I had a client who was fundamentally unhappy with me, would be uncomfortable in different surroundings, or would not be able to offer a realistic suggestion, I probably wouldn't proceed this way. And in every case I would reserve the right to negotiate an idea that for some reason was not appropriate, like spending an evening at my apartment. But in general I think this is a good way to allow the client to devise his or her own ritual.

Black Coffee

This next example provides an amusing twist to the one just related.

While working in a Child Protective Services agency I counseled two adolescent girls for several months. They had been placed with an extended family member, a grandfather, because of their mother's neglect. They were good girls and made steady progress in learning to cope with the disrupted family situation. They were outgoing by nature, and when it was time to end our work they asked me to come to their home for a social visit. They were excited about having a chance to do something for me and having me meet their grandfather. I never made home visits in that job, but it seemed to be an appropriate way to end our relationship—a nice farewell ritual.

Well, I knew they came from a poor family, but I was not prepared for what I saw. The home was small and one of the dirtiest I had seen in my life. Clothes, dishes, boxes, and old furniture were strewn everywhere. I didn't want to stay long, but the girls were so pleased to be my hosts! Of course, I laugh about this now. The low point came when they asked if I would like some coffee. I loved black coffee and asked for a cup. Grandfather insisted on making it—and pulled out some dirty dishes and a large, stained cup for the job. Grandfather forgot my specific request and filled the sixteen-ounce cup with weak coffee and about six teaspoons of sugar. And I drank it! It really was a nice ending, but it was difficult to enjoy at the time.

The Invisible Gift

This activity celebrates the client's accomplishments. It is compatible with ego psychology, cognitive theory, behavior theory, structural family theory, and narrative theory. The activity affirms clients' goal achievement and the significance of the process to the practitioner.

I know that many agencies prohibit the giving and receiving of material gifts when practitioners finish working with clients. So I thought of an alternative—the "invisible gift." It may seem like a hokey idea, but it worked well for me.

I once took a psychology class that required students to spend one day per week providing services to the residents of a juvenile detention center. I was a mentor and met with a number of adolescent boys individually each week to tutor them in their schoolwork. I also spent time talking with them informally, acting as a "big sister," and trying to be a positive support. I came every week for two semesters.

The school year was ending, and my final day with the boys was approaching. I decided to give them mementos of our time together. I made a greeting card for each boy and distributed them during our last meetings. On the front was a drawing of a gift package with the words "your invisible gift." Inside the card was a special wish I had written for each of them. These were simple but personalized hopes for them to have successful lives. I am no artist, but the boys seemed to like the cards. They had not expected anything from me. I think it is important that the cards were handmade, because it showed that I had taken some time to prepare them. They also liked the fact that I included a special wish for each of them. The cards were a good way to help us review our time together that year. It was a nice ending ritual that cost me next to nothing.

The Tea Party

Some activities of this type may have unintended negative consequences for clients, as in the following example.

I supervised a graduate student who came from a conservative, affluent Southern family. She had been the coleader of a recovery group for alcoholic men at a mental health center. She loved her clients and worked hard for them throughout her nine months in that field practicum. On her last day with the group, she brought in her expensive silver tea service and hosted a tea party for the men. I wasn't sure this was an appropriate activity. It highlighted the social class differences between the student and her clients, and it also might have felt condescending to them. The student saw it differently. She saw the activity as her way of honoring the men by sharing with them her fine silver.

Silk Cat in a Sewer: A Letter about a Premature Ending

To affirm, achieve closure with, and provide support to a client who is dropping out of the intervention, a practitioner may write a letter to the client. This activity is derived from narrative theory.

The practitioner whose story follows often writes letters to her clients, frequently as an ending exercise.

Jessica was a seventeen-year-old who had sought help at the insistence of her mother after being sexually assaulted by a stranger. Her mother had problems of her own related to bipolar disorder. Jessica and her mother lived with Jessica's grandmother, who often asked Jessica for advice on how to manage her mother. It was a confusing family situation—the client was not sure if she should act as her mother's daughter or her grandmother's mother! Jessica was not a willing participant in the intervention process from the beginning. I wrote this letter and sent it to her after our fourth session, when I thought she might not come back. I hoped that it might be helpful to her in the future, because she might keep it and reread it. Jessica came to see me one more time but then dropped out.

Jessica,

I know you have a hard time accepting compliments. So how can I say that I see in you so much creative energy and talent without getting a brush-off? You are being held back by a lot of double-talk. Can you hear both voices when people talk to you? Your mom says, "I'll be alright," but she sits there crying. She stands and tells you, "You don't need to take care of me," but she sits back down like a child, whispering, "I need someone to watch over me." She says, "I want you to go out on your own," and then, "but you can always live with me." She says, "I can take care of grandma, but she'll listen better to you." She says, "I'm the mom, and I want you to be an independent daughter," but she acts like you're the mom and she's the child. Which voice do you believe?

Your grandfather used to recognize your beauty and compliment you, but later he made you feel creepy because of that beauty. Your grandmother never defended you, so how can you discover that you're worth anyone's respect? I think these double-talk voices are locking you up. They are locking you into being someone you're not. When you dressed in the clothes you liked last week, I thought you looked majestic. Of course, with all these conflicting messages you might still feel like a sewer rat in silk. But what I see is a silk cat in a sewer, looking for a way out. I'm here for that. I hope you understand this and will let me inside your thoughts rather than push me aside.

Additional Ending Activities for Families

The activities presented in this section are drawn from the literature rather than from my interviews with clinical practitioners.

The Wake-Up Call

Practitioners are sometimes faced with the dilemma of how to proceed when a family does not appear to be making progress toward its stated goals. The flexible practitioner will use a variety of intervention strategies in an effort to help the family move forward. There are times, however, when it seems that the family, for whatever reasons, is not able to work constructively on change activities. In these situations the practitioner may give a paradoxical recommendation that the family stop participating in treatment (Mitchell, 1993). The recommendation is intended as a wake-up call to the family, a warning that they may have to continue living with the problem for which they have sought help. It is derived from behavior theory and is suitable when intervention goals are not being met. The practitioner may state, "I have decided that your lack of communication is not really a concern, but rather the way you all prefer to interact. Apparently it is more comfortable than any alternatives we have considered." This statement is intended to force the family to redefine the problem as something that they are willing to work on, promote new motivation by heightening member awareness that outside support may not be available, or result in the end of an intervention that has not been productive anyway.

Symbolic Objects

This symbolic gift exchange provides a way for family members to celebrate the end of a successful intervention and reinforce changes they have made (Roberts, 1993). It is compatible with all theoretical perspectives. For the last family meeting, the practitioner assigns members to bring in an object that symbolizes their feelings about other members of the family and what the intervention has meant to them. These items are not to be purchased—they can be either handmade or selected from a member's own possessions. The items should not be expensive but should reflect thought. For example, one person may bring in postcards to share with the others if improved communication has been an intervention goal, and some members live apart from one another. Another member might bring in a paper bag with cutout "feeling words" inside it. During the session the person can take the words out of the bag and tape them to the outside to demonstrate each member's new ability to express feelings and thoughts. As these examples indicate, members can be creative with their gifts, and the unpredictability of their choices can make this an enjoyable interaction.

Shared family interests can be a source of creative gift-giving ideas. In an attempt to reinforce the changes each member had made during therapy, one family used a beach vacation to test and reinforce new patterns of interaction. The practitioner suggested that each person select a shell that embodied the characteristics they saw either in another family member or in his or her relationship with that person. Upon their return, they told the practitioner about the shell collecting they had done, and each shell served as a metaphor for positive outcomes of the intervention. For example, a conch shell that had broken showed its many chambers, and one family member likened this shell to the inner complexity of a sibling who had a "smooth and shiny" exterior.

Organizing Setbacks

This paradoxical technique, compatible with the cognitive, behavior, and structural family theories, may be suitable when the practitioner recognizes an increase in family member anxiety caused by the clinical ending, even when progress has been significant (McCollum, 1993). It reduces the chances for recurrence of the problems. Family members need reassurance that they are likely to experience ongoing healthy functioning. Toward this end, the practitioner engages them in a process of considering and even practicing the steps they would need to take to bring the problem back again. He or she asks what would be required of each person to contribute to a resurgence of the problem issue. With this information the practitioner organizes role plays in which the members engage in old behavioral patterns and then process afterward what thoughts and feelings they experienced when doing so. The practitioner's intention is for the family to experience discomfort when assuming their former behaviors, which will help to increase their confidence that they can avoid those behaviors in the future.

Sculpting Progress and Change

This activity can be used to evaluate progress and change and to encourage motivation for ongoing change. Derived from structural theory, it is useful for families with young children or members who are not openly expressive.

During the final family session, the practitioner draws an imaginary line that extends from one wall of the room to a point just outside the door (Marquez, 1993). The point on the wall is identified as the beginning of intervention, when certain significant problems were occurring. The point outside the room is identified as the ending, where concerns related to family life no longer exist. Each family member is asked to identify two places along the line—where they are now, with regard to the quality of family functioning, and where they would like to be. After all family members select two positions, the practitioner points to each choice and leads a discussion about it. He or she asks questions of the family members, such as: "Were you aware of the perspectives of other family members?" "How does seeing where they are make you feel?" "Do you agree that this is where they really are, or do you see them as somewhere else?" "Do you feel that you are stuck where you are now?" The practitioner emphasizes that all members of the family have worked hard and made progress. Still, each member's two selected places on the line can symbolize his or her need to make additional changes after the intervention ends.

The Family Consultation

Families who achieve their goals can be empowered during the end stage by the practitioner's moving them toward an egalitarian position (Wetchler, 1993). With this activity, the practitioner not only praises the family for its accomplishments but also affirms that members have demonstrated good therapeutic judgment in finding solutions to its problems. The practitioner then shares a clinical problem involving a real or fictitious family that is similar to what the current family presented and asks the members for guidance in resolving it. This recognition of a family's expertise can be a powerful affirmation of its growth.

Letters to Families That Leave Intervention Prematurely

This strategy, compatible with cognitive theory and structural theory, may be useful when a family decides to terminate an intervention but the practitioner suspects that the family may experience further difficulty related to the problem issue (Jurich, 1993). Three or four weeks after the family has left (or dropped out), the practitioner writes a friendly and positive letter to the family. The practitioner hopes that all is well with the family, reviews the presenting problems and goals that were set, and adds an imagined description of how much better life must be now that their major concerns have been resolved. The practitioner adds a few warning signs of problem resurgence and concludes with an invitation for the family to return if they wish to. While this may appear to be a manipulative strategy, the letter assumes healthy functioning. The family can concur with the positive scenario painted by the social worker, in which case they did not end prematurely, or feel welcomed to return for more assistance.

Additional Ending Activities for Groups

The Compliment Box

This activity is particularly useful with children and adolescents. It helps to affirm self-esteem and review group content. It fits with all practice theories.

> I once co-led a six-week support and self-esteem group for children whose parents were incarcerated in jails or prisons. The kids, usually between six and eight years old, understandably had difficulty adjusting to their loss, and the purpose of the group was to help them through the adjustment process. I brought a small wooden box with a mail slot in the top to each meeting—this was called the "compliment box." At the end of each meeting the children were given sheets of paper and pencils, and we asked them to think about one good thing they wanted to write down about that meeting. They could write about another person or about something that happened that was helpful to them. We folded these into envelope-sized sheets and put them in the box for safekeeping.
>
> As one part of our final meeting we opened the box and read each of the papers that had been put in during the previous five weeks. My co-leader and I went through the contents of the box prior to that meeting to make sure that all members were represented with positive comments. Sometimes, but not often, we added a few additional notes to ensure this balance. The children absolutely loved hearing all the comments that had been written about them and the group topics. It made them feel good to

be mentioned by their peers in a positive way, and it reminded them of the important things they had learned during the program.

The Review Sheet

The objective of this activity is to help inpatient group members make a positive transition to community life. It helps clients review and retain awareness of their intervention gains and is compatible with ego psychology and cognitive and behavioral theories.

Psychiatric hospital discharge is a transition period that usually represents positive developments. It may also provoke anxiety in the client, who will be resuming a "normal" life that had most recently been experienced as difficult. This ending activity includes an extensive summary of the departing member's group experience (Brabender & Fallon, 1996). During this structured activity the practitioner and other members of the group share their perceptions of the client's strengths and positive changes. What makes this activity unique is that the practitioner or client records the feedback on paper as it is shared. The practitioner asks the client to take the written feedback home and place it in a prominent location there. The discharged member is encouraged to refer to it at difficult times during the posthospital adjustment period.

End of the Semester

The following example describes ending activities with classes that could be used with a variety of treatment groups. It affirms the significance of the personal bonds that have developed during the group process.

There are two ceremonies that I like to use with the graduating students in my clinical practice courses. These are year-long courses, and over nine months we meet thirty times for three-hour sessions. One of my ongoing themes with students is that we can learn much about group processes from monitoring how our relationships develop through the year. I make a point of talking with them about our unfolding ending process every week after our spring break, when we have seven meetings left. I remind them that their ending process is different from mine. They are looking forward to the excitement and relief that graduation brings, while I reflect with melancholy about the cycles of academia and the students who come and go in my life.

During the second-to-last class period I take a group picture, and one week later I give each student a copy as a gift. I tell them that I will put the picture on my office wall to help me remember them over the years. Also, during our last class meeting, I give the students a brief lecture about the importance of rituals as ways of celebrating rites of passage. I then divide them into five groups of five members and instruct them to develop, in fifteen minutes, an ending ritual for the class. After they have done so, they need to implement the ritual. This is always a lot of fun as well as an effective ending activity. Students surprise me with their creativity. Some examples of their rituals include:

Composing a poem and reading it to the class

Conducting a sing-along involving a popular song with new words

Initiating a chalk drawing on the board to which each student makes a contribution to a final picture

A symbolic dance

The request that each student share his or her future plans

Placing a sheet of paper on everyone's desk and taking time to stroll about the room, writing goodbye comments

The rock concert tradition of turning out the lights and flicking cigarette lighters to call for an encore

This activity loosens up the students considerably, and they usually leave the room laughing and in animated conversations with one another. I think that part of the reason this activity works so well is the age of the students (early to mid-twenties on average). They are young enough to risk being goofy but old enough to be able to reflect on the symbolism of their rituals.

References

Alexander, J. F., & Abeles, N. (1968). Dependency changes in psychotherapy as related to interpersonal relationships. *Journal of Counseling and Clinical Psychology, 32*(6), 685-689.

American Psychiatric Association. (2001). *Diagnostic and statistical manual of mental disorders* (4th ed.). Washington, DC: Author.

Anderson, J. (1997). *Social work with groups: A process model.* New York: Longman.

Anthony, S., & Pagano, G. (1998). The therapeutic potential for growth during the termination process. *Clinical Social Work Journal, 26*(3), 281-296.

April, D., & Nicholas, L. J. (1997). Premature termination of counselling at a university counselling centre. *International Journal for the Advancement of Counselling, 19,* 379-387.

Bassett, H., & Lloyd, C. (2001). Occupational therapy in mental health: Managing stress and burnout. *British Journal of Occupational Therapy, 64*(8), 406-411.

Baum, N. (2005). Correlates of clients' emotional and behavioral responses to treatment termination. *Clinical Social Work Journal, 33*(3), 309-325.

Beck, J. S. (1995). *Cognitive therapy: Basics and beyond.* New York: Guilford.

Bein, A., Torres, S., & Kurilla, V. (2000). Service delivery issues in early termination of Latino clients. *Journal of Human Behavior in the Social Environment, 3*(2), 43-59.

Ben-Ze'ev, A. (2000). *The subtlety of emotions.* Cambridge, MA: MIT Press.

Birnbaum, M., & Cicchetti, A. (2000). The power of purposeful sessional endings in each group encounter. *Social Work with Groups, 23*(3), 37-52.

Black, E. I. (1993). The giving of gifts: A therapeutic ritual. In T. Nelson & T. Tepper (Eds.), *101 interventions in family therapy* (pp. 120-125). New York: Haworth.

Blanck, G., & Blanck, R. (1979). *Ego psychology II: Psychoanalytic developmental psychology.* New York: Columbia University Press.

Blask, R. A. (1998). Criteria counselors use to classify terminations as premature or appropriate. *Dissertation Abstracts International, 58,* 8A.

Blechner, M. J. (1995). Schizophrenia. In M. Lionells, J. Fiscalini, C. H. Mann, & D. B. Sterno (Eds.), *Handbook of interpersonal psychoanalysis* (pp. 375-396). Hillsdale, NJ: Analytic Press.

Bloom, V. (1997). Interminable analysis? *Journal of the American Academy of Psychoanalysis, 25*(2), 313-316.

Bowen, M. (1978). *Family therapy in clinical practice.* New York: Jason Aronson.

Brabender, V., & Fallon, A. (1996). Termination in inpatient groups. *International Journal of Group Psychotherapy, 46*(1), 81-98.

Brill, M., & Nahamani, N. (1993). Clients' responses to separation from social work trainees. *Journal of Teaching in Social Work, 7*(2), 97-111.

Bruhn, J. G., Levine, H. G., & Levine, P. L. (1993). *Managing boundaries in the helping professions.* Springfield, IL: Charles C. Thomas.

Chambless, D. L. (1998). Empirically validated treatments. In G. P. Koocher, J. C. Norcross, & S. S. Hill (Eds.), *Psychologists' desk reference* (pp. 209-219). New York: Oxford University Press.

Chiaramonte, J. A. (1986). Therapist pregnancy and maternity leave: Maintaining and furthering therapeutic gains in the interim. *Clinical Social Work Journal, 14*(4), 335-348.

Conway, P. S. (1999). When all is said... A phenomenological inquiry into posttermination experience. *International Journal of Psychoanalysis, 80,* 563-574.

Corcoran, J. (2000). Brief solution-focused therapy. In N. Coady & P. Lehman (Eds.), *Theoretical perspectives in direct social work practice: An eclectic-generalist approach* (pp. 326-343). New York: Springer.

Dallen, B. (1986). Art break: A 2 day expressive art therapy program using art and psychodrama to further the termination process. *The Arts in Psychotherapy, 13,* 137-142.

Davis, N. (1990). *Once upon a time: Therapeutic stories to heal abused children* (rev. ed.). Oxon Hill, MD: Psychological Associates of Oxen Hill.

DeJong, P., & Berg, I. K. (2002). *Interviewing for solutions* (2nd ed.). Pacific Grove, CA: Brooks/ Cole.

Duehn, W. D., & Proctor, E. K. (1977). Initial clinical interaction and premature discontinuance in treatment. *American Journal of Orthopsychiatry, 47*(2), 284-290.

Epstein, M. (1989). Mental representation of the psychotherapeutic relationship during the post-termination period. *Dissertation Abstracts International, 25,* 3.

Epston, D., & White, M. (1995). Termination as a rite of passage: Questioning strategies for a therapy of inclusion. In R. A. Niemeyer & M. J. Mahoney (Eds.), *Constructivism in psychotherapy* (pp. 339-353). Washington, DC: American Psychological Association.

Epston, D., White, M., & "Ben." (1995). Consulting your consultants: A means to the co-construction of alternative knowledges. In S. Friedman (Ed.), *The reflecting team in action* (pp. 277-313). New York: Guilford.

Erikson, E. (1968). *Identity: Youth and crisis.* New York: W. W. Norton.

Everson, D. K. (1999). Prediction of treatment attrition in a psychological training clinic using the Personality Assessment Inventory, client variables, and therapist variables. *Dissertation Abstracts International, 60,* 2B.

Fabricius, J., & Green, V. (1995). Termination in child analysis: A child-led process? In A. J. Solnit, P. B. Neubauser, S. Abrams, & A. S. Dowling (Eds.), *The psychoanalytic study of the child* (pp. 205-226). New Haven, CT: Yale University Press.

Farberow, N. L. (2005). The mental health professional as suicide survivor. *Clinical Neuropsychiatry: Journal of Treatment Evaluation, 2*(1), 13-20.

Firestein, S. K. (2001). *Termination in psychoanalysis and psychotherapy* (rev. ed.). Madison, CT: International Universities Press.

Fong, R., & Furuto, S. (Eds.). (2001). *Culturally competent practice: Skills interventions, and evaluations.* Boston: Allyn & Bacon.

Forsyth, D. R. (2002). *Group dynamics* (3rd ed.). Pacific Grove, CA: Brooks/Cole.

Fortune, A. E. (1985). Planning duration and termination of treatment. *Social Service Review, 59*(4), 647-661.

Fortune, A. E. (1987). Grief only? Client and social worker reactions to termination. *Clinical Social Work Journal, 15*(2), 159-171.

Fortune, A. E. (1994). Termination in direct practice. In R. L. Edwards (Ed.), *Encyclopedia of social work* (pp. 2398-2404). Silver Spring, MD: National Association of Social Workers.

Fortune, A. E., Pearlingi, B., & Rochelle, C. D. (1991). Criteria for terminating treatment. *Families in Society, 72*(6), 366-371.

Frank, G. (1999). Termination revisited. *Psychoanalytic Psychology, 16*(1), 119-129.

Frank. J. D., & Frank, J. B. (1993). *Persuasion and healing: A comparative study of psychotherapy* (3rd ed.). Baltimore, MD: Johns Hopkins University Press.

Frankl, V. E. (1988). *The will to meaning: Foundations and applications of logotherapy.* New York: Meridian.

Franklin, C., Streeter, D. L., & Springer, D. W. (2001). Validity of the FACES IV family assessment measure. *Research on Social Work Practice, 11*(5), 576-596.

Freedman, J., & Combs, J. (1996). *Narrative therapy: The social construction of preferred realities.* New York: W. W. Norton.

Freud, S. (1937). Analysis terminable and interminable. *Standard edition of the works of Sigmund Freud, 23,* 209-254. London: Hogarth.

Fromm, E. (1967). *Psychoanalysis and religion.* New Haven, CT: Yale University Press.

Gabbard, G. O. (1995). Countertransference: The emerging common ground. *International Journal of Psychoanalysis, 76,* 475-485.

Goldstein, E. (1995). *Ego psychology and social work practice* (2nd ed.). New York: Free Press.

Gottesman, I. I. (1991). *Schizophrenia genesis: The origins of madness.* New York: W.H. Freeman.

Granvold, D. K. (Ed.). (1994). *Cognitive and behavioral treatment: Methods and applications.* Pacific Grove, CA: Brooks/Cole.

Greenberger, D., & Padesky, C. A. (1995). *Mind over mood: A cognitive therapy treatment manual for clients.* New York: Guilford.

Groves, J. E., & Newman, A. E. (1996). Terminating psychotherapy: Calling it quits. In J. Edwards & J. B. Sanville (Eds.), *Fostering healing and growth: A psychoanalytic social work approach* (pp. 339–358). Northvale, NJ: Jason Aronson.

Gutheil, I. A. (1993). Rituals and termination procedures. *Smith College Studies in Social Work, 63*(2), 163–176.

Guy, J. D., French, R. J., Poelstra, P. L., & Brown, C. K. (1993). Therapeutic terminations: How psychotherapists say good-bye. *Psychotherapy in Private Practice, 12*(2), 73–82.

Harper, K. V., & Lantz, J. (1996). *Cross-cultural practice: Social work with diverse populations.* Chicago: Lyceum Books.

Harrigan, M. P., Fauri, D. P., & Netting, F. E. (1998). Termination: Extending the concept for macro social work practice. *Journal of Sociology and Social Welfare, 25*(4), 61–80.

Hartmann, H. (1964). *Essays on ego psychology.* Madison, CT: International Universities Press.

Hasselkus, B. R., & LaBelle, A. (1998). Dementia day care endings: The uncertain limits of care. *Journal of Applied Gerontology, 17*(1), 1–14.

Hatchett, G. T. (2004). Reducing premature termination in university counseling centers. *Journal of College Student Psychotherapy, 19*(2), 13–27.

Hepworth, D. H., Rooney, R. H., Larsen, J. A. (2002). *Direct social work practice: Theory and skills* (6th ed.). Pacific Grove, CA: Brooks/Cole.

Herlihy, B., & Corey, G. (1997). *Boundary issues in counseling: Multiple roles and responsibilities.* Alexandria, VA: American Counseling Association.

Hertz, P. (1996). The psychoses, with a special emphasis on schizophrenia. In J. Berzoff (Ed.), *Inside out and outside in: Psychodynamic clinical theory and practice in contemporary multicultural contexts* (pp. 267–298). Northvale, NJ: Jason Aronson.

Hilsenroth, M. J., Holdwick, D. J., Castlebury, F. D., & Blais, X. (1998). The effects of DSM-IV cluster B personality disorder symptoms on the termination and continuation of psychotherapy. *Psychotherapy, 35*(2), 163–176.

Holmes, J. (1997). "Too early, too late": Endings in psychotherapy—an attachment perspective. *British Journal of Psychotherapy, 14*(2), 159–171.

Hoper, J. H. (1999). Families who unilaterally discontinue narrative therapy: Their story, a qualitative study. *Dissertation Abstracts International, 60,* 6B.

Hora, T. J. (1996). *Beyond the dream: Awakening to reality* (2nd ed.). New York: Crossroad.

Hudson, W. W., & Faul, A. C. (1998). *The clinical measurement package: A field manual* (2nd ed.). Tallahassee, FL: WALMYR.

Huey, S. J. (1999). Therapy termination among Black, Caucasian, and Latino children referred to community mental health clinics. *Dissertation Abstracts International, 59,* 9B.

Hunsley, J., Aubrey, T., Vestervelt, C. M., & Vito, D. (1999). Comparing therapist and client perspectives on reasons for psychotherapy termination. *Psychotherapy, 36*(4), 380–388.

Hutchison, E. D. (1999). *Dimensions of human behavior: Person and environment.* Thousand Oaks, CA: Pine Forge.

Imber-Black, E. (1993). The giving of gifts—a therapeutic ritual. In T. Nelson & T. Tepper (Eds.), *101 interventions in family therapy* (pp. 120–125). New York: Haworth.

Jacobs, T. J. (1999). Countertransference past and present: A review of the concept. *International Journal of Psychoanalysis, 80,* 575–594.

Jurich, A. P. (1993). Letters to families who leave therapy prematurely. In T. Nelson & T. Tepper (Eds.), *101 interventions in family therapy* (pp. 332–340). New York: Haworth.

Kacen, L. (1999). Anxiety levels, group characteristics, and members' behaviors in the termination stage of support groups for patients recovering from heart attacks. *Research on Social Work Practice, 9*(6), 656–672.

Kanter, J. (1988). Clinical issues in the case management relationship. In M. Harris & L. L. Bachrach (Eds.), *Clinical case management* (pp. 15-26). New Directions for Mental Health Services, 40. San Francisco: Jossey-Bass.

Kazdin, A. E., & Wassell, G. (1998). Treatment completion and therapeutic change among children referred for outpatient therapy. *Professional Psychology: Research and Practice, 29*(4), 332-340.

Kelley, P. (1996). Narrative theory and social work practice. In F. Turner (Ed.), *Social work treatment* (4th ed.; pp. 461-479). New York: Free Press.

Kendall, P. C. (1900). *Child and adolescent therapy: Cognitive/behavioral procedures* (2nd ed.). New York: Guilford.

Kerr, M. E., & Bowen, M. (1988). *Family evaluation: An approach based on Bowen theory.* New York: W. W. Norton.

Kieffer, C. C. (2006). Why ending psychotherapy is the most important part of the treatment [Abstract]. *PsyCritiques, 51*(4).

Kilburg, R. R., & Nathan, P. E. (Eds.). (1986). *Professionals in distress: Issues, syndromes, and solutions in psychology.* Washington, DC: American Psychological Association.

Kocan, M. (1988). *Transference and countertransference in clinical work.* Workshop sponsored by the American Healthcare Institute.

Kramer, S. A. (1990). *Positive endings in psychotherapy: Bringing meaningful closure to therapeutic relationships.* San Francisco: Jossey-Bass.

Krill, D. F. (1996). Existential social work. In F. J. Turner (Ed.), *Social work treatment* (4th ed.; pp. 250-281). New York: Free Press.

Kupers, T. A. (1988). *Ending therapy: The meaning of termination.* New York: New York University Press.

Lantz, J. (1996). Cognitive theory and social work treatment. In F. J. Turner (Ed.), *Social work treatment* (4th ed.; pp. 94-115). New York: Free Press.

Lanyado, M. (1999). Holding and letting go: Some thoughts about the process of ending therapy. *Journal of Child Psychotherapy, 25*(3), 357-378.

Lazaratou, H., Anagnostopoulos, D. C., & Viassopoulos, M. (2006). Treatment compliance and early termination of therapy. *Psychotherapy and Psychosomatics, 75*(2), 113-121.

Lazarus, R. S., & Lazarus, B. N. (1994). *Passion and reason: Making sense of our emotions.* New York: Oxford University Press.

Levenson, L. N. (1998). Superego defense analysis in the termination phase. *Journal of the American Psychoanalytic Association, 46*(3), 847-866.

Levin, D. (1998). Unplanned termination: Pain and consequences. *Journal of Analytic Social Work, 5*(2), 35-46.

Lieberman, E. J. (1985). *Acts of will: The life and work of Otto Rank.* New York: Free Press.

Ludgate, J. L. (1995). *Maximizing psychotherapeutic gains and preventing relapse in emotionally distressed clients.* Sarasota, FL: Professional Resource Press.

Mackenzie, K. R. (1996). Time-limited group psychotherapy. *International Journal of Group Psychotherapy, 46*(1), 41-60.

Maddi, S. R. (1996). *Personality theories: A comparative analysis* (6th ed.). Pacific Grove, CA: Brooks/Cole.

Maier, H. W. (1978). *Three theories of child development* (3rd ed.). New York: Harper & Row.

Malmquist, C. P., & Notman, M.T. (2001). Psychiatrist-patient boundary issues following treatment termination. *American Journal of Psychiatry, 158*(7), 1010-1018.

Marini, M., Semenzin, M., & Vignaga, F. (2005). Dropout in institutional emotional crisis counseling and brief focused intervention. *Brief Treatment and Crisis Intervention, 5*(4), 356-367.

Marks, I. M. (1987). *Fears, phobias, and rituals: Panic, anxiety, and their disorders.* New York: Oxford University Press.

Marquez, M. G. (1993). Sculpting progress and change. In T. Nelson & T. Tepper (Eds.), *101 interventions in family therapy* (pp. 33-36). New York: Haworth.

Maslow, A. H. (1968). *Toward a psychology of being* (2nd ed.). Princeton, NJ: Van Nostrand.

Mathews, B. (1989). Terminating therapy: Implications for the private practitioner. *Psychotherapy in Private Practice, 7*(3), 29–39.

Mattaini, M. A. (1997). Should social workers rely on genograms and ecomaps? Yes. In B. Thyer (Ed.), *Controversial issues in social work practice* (pp. 217–225). Needham Heights, MA: Allyn & Bacon.

May, R., & Yalom, I. (1995). Existential psychotherapy. In R. J. Corsini & D. Wedding (Eds.), *Current psychotherapies* (5th ed.; pp. 262–292). Itasca, IL: F. E. Peacock.

McClelland, D. C. (1985). *Human motivation.* Glenview, IL: Scott, Foresman.

McCollum, E. E. (1993). Termination rituals. In T. Nelson & T. Tepper (Eds.), *101 interventions in family therapy* (pp. 154–157). New York: Haworth.

McGoldrick, M., Gerson, R., & Shellenberger, S. (1999). *Genograms: Assessment and intervention* (2nd ed.). New York: W. W. Norton.

McRoy, R. G., Freeman, E. M., & Logan, S. (1986). Strategies for teaching students about termination. *The Clinical Supervisor, 4*(4), 45–56.

Mehlman, E., & Glickauf-Hughes, C. (1994). The underside of psychotherapy: Confronting hateful feelings toward clients. *Psychotherapy, 31*(3), 434–439.

Metcalf, L., & Thomas, F. (1994). Client and therapist perceptions of solution focused brief therapy: A qualitative analysis. *Journal of Family Psychotherapy, 5*(4), 49–66.

Millon, T., Millon, C., & Antoni, M. (1986). Sources of emotional support and mental disorders among psychologists: A career development perspective. In R. Kilburg & P. Nathan (Eds.), *Professionals in distress: Issues, syndromes, and solutions in psychology* (pp. 119–134). Washington, DC: American Psychological Association.

Minkoff, K. (1987). Resistance of mental health professionals to working with the chronic mentally ill. In A. T. Meyerson (Ed.), *Barriers to treating the chronic mentally ill* (pp. 3–20). San Francisco: Jossey-Bass.

Minnix, J. A., Reitzel, L. R., & Repper, K. A. (2005). Total number of MMPI-2 clinical scale elevations predicts premature termination after controlling for intake symptom severity and personality disorder diagnosis. *Personality and Individual Differences, 38*(8), 1745–1755.

Minuchin, S. (1978). *Families and family therapy.* Cambridge, MA: Harvard University Press.

Minuchin, S., Lee, W., & Simon, G. M. (1996). *Mastering family therapy: Journeys of growth and transformation.* New York: Wiley.

Mitchell, M. E. (1993). Termination as a therapeutic technique. In T. Nelson & T. Tepper (Eds.), *101 interventions in family therapy* (pp. 211–213). New York: Haworth.

Monk, G., Winslade, J., Crocket, K., & Epston, D. (Eds.). (1997). *Narrative therapy in practice.* San Francisco: Jossey-Bass.

Morse, B. A., Bartolotta, C. N., Cushman, L. G., & Rubin, P. T. (1982). End of term blues: An annual dilemma. *Social Work in Education, 5*(1), 26–39.

Mosher-Ashley, P. M. (1994). Therapy termination and persistence patterns of elderly clients in a community mental health center. *The Gerontologist, 34*(2), 180–189.

National Association of Social Workers. (1996). *Code of ethics.* Washington, DC: Author.

Nehls, N. (2000). Being a case manager for persons with borderline personality disorder: Perspectives of community mental health center clinicians. *Archives of Psychiatric Nursing, 14*(1), 12–18.

Nelson, W. M., & Politano, P. M. (1993). The goal is to say "goodbye" and have the treatment effects generalize and maintain: A cognitive-behavioral view of termination. *Journal of Cognitive Psychotherapy: An International Quarterly, 7*(4), 251–257.

Netting, F. E., Kettner, P. M., & McMurtry, S. L. (1998). *Social work macro practice* (2nd ed.). New York: Longman.

Nichols, M. P., & Schwartz, R. C. (2001). *Family therapy: Concepts and methods* (5th ed.). Needham Heights, MA: Allyn & Bacon.

Northen, H. (1994). *Clinical social work: Knowledge and skills* (2nd ed.). New York: Columbia University Press.

Noy-Sharav, D. (1998). Who is afraid of STDP? Termination in STDP and therapist's personality. *Psychotherapy, 35*(1), 69–77.

O'Connell, B. (1998). *Solution-focused therapy.* Thousand Oaks, CA: Sage.

O'Hanlon, W. H., & Weiner-Davis, M. (1989). *In search of solutions: A new direction in psychotherapy.* New York: W. W. Norton.

Orgel, S. (2000). Letting go: Some thoughts about termination. *Journal of the American Psychoanalytic Association, 48*(3), 719–738.

Pearson, Q. M. (1998). Terminating before counseling has ended: Counseling implications and strategies for counselor relocation. *Journal of Mental Health Counseling, 20*(1), 55–63.

Pekarik, G. (1983). Improvement in clients who have given different reasons for dropping out of treatment. *Journal of Clinical Psychology, 39*(6), 909–913.

Pekarik, G., & Finney-Owen, K. (1987). Outpatient clinic therapist attitudes and beliefs relevant to client dropout. *Community Mental Health Journal, 23*(2), 120–130.

Pekarik, G., & Guidry, L. L. (1999). Relationship of satisfaction to symptom change, follow-up adjustment, and clinical significance in private practice. *Professional Psychology—Research & Practice, 30*(5), 474–478.

Perkins, R. (2001). What constitutes success? The relative priority of service users' and clinicians' views of mental health services. *British Journal of Psychiatry, 179*, 9–10.

Philip, C. E. (1994). Letting go: Problems with termination when a therapist is seriously ill or dying. *Smith College Studies in Social Work, 64*(2), 169–179.

Pietro, B. B. (1998). Loss history, anxiety, and the use of defense mechanisms as predictors of counselor termination behaviors. *Dissertation Abstracts International, 58,* 12A.

Ramon, S. (1989-90). The relevance of symbolic interactionism perspectives to the conceptual and practice construction of leaving a psychiatric hospital. *Social Work and Social Sciences Review, 1*(3), 163–176.

Rauch, J. B. (1993). *Assessment: A sourcebook for social work practice.* Milwaukee, WI: Families International.

Reid, K. E. (1997). *Social work practice with groups: A clinical perspective* (2nd ed.). Pacific Grove, CA: Brooks/Cole.

Reis, B. F., & Brown, L. G. (1999). Reducing psychotherapy dropouts: Maximizing perspective convergence in the psychotherapy dyad. *Psychotherapy, 36*(2), 123–136.

Resnick, C., & Dziegielewski, S. F. (1996). The relationship between therapeutic termination and job satisfaction among medical social workers. *Social Work in Health Care, 23*(3), 17–33.

Robb, M., & Cameron, P. M. (1998). Supervision of termination in psychotherapy. *Canadian Journal of Psychiatry, 43*(4), 397–402.

Roberts, J. (1993). Termination rituals. In T. Nelson & T. Tepper (Eds.), *101 interventions in family therapy* (pp. 38–42). New York: Haworth.

Robinson, M. V., & Flaherty, J. A. (1982). Self-regulation of distance in supportive psychotherapy. *Clinical Social Work Journal, 10*(3), 209–217.

Rodwell, M. K. (1998). *Social work constructivist research.* New York: Garland.

Rouse, T. P. (1996). Conditions for a successful status elevation ceremony. *Deviant Behavior, 17*(1), 21–42.

Sander, R. L. (1998). College students' use of psychotherapeutic services as a function of year in school. *Dissertation Abstracts International, 59,* 4A.

Sanville, J. (1982). Partings and impartings: Toward a nonmedical approach to interruptions and terminations. *Clinical Social Work Journal, 10*(2), 123–131.

Savage, C. (1987). Countertransference in the therapy of schizophrenics. In E. Slakter (Ed.), *Countertransference* (pp. 115–130). Northvale, NJ: Jason Aronson.

Sawin, K. J., & Harrigan, M. P. (1995). *Measures of family functioning for research and practice.* New York: Springer.

Schacter, J., Martin, G. C., Gundle, M. J., & O'Neil, M. K. (1997). Clinical experience with psychoanalytic posttermination meetings. *International Journal of Psychoanalysis, 78*(6), 1183–1198.

Schamess, G. (1996). Ego psychology. In J. Berzoff, L. M. Flanagan, & P. Hertz (Eds.). *Inside out and outside in: Psychodynamic clinical theory and practice in contemporary multicultural contexts* (pp. 67–101). Northvale, NJ: Jason Aronson.

Schermer, V. L., & Klein, R. H. (1996). Termination in group psychotherapy from the perspectives of contemporary object relations theory and self psychology. *International Journal of Group Psychotherapy, 46*(1), 99–115.

Schoenwolf, G. (1993). *Counterresistance: The therapist's interference with the therapeutic process*. Northvale, NJ: Jason Aronson.

Schulz, C. G. (1984). The struggle toward ambivalence. *Psychiatry, 47,* 28–36.

Sczecsody, I. (1999). How can we end psychoanalysis—and still have a follow-up of it? *Scandinavian Psychoanalytic Review, 22,* 48–66.

Shapiro, R. J. (1974). Therapist attitudes and premature termination in family and individual therapy. *The Journal of Nervous and Mental Disease, 159*(2), 101–107.

Shulman, L. (1999). *The skills of helping individuals, families, groups, and communities* (4th ed.). Itasca, IL: F. E. Peacock.

Shulman, S. R. (1999). Termination of short-term and long-term psychotherapy: Patients' and therapists' affective reactions and therapists' technical management (attachment style, therapy model). *Dissertation Abstracts International, 60,* 6B.

Siebold, C. (1991). Termination: When the therapist leaves. *Clinical Social Work Journal, 19*(2), 191–204.

Siebold, C. (1992). Forced termination: Reconsidering theory and technique. *Smith College Studies in Social Work, 63*(1), 325–341.

Stallard, P. (1996). The role and use of consumer satisfaction surveys in mental health services. *Journal of Mental Health, 5*(4), 333–348.

St. Clair, M. (1999). *Object relations and self-psychology: An introduction* (3rd ed.). Pacific Grove, CA: Brooks/Cole.

Strean, H. S. (1986). Why therapists lose clients. *Journal of Independent Social Work, 1*(1), 7–17.

Super, S. I. (1982). Successful termination: Therapeutic interventions with the transferred client. *Clinical Social Work Journal, 10*(2), 113–122.

Sutton, J. R. (1998). Fostering client engagement in counseling through the use of videotape. *Dissertation Abstracts International, 59,* 4A.

Sweet, C., & Noones, J. (1989). Factors associated with premature termination from outpatient treatment. *Hospital and Community Psychiatry, 40*(9), 947–951.

Thomlinson, B. (2002). *Family assessment handbook: An introductory practice guide to family assessment and intervention*. Pacific Grove, CA: Brooks/Cole.

Titelman, P. (Ed.). (1998). *Clinical applications of Bowen family systems theory*. New York: Haworth.

Toseland, R. W., & Rivas, R. F. (2001). *An introduction to group work practice* (4th ed.). Boston: Allyn & Bacon.

Vaux, A. (1988). *Social support: Theory, research, and intervention*. New York: Praeger.

Wadeson, H. (1989). The art therapy termination group. In H. Wadeson, J. Durkin, & D. Perach (Eds.), *Advances in art therapy* (pp. 433–451). New York: Wiley.

Walsh, F. (1993). *Normal family processes* (2nd ed.). New York: Guilford.

Walsh, J., & Connelly, P. R. (1996). Supportive behaviors in natural support networks of people with serious mental illness. *Health and Social Work, 21*(4), 296–303.

Walsh, J., Hewitt, H. E., & Londeree, A. (1996). The role of the facilitator in support group development. *Social Work with Groups, 19*(3/4), 83–91.

Webb, N. B. (1985). A crisis intervention perspective on the termination process. *Clinical Social Work Journal, 13*(4), 329–340.

Werbart, A. (1997). Separation, termination process, and long-term outcome in psychotherapy with severely disturbed patients. *Bulletin of the Menninger Clinic, 61*(1), 16–43.

West, J. (1984). Ending or beginning? A discussion of the theory and practice of termination procedures in play therapy. *Journal of Social Work Practice, 1*(2), 49–65.

Wetchler, J. L. (1993). The family as consultant to the therapist: A technique for facilitating termination with reluctant families. In T. Nelson & T. Tepper (Eds.), *101 interventions in family therapy* (pp. 137–140). New York: Haworth.

Wetchler, J. L., & Ofte-Atha, G. R. (1993). Empowering families at termination: A structural/strategic orientation. *Journal of Family Psychotherapy, 4*(1), 33–44.

Wexler, J. M., & Steele, T. E. (1978). Termination of one therapist in co-led psychotherapy. *Clinical Social Work Journal, 6*(3), 211–220.

White, M., & Epston, D. (1990). *Narrative means to therapeutic ends.* New York: W. W. Norton.

Williams, B., Coyle, J., & Healy, D. (1998). The meaning of patient satisfaction: An explanation of high reported levels. *Social Science and Medicine, 47*(9), 1351–1358.

Williams, B., & Wilkinson, G. (1995). Patient satisfaction in mental health care: Evaluating an evaluative method. *British Journal of Psychiatry, 166*(5), 559–562.

Williams, S. L., Ketring, S. A., & Salts, C. (2005). Premature termination as a function of intake data based on ethnicity, gender, socioeconomic status, and income. *Contemporary Family Therapy, 27*(2), 213–231.

Willis, R. J. (1994). *Transcendence in relationship: Existentialism and psychotherapy.* Norwood, NJ: Ablex.

Wilson, G. T. (2000). Behavior therapy. In R. J. Corsini & D. Wedding (Eds.), *Current psychotherapies* (6th ed.; pp. 205–240). Itasca, IL: F. E. Peacock.

Wodarski, J. S., & Bagarozzi, D. A. (1979). *Behavioral social work.* New York: Human Sciences Press.

Woods, M. E., & Hollis, F. H. (2000). *Casework: A psychosocial therapy* (5th ed.). New York: McGraw-Hill.

Yalom, I. D. (1980). *Existential psychotherapy.* New York: Basic Books.

Yalom, I. D. (1995). *The theory and practice of group psychotherapy* (4th ed.). New York: Basic Books.

Zagayko, K. L. (1994). *Premature termination in child and adolescent therapy cases: Predictors of termination status and relationship to outcome.* Ph.D. dissertation, Virginia Commonwealth University, Richmond.

Index